# First World War
and Army of Occupation
# War Diary
France, Belgium and Germany

39 DIVISION
116 Infantry Brigade
East Yorkshire Regiment 1/4th Battalion,
Alexandra, Princess of Wales's Own (Yorkshire Regiment)
4th and 5th Battalion,
South Staffordshire Regiment 4th Special Reserve Battalion,
Prince of Wales's (North Staffordshire Regiment) 1/5
Battalion,
Hampshire Regiment 14th (Service) Battalion,
Brigade Machine Gun Company
and Brigade Trench Mortar Battery
1 March 1916 - 26 September 1916

WO95/2583

The Naval & Military Press Ltd
www.nmarchive.com
Published in association with The National Archives

Published by

## The Naval & Military Press Ltd

Unit 10 Ridgewood Industrial Park,
Uckfield, East Sussex,
TN22 5QE England
Tel: +44 (0) 1825 749494

www.naval-military-press.com
www.nmarchive.com

*This diary has been reprinted in facsimile from the original. Any imperfections are inevitably reproduced and the quality may fall short of modern type and cartographic standards.*

© **Crown Copyright**
**Images reproduced by permission of The National Archives, London, England, 2015.**

# Contents

| Document type | Place/Title | Date From | Date To |
|---|---|---|---|
| Heading | Training Cadre 39th Division 116th Infy Bde 4th Bn East Yorks Aug-Nov 1918 From 50 Div 150 Bde. | | |
| War Diary | | 10/08/1918 | 31/08/1918 |
| Heading | War Diary. 4th Bn. East Yorkshire Regt. September 1918. Volume XLII | | |
| War Diary | | 01/09/1918 | 30/09/1918 |
| Heading | War Diary. 4th Bn. E. Yorkshire Regt. October 1918. Volume XLIII. | | |
| War Diary | | 01/10/1918 | 01/11/1918 |
| Miscellaneous | 4 E York | | |
| Miscellaneous | | | |
| War Diary | Rouxmesnil | 01/08/1916 | 15/08/1916 |
| War Diary | Cucq | 16/08/1916 | 20/08/1916 |
| War Diary | Le Touquet | 20/08/1916 | 31/08/1916 |
| War Diary | Stella Plage (Le Touquet) | 01/09/1916 | 31/10/1916 |
| Miscellaneous | Yorks. | | |
| Heading | Training Cadre 39th Division 116th Infy Bde 5th Bn Yorkshire Regt Aug-Nov 1918 50 Div 150 Bde Nov 1918 | | |
| War Diary | In The Field | 01/08/1918 | 06/11/1918 |
| Miscellaneous | 5 Yorks | | |
| Heading | Training Cadre 39th Division 116th Infy Bde 4th Bn Sth Staffs Aug-Nov 1918 From 25 Div-7 Bde. | | |
| War Diary | Rouxmesnil Camp Dieppe. | 01/08/1918 | 15/08/1918 |
| War Diary | Cucq Camp Etaples | 16/08/1918 | 19/08/1918 |
| War Diary | Le Touquet | 19/08/1918 | 31/10/1918 |
| War Diary | Stella Plage | 01/11/1918 | 08/11/1918 |
| Heading | 4th S Staffs | | |
| Heading | ?Training Cadre ?th Division ?th Infy Bde 6 Bde ?th Bn Nth Staffs Aug-Nov 1918 ?Demobilised Nov 1918 ?Div 176 Bde | | |
| Miscellaneous | To:- Headquarters, 116th Infantry Brigade. | 30/09/1918 | 30/09/1918 |
| War Diary | La Panne | 01/08/1918 | 14/08/1918 |
| War Diary | Cucq Common | 15/08/1918 | 18/08/1918 |
| War Diary | Etaples Administrative District | 19/08/1918 | 22/08/1918 |
| War Diary | Etaples A District | 23/08/1918 | 31/08/1918 |
| War Diary | Etaples Administrative District | 01/09/1918 | 06/11/1918 |
| Miscellaneous | S.N. Staffs. | | |
| Miscellaneous | | | |
| Heading | S N. Staff July 1918 Went to 116 Bde 12.8.18 | | |
| War Diary | Clarques | 01/07/1916 | 02/07/1916 |
| War Diary | Preures | 03/07/1916 | 06/07/1916 |
| War Diary | Aix-En-Ergny | 07/07/1916 | 10/07/1916 |
| War Diary | Bout de Haut. | 11/07/1916 | 31/07/1916 |
| Miscellaneous | Table "A" Lewis Gun Course. | | |
| Miscellaneous | Table "C" Bombing Course. | | |
| Miscellaneous | 5.N. Staff | | |
| Miscellaneous | | | |

| | | | |
|---|---|---|---|
| Heading | 116th Brigade. 39th Division. Battalion Disembarked Havre 6.3.16, 1/14th Battalion Hampshire Regiment March 1916 | | |
| War Diary | Wittey Camp | 05/03/1916 | 05/03/1916 |
| War Diary | Southampton | 05/03/1916 | 05/03/1916 |
| War Diary | Dochs | 05/03/1916 | 05/03/1916 |
| War Diary | Havre | 06/03/1916 | 07/03/1916 |
| War Diary | Morbec | 08/03/1916 | 08/03/1916 |
| War Diary | Estaires | 08/03/1916 | 08/03/1916 |
| War Diary | Mosbeck | 09/03/1916 | 09/03/1916 |
| War Diary | Moshe | 10/03/1916 | 11/03/1916 |
| War Diary | Estaires | 12/03/1916 | 19/03/1916 |
| War Diary | Bac-Se-Maux | 20/03/1916 | 20/03/1916 |
| War Diary | Heurbaix | 21/03/1916 | 23/03/1916 |
| War Diary | Estaires | 24/03/1916 | 25/03/1916 |
| War Diary | La Gorgue. | 26/03/1916 | 01/04/1916 |
| War Diary | Caudresac | 03/04/1916 | 03/04/1916 |
| Heading | 116th Brigade. 39th Division. 1/14th Battalion Hampshire Regiment April 1916 | | |
| War Diary | Caudescure | 04/04/1916 | 14/04/1916 |
| War Diary | La. Pannerie | 15/04/1916 | 15/04/1916 |
| War Diary | Gwenchy | 16/04/1916 | 27/04/1916 |
| War Diary | Gorre. | 28/04/1916 | 30/04/1916 |
| Heading | 116th Brigade. 39th Division. 1/11th Battalion Hampshire Regiment May 1916 | | |
| Miscellaneous | D.A.G. 3rd Echelon. | 03/06/1916 | 03/06/1916 |
| War Diary | Gorre. | 02/05/1916 | 02/05/1916 |
| War Diary | Riez De Vinage. | 03/05/1916 | 09/05/1916 |
| War Diary | Festubert O.B.L. | 10/05/1916 | 12/05/1916 |
| War Diary | Festubert. | 13/05/1916 | 13/05/1916 |
| War Diary | Village Line. | 14/05/1916 | 17/05/1916 |
| War Diary | Festubert O.B.L. | 18/05/1916 | 21/05/1916 |
| War Diary | Le Touret | 22/05/1916 | 25/05/1916 |
| War Diary | Riez du Vinage | 26/05/1916 | 26/05/1916 |
| War Diary | Festubert | 27/05/1916 | 27/05/1916 |
| War Diary | Riez De Vinage | 28/05/1916 | 28/05/1916 |
| War Diary | Cuinchy Right | 29/05/1916 | 31/05/1916 |
| Heading | 116th Brigade. 39th Division. 1/14th Battalion The Hampshire Regiment June 1916, Report On Raid 7/8th June Attached. | | |
| Miscellaneous | D.A.G. Base. | 03/07/1916 | 03/07/1916 |
| War Diary | Annequin North. | 02/06/1916 | 05/06/1916 |
| War Diary | Cuinchy Right | 06/06/1916 | 08/06/1916 |
| War Diary | Cuinchy Village Line | 09/06/1916 | 10/06/1916 |
| War Diary | Riez De Vinage | 11/06/1916 | 15/06/1916 |
| War Diary | Richbourg St Vaast | 16/06/1916 | 21/06/1916 |
| War Diary | Ferme Du Bois Right. Section. | 22/06/1916 | 22/06/1916 |
| War Diary | Ferme Du Bois Right. | 23/06/1916 | 28/06/1916 |
| War Diary | Croix Barbee | 29/06/1916 | 29/06/1916 |
| War Diary | Ferme Du Bois Right. | 30/06/1916 | 30/06/1916 |
| Miscellaneous | XIth Corps. 8th June, 1916. The O.C. 14th Hampshire Regt. | 08/06/1916 | 08/06/1916 |
| Miscellaneous | Report On Raid On Enemy Trench At A 22 A 2 Carried Out By 14th Battalion Hampshire Regiment On The Night Of 7th/8th June 1916 | 08/06/1916 | 08/06/1916 |

| | | | |
|---|---|---|---|
| Heading | 116th Brigade 39th Division. 1/14th Battalion Hampshire Regiment July 1916 | | |
| War Diary | Ferme Du Bois Right. | 01/07/1916 | 01/07/1916 |
| War Diary | Le. Touret. | 02/07/1916 | 06/07/1916 |
| War Diary | Le Quesnoy | 07/07/1916 | 07/07/1916 |
| War Diary | Cuinchy (Left) | 08/07/1916 | 11/07/1916 |
| War Diary | Maison Rouge | 12/07/1918 | 12/07/1918 |
| War Diary | Cuinchy (Left) | 13/07/1916 | 14/07/1916 |
| War Diary | Gorre | 15/07/1916 | 19/07/1916 |
| War Diary | Gorre & Ferme du Bois | 20/07/1916 | 20/07/1916 |
| War Diary | Ferme du Bois | 21/07/1916 | 23/07/1916 |
| War Diary | Ferme du Bois | 24/07/1916 | 24/07/1916 |
| War Diary | Festubert Right. | 25/07/1916 | 28/07/1916 |
| War Diary | Festubert Village Line | 29/07/1916 | 31/07/1916 |
| Heading | 116th Brigade. 39th Division. 1/14th Battalion The Hampshire Regiment August 1916 | | |
| War Diary | Festubert Village Line. & Les Choquaux | 01/08/1916 | 01/08/1916 |
| War Diary | Les Choquaux | 02/08/1916 | 06/08/1916 |
| War Diary | Givenchy (Left) | 07/08/1916 | 11/08/1916 |
| War Diary | Allouagne | 12/08/1916 | 13/08/1916 |
| War Diary | Magnicourt En. Comte. | 14/08/1916 | 21/08/1916 |
| War Diary | Magnicourt | 22/08/1916 | 24/08/1916 |
| War Diary | Le Souich. | 25/08/1916 | 25/08/1916 |
| War Diary | Bois Du Warnimont | 26/08/1916 | 27/08/1916 |
| War Diary | P.18 | 28/08/1916 | 31/08/1916 |
| Heading | 116th Brigade. 39th Division. 1/14th Battalion The Hampshire Regiment September 1916 | | |
| War Diary | Mailly Wood | 01/09/1916 | 06/09/1916 |
| War Diary | Bertrancourt. | 07/09/1916 | 10/09/1916 |
| War Diary | Mailly | 11/09/1916 | 14/09/1916 |
| War Diary | Auchonvillers | 15/09/1916 | 30/09/1916 |
| Miscellaneous | Conversation Of 2nd. Lt. Bartlett, 14th. Bn. Hamp. R. Taken Down By Major Lytton At No. C.C.S. Gezaincourt, Sept. 6th. 1916 | 06/09/1916 | 06/09/1916 |
| Heading | 116th Brigade. 39th Division. 1/14th Battalion The Hampshire Regiment October 1916 | | |
| War Diary | Auchonvillers | 01/10/1916 | 06/10/1916 |
| War Diary | Englebelmer | 07/10/1916 | 10/10/1916 |
| War Diary | Y. Ravine | 11/10/1916 | 16/10/1916 |
| War Diary | Englebelmer | 17/10/1916 | 17/10/1916 |
| War Diary | Schwaben Redoubt | 18/10/1916 | 21/10/1916 |
| War Diary | Pioneer Road. | 22/10/1916 | 22/10/1916 |
| War Diary | Wood Post. | 22/10/1916 | 23/10/1916 |
| War Diary | Senlis | 24/10/1916 | 25/10/1916 |
| War Diary | Pioneer Rd | 28/10/1916 | 30/10/1916 |
| War Diary | Thiepval | 31/10/1916 | 31/10/1916 |
| Heading | 116th Brigade. 39th Division. 14th Battalion The Hampshire Regiment November 1916 | | |
| War Diary | Thiepval Post | 01/11/1916 | 01/11/1916 |
| War Diary | Pioneer Road. | 02/11/1916 | 02/11/1916 |
| War Diary | Martinsart Wood. | 03/11/1916 | 04/11/1916 |
| War Diary | Point 70 | 05/11/1916 | 05/11/1916 |
| War Diary | Senlis. | 06/11/1916 | 09/11/1916 |
| War Diary | Point 29 | 10/11/1916 | 12/11/1916 |
| War Diary | Point 65 | 13/11/1916 | 13/11/1916 |
| War Diary | Pioneer Road. | 14/11/1916 | 14/11/1916 |

| | | | |
|---|---|---|---|
| War Diary | Warloy. | 15/11/1916 | 15/11/1916 |
| War Diary | Doullens | 16/11/1916 | 17/11/1916 |
| War Diary | Y Camp | 18/11/1916 | 30/11/1916 |
| Miscellaneous | Report of Operations Carried Out by 14th Hants Regt During Period | 13/11/1916 | 13/11/1916 |
| Heading | 116th Brigade. 39th Division. 1/14th Battalion The Hampshire Regiment December 1916 | | |
| War Diary | Y Camp | 01/10/1916 | 01/10/1916 |
| War Diary | Poperinghe | 02/10/1916 | 12/10/1916 |
| War Diary | Canal Bank | 13/10/1916 | 16/10/1916 |
| War Diary | Hilltop | 17/10/1916 | 20/10/1916 |
| War Diary | Canal Bank | 21/10/1916 | 23/10/1916 |
| War Diary | P Camp | 24/10/1916 | 30/10/1916 |
| War Diary | Boesinghe Support. | 31/10/1916 | 31/10/1916 |
| Miscellaneous | G.S.O.I 39th Division. | | |
| Heading | 14th Bn Hampshire Regt War Diary For The Month Of January 1917 Vol XI. | | |
| War Diary | Boesinghe Support | 01/01/1917 | 03/01/1917 |
| War Diary | Front Line Boesinghe Sector | 04/01/1917 | 07/01/1917 |
| War Diary | Boesinghe Support | 08/01/1917 | 11/01/1917 |
| War Diary | Boesinghe Front Line | 12/01/1917 | 14/01/1917 |
| War Diary | Bleuet Farm | 15/01/1917 | 16/01/1917 |
| War Diary | Ypres. | 17/01/1917 | 20/01/1917 |
| War Diary | Railway Wood Left Sector. | 21/01/1917 | 24/01/1917 |
| War Diary | Ypres. | 25/01/1917 | 28/01/1917 |
| War Diary | Railway Wood Left Sector. | 29/01/1917 | 31/01/1917 |
| Heading | War Diary For The Month Of February 17 Bn Hampshire Bn Vol XII | | |
| War Diary | Railway Wood Left Sector. | 01/02/1917 | 01/02/1917 |
| War Diary | Ypres | 02/02/1917 | 03/02/1917 |
| War Diary | C Camp. | 04/02/1917 | 16/02/1917 |
| War Diary | Bollezeele. | 17/02/1917 | 24/02/1917 |
| War Diary | Toronto Camp | 25/02/1917 | 25/02/1917 |
| War Diary | Observatory Ridge. | 26/02/1917 | 28/02/1917 |
| Heading | War Diary of 14th Bn. Hants Reg For March 1917. Vol 13 | | |
| War Diary | Kruisstraat. | 01/03/1917 | 03/03/1917 |
| War Diary | Toronto Camp (G.18.0.37) | 04/03/1917 | 09/03/1917 |
| War Diary | In The Line (Observatory Ridge) | 10/03/1917 | 13/03/1917 |
| War Diary | Bund (Zillebeke) | 14/03/1917 | 17/03/1917 |
| War Diary | In The Line (Observatory Ridge) | 18/03/1917 | 20/03/1917 |
| War Diary | Observatory Ridge. | 20/03/1917 | 22/03/1917 |
| War Diary | Toronto Camp. | 23/03/1917 | 28/03/1917 |
| War Diary | Kruisstraat. | 29/03/1917 | 31/03/1917 |
| Heading | War Diary of 4th Bn Hants Regt For April 1917. Vol 14 | | |
| War Diary | In The Line (Observatory Ridge) | 01/04/1917 | 04/04/1917 |
| War Diary | Bund. | 05/04/1917 | 06/04/1917 |
| War Diary | Erie Camp | 07/04/1917 | 11/04/1917 |
| War Diary | Observatory Ridge | 12/04/1917 | 15/04/1917 |
| War Diary | Erie Camp. | 16/04/1917 | 17/04/1917 |
| War Diary | Canal Bank | 18/04/1917 | 22/04/1917 |
| War Diary | Hilltop Sector. | 24/04/1917 | 28/04/1917 |
| War Diary | Y Camp | 29/04/1917 | 01/05/1917 |
| War Diary | Argues | 02/04/1917 | 02/05/1917 |
| Miscellaneous | Headquarters, 116 Infy Bde. | 01/05/1917 | 01/05/1917 |
| War Diary | Moringhem | 01/05/1917 | 14/05/1917 |

| | | | |
|---|---|---|---|
| War Diary | Arques | 15/05/1917 | 15/05/1917 |
| War Diary | Arneke. | 16/05/1917 | 16/05/1917 |
| War Diary | Wormhoudt | 17/05/1917 | 27/05/1917 |
| War Diary | Wieltje Sector | 28/05/1917 | 31/05/1917 |
| War Diary | Weiltje | 31/05/1917 | 31/05/1917 |
| War Diary | Canal Bank | 01/06/1917 | 04/06/1917 |
| War Diary | Hill Top | 05/06/1917 | 10/06/1917 |
| War Diary | Canal Bank | 11/06/1917 | 15/06/1917 |
| War Diary | C Camp. | 16/06/1917 | 21/06/1917 |
| War Diary | Houlle | 22/06/1917 | 16/07/1917 |
| War Diary | Y Camp | 17/07/1917 | 22/07/1917 |
| War Diary | O Camp. | 23/07/1917 | 29/07/1917 |
| War Diary | Canal Bank | 30/07/1917 | 30/07/1917 |
| War Diary | Hill Top Sector. | 31/07/1917 | 02/08/1917 |
| War Diary | Canal Bank. | 03/08/1917 | 04/08/1917 |
| War Diary | School Camp. | 05/08/1917 | 08/08/1917 |
| War Diary | Meteren | 09/08/1917 | 12/08/1917 |
| War Diary | Ridgewood | 13/08/1917 | 13/08/1917 |
| War Diary | Hollebeke | 14/08/1917 | 16/08/1917 |
| War Diary | Spoil Bank | 17/08/1918 | 21/08/1918 |
| War Diary | Hollebeke | 22/08/1917 | 23/08/1917 |
| War Diary | Ridgewood | 24/08/1917 | 27/08/1917 |
| War Diary | Gordon Lane | 28/08/1917 | 31/08/1917 |
| War Diary | Keien Zillebeke | 01/09/1917 | 02/09/1917 |
| War Diary | Ridgewood | 03/09/1917 | 04/09/1917 |
| War Diary | Chippewa Camp | 05/09/1917 | 08/09/1917 |
| War Diary | Larch Wood Area | 09/09/1917 | 10/09/1917 |
| War Diary | Chippewa Camp. | 11/09/1917 | 13/09/1917 |
| War Diary | Cottage Camp. | 01/09/1917 | 01/09/1917 |
| War Diary | Shrewsbury Forest | 15/09/1917 | 17/09/1917 |
| War Diary | Cottage Camp (Nqb) | 18/09/1917 | 18/09/1917 |
| War Diary | Curragh Camp | 19/09/1917 | 20/09/1917 |
| War Diary | Cottege Camp (Nqb) | 21/09/1917 | 22/09/1917 |
| War Diary | Shrewsbury Forest | 23/09/1917 | 24/09/1917 |
| War Diary | Cottage Camp Nqb | 25/09/1917 | 25/09/1917 |
| War Diary | Shrewsbury Forest | 26/09/1917 | 28/09/1917 |
| War Diary | Mount Cockereel | 29/09/1917 | 30/09/1917 |
| War Diary | Mount Kokereel (R18c.8.5) | 01/10/1917 | 14/10/1917 |
| War Diary | Tower Hamlets. | 15/10/1917 | 23/10/1917 |
| War Diary | Carnarvon Camp M 10 B 7.3 | 24/10/1917 | 24/10/1917 |
| War Diary | Chippewa Camp | 01/11/1917 | 03/11/1917 |
| War Diary | Canada Tunnels | 04/11/1917 | 06/11/1917 |
| War Diary | Line | 07/11/1917 | 08/11/1917 |
| War Diary | Chippewa Camp | 09/11/1917 | 11/11/1917 |
| War Diary | Ridgewood | 12/11/1917 | 12/11/1917 |
| War Diary | Hedge St | 13/11/1917 | 17/11/1917 |
| War Diary | Front Line | 18/11/1917 | 24/11/1917 |
| War Diary | Carnarvon Camp M 10 B 7.3 | 25/11/1917 | 27/11/1917 |
| War Diary | Chippewa Camp | 28/11/1917 | 31/11/1917 |
| War Diary | Line | 20/11/1917 | 31/11/1917 |
| War Diary | Weiltje Ypres | 01/12/1917 | 08/12/1917 |
| War Diary | Winnizeele Area | 09/12/1917 | 10/12/1917 |
| War Diary | Bayenghem | 11/12/1917 | 28/12/1917 |
| War Diary | Quesques | 29/12/1917 | 29/12/1917 |
| War Diary | Bayenghem | 30/12/1917 | 30/12/1917 |
| War Diary | Dambre Camp | 31/12/1917 | 07/01/1918 |

| | | | |
|---|---|---|---|
| War Diary | Canal Bank | 08/01/1918 | 15/01/1918 |
| War Diary | Hilltop Farm | 16/01/1918 | 18/01/1918 |
| War Diary | Westroosebeke (Left Sector) | 19/01/1918 | 21/01/1918 |
| War Diary | School Camp | 22/01/1918 | 27/01/1918 |
| War Diary | Sailly-Le-Sec | 28/01/1918 | 30/01/1918 |
| War Diary | Haut Allaines | 31/01/1918 | 01/02/1918 |
| War Diary | Gauche Wood | 02/02/1918 | 03/02/1918 |
| War Diary | Revelon Farm | 04/02/1918 | 09/02/1918 |
| War Diary | Heudicourt | 10/02/1918 | 20/02/1918 |
| War Diary | Heudicourt. | 02/02/1918 | 02/02/1918 |
| War Diary | Haut Allaines | 21/02/1918 | 23/02/1918 |
| Heading | 39th Division 116th Machine Gun Coy Mar 1916-Feb 1918 | | |
| Heading | 116th Brigade. 39th Division. Disembarked France 16.5.16<br>116th Brigade Machine Gun Company March To July 1916<br>Attached:- Report On Operations 29/30 June. | | |
| War Diary | Grantham | 01/03/1916 | 01/03/1916 |
| War Diary | Festubert | 01/03/1916 | 01/03/1916 |
| War Diary | Cuinchy | 28/05/1916 | 30/05/1916 |
| War Diary | Ferme du Bois | 30/06/1916 | 05/07/1916 |
| War Diary | Beuvry | 06/07/1916 | 06/07/1916 |
| War Diary | Auchy | 07/07/1916 | 07/07/1916 |
| War Diary | Lacouture | 13/07/1916 | 13/07/1916 |
| War Diary | Ferme Du Bois | 19/07/1916 | 19/07/1916 |
| War Diary | Festubert | 23/07/1916 | 23/07/1916 |
| War Diary | Bethune | 22/07/1916 | 22/07/1916 |
| Miscellaneous | Operation Report 116 M.G. Coy. | | |
| Heading | 116th Brigade. 39th Division. 116th Brigade Machine Gun Company August 1916 | | |
| War Diary | Festubert | 01/08/1916 | 01/08/1916 |
| War Diary | Bethune | 01/08/1916 | 01/08/1916 |
| War Diary | Givenchy | 06/08/1916 | 06/08/1916 |
| War Diary | Gorre. | 06/08/1916 | 06/08/1916 |
| War Diary | Gorre. | 02/08/1916 | 02/08/1916 |
| War Diary | Allouagne. | 11/08/1916 | 11/08/1916 |
| War Diary | Canchy A La Tour | 12/08/1916 | 12/08/1916 |
| War Diary | Rocourt | 13/08/1916 | 23/08/1916 |
| War Diary | Ivergny | 23/08/1916 | 23/08/1916 |
| War Diary | Warnimont | 25/08/1916 | 27/08/1916 |
| War Diary | Ancre | 27/08/1916 | 02/09/1916 |
| War Diary | Festubert | 01/08/1916 | 01/08/1916 |
| War Diary | Bethune | 01/08/1916 | 01/08/1916 |
| War Diary | Givenchy | 06/08/1916 | 06/08/1916 |
| War Diary | Gorre | 06/08/1916 | 06/08/1916 |
| War Diary | Gorre. | 02/08/1916 | 02/08/1916 |
| War Diary | Allouagne | 11/08/1916 | 11/08/1916 |
| War Diary | Cauchy A La Tour | 11/08/1916 | 12/08/1916 |
| War Diary | Rocourt. | 13/08/1916 | 23/08/1916 |
| War Diary | Ivergny | 23/08/1916 | 23/08/1916 |
| War Diary | Warnimont | 25/08/1916 | 27/08/1916 |
| War Diary | Ancre | 27/08/1916 | 02/09/1916 |
| Heading | 116th Brigade. 39th Division. 116th Brigade Machine Gun Company September 1916 | | |
| War Diary | Mailly-Maillet Wood | 02/09/1916 | 02/09/1916 |
| War Diary | Louvencourt | 02/09/1916 | 02/09/1916 |

| | | | |
|---|---|---|---|
| War Diary | Le Hamel | 02/09/1916 | 02/09/1916 |
| War Diary | Ancre | 03/09/1916 | 03/09/1916 |
| War Diary | Englebelmer | | |
| War Diary | Betrancourt | 06/09/1916 | 06/09/1916 |
| War Diary | Beaumont Hamel | 10/09/1916 | 28/09/1916 |
| Heading | 116th Brigade 39th Division. 116th Brigade Machine Gun Company October 1916 | | |
| War Diary | Mailly-Maillet | 03/10/1916 | 03/10/1916 |
| War Diary | Englebelmer | 04/10/1916 | 04/10/1916 |
| War Diary | Auchonvillers | 04/10/1916 | 04/10/1916 |
| War Diary | Schwaben | 17/10/1916 | 17/10/1916 |
| War Diary | Redoubt | 23/10/1916 | 23/10/1916 |
| War Diary | Stuff Trench | 21/10/1916 | 22/10/1916 |
| War Diary | Aueluy Wood | 22/10/1916 | 22/10/1916 |
| War Diary | Jacob's Ladder | 22/10/1916 | 22/10/1916 |
| War Diary | Martinsart | 22/10/1916 | 22/10/1916 |
| War Diary | River Sector | 22/10/1916 | 22/10/1916 |
| War Diary | Authville | 22/10/1916 | 22/10/1916 |
| War Diary | 116th Brigade 39th Division. 116th Brigade Machine Gun Company November 1916 | | |
| War Diary | Authuile | 01/11/1916 | 01/11/1916 |
| War Diary | Martinsart | 02/11/1916 | 04/11/1916 |
| War Diary | Authville | 05/11/1916 | 05/11/1916 |
| War Diary | Martinsart | 06/11/1916 | 09/11/1916 |
| War Diary | Authuile | 10/11/1916 | 11/11/1916 |
| War Diary | Mesnil (Jacobs Ladder) | 12/11/1916 | 13/11/1916 |
| War Diary | Martinsart | 14/11/1916 | 14/11/1916 |
| War Diary | Warloy | 15/11/1916 | 15/11/1916 |
| War Diary | Freschvillers | 17/11/1916 | 17/11/1916 |
| War Diary | St. Jan-Ter-Bezen (Y Camp) | 19/11/1916 | 30/11/1916 |
| Heading | 116th Brigade. 39th Division 116th Brigade Machine Gun Company. December 1916 | | |
| Heading | 116th Coy., Machine Gun Corps 1st Dec-31st December 1916 | | |
| War Diary | 'Y' Camp And Poperinghe | 01/12/1916 | 11/12/1916 |
| War Diary | Canal Bank C 19c25.60 | 13/12/1916 | 23/12/1916 |
| War Diary | 'S' Camp In Poperinghe Elverdinghe Road (A3.31.4.) | 24/12/1916 | 24/12/1916 |
| War Diary | 'S' Camp In Poperinghe Elverdinghe Road. | 24/12/1916 | 30/12/1916 |
| War Diary | B13b.2.8.on the Elverdinghe Poperinghe | 30/12/1916 | 31/12/1916 |
| Heading | 116th Coy M.G. Corps War Diary The Month Of January 1917 Vol XI. | | |
| Heading | 116 Company M.G. Corps. Jan 1st-31st 1917 | | |
| War Diary | B13.b.20.80. Boesinghe Sector | 01/01/1917 | 17/01/1917 |
| War Diary | Railway Wood | 17/01/1917 | 17/01/1917 |
| War Diary | Ecole Ypres. | 17/01/1917 | 17/01/1917 |
| War Diary | I.9.C.15.00. (Zillebeke 28 NW & N.E). | 17/01/1917 | 17/01/1917 |
| War Diary | Ecole Ypres | 18/01/1917 | 31/01/1917 |
| Heading | War Diary For The Month Of February 1917, 116th Machine Gun Co Vol 12 | | |
| War Diary | Railway Wood Sector | 01/02/1917 | 02/02/1917 |
| War Diary | Railway Wood. | 03/02/1917 | 04/02/1917 |
| War Diary | Brandhoek | 04/02/1917 | 19/02/1917 |
| War Diary | Bollezeele | 18/02/1917 | 24/02/1917 |
| War Diary | Erie Camp | 25/02/1917 | 25/02/1917 |
| War Diary | The Bund Zillebeke Sector I.15.d.1.2 | 26/02/1917 | 26/02/1917 |
| War Diary | The Bund Zillebeke Sector | 26/02/1917 | 28/02/1917 |

| | | | |
|---|---|---|---|
| War Diary | Observatory Ridge Sector Zillebeke | | |
| Heading | War Diary of 116th Co. M.G. Corps For March 1917 Vol 13 | | |
| War Diary | Observatory | 01/03/1917 | 01/03/1917 |
| War Diary | Ridge Section. | 02/03/1917 | 02/03/1917 |
| War Diary | Zillebeke | 03/03/1917 | 04/03/1917 |
| War Diary | Erie Camp | 04/03/1917 | 31/03/1917 |
| Heading | War Diary of 116th Machine Gun Co For April 1917 Vol 14 | | |
| War Diary | Observatory | 01/04/1917 | 01/04/1917 |
| War Diary | Ridge Sector. | 01/04/1917 | 01/04/1917 |
| War Diary | Zillebeke | 01/04/1917 | 01/04/1917 |
| War Diary | HQ Bund | 02/04/1917 | 16/04/1917 |
| War Diary | Canal Bank | | |
| War Diary | | 17/04/1917 | 30/04/1917 |
| Miscellaneous | To H.Q. 116th Infantry Bde | 01/06/1917 | 01/06/1917 |
| Heading | From 1st-31st May 1917 116 Goy., Machine Gun Corps Vol 15 | | |
| War Diary | 'S' Camp | 01/05/1917 | 01/05/1917 |
| War Diary | Wizernes | 02/05/1917 | 02/05/1917 |
| War Diary | Le Val D'Acquin | 03/05/1917 | 07/05/1917 |
| War Diary | Val D'Acquin | 08/05/1917 | 14/05/1917 |
| War Diary | Wizernes | 15/05/1917 | 15/05/1917 |
| War Diary | Nordpeene | 16/05/1917 | 16/05/1917 |
| War Diary | Wormhoudt | 17/05/1917 | 23/05/1917 |
| War Diary | D Camp Ref Map Belgium 28. N.W. B.30. Central. | 24/05/1917 | 28/05/1917 |
| War Diary | D Camp B.30 Central | 29/05/1917 | 30/05/1917 |
| War Diary | Canal Bank Hill Top Sector C.25.a.8.2 | 31/05/1917 | 31/05/1917 |
| Heading | War Diary of 116 Company M.G. Corps From June 1st 1917-June 30th 1917 Vol 16 | | |
| War Diary | Canal-Bank Hill Top Sector C25a8.2 | 01/06/1917 | 03/06/1917 |
| War Diary | Canal-Bank Hill Top Sector H.Q C25a8.2 | 03/06/1917 | 06/06/1917 |
| War Diary | Canal-Bank Hill Top Sector H.Q C25a8.2 St-Julian. | 07/06/1917 | 08/06/1917 |
| War Diary | Canal-Bank Hill Top Sector St-Julian. | 08/06/1917 | 09/06/1917 |
| War Diary | Hill Top Sector. St Julian 28 NW.2 | 10/06/1917 | 14/06/1917 |
| War Diary | Hill Top Sector. | 15/06/1917 | 21/06/1917 |
| War Diary | Moulle | 22/06/1917 | 30/06/1917 |
| Miscellaneous | | | |
| Heading | War Diary of 116 Company M.G. Corps From July 1st To July 31st 1917 Vol 17 | | |
| War Diary | Moule | 01/07/1917 | 13/07/1917 |
| Miscellaneous | Indirect Overhead Fire. | 13/07/1917 | 13/07/1917 |
| Miscellaneous | Barrage Scheme | | |
| War Diary | | 14/07/1917 | 16/07/1917 |
| War Diary | Z Camp | 17/07/1917 | 22/07/1917 |
| War Diary | C Camp | 23/07/1917 | 29/07/1917 |
| War Diary | Canal Bank No 90 Dugout | 29/07/1917 | 31/07/1917 |
| Heading | War Diary of 116 Coy. M.G. Corps. August 1st-31st 1917. Vol 18 | | |
| War Diary | Calf Reserve Tr. | 01/08/1917 | 08/08/1917 |
| War Diary | Billets X 4.C.4.4. (Belg & France Sheet 27) | 09/08/1917 | 12/08/1917 |
| War Diary | Ridge Wood N.5.a. | 13/08/1917 | 13/08/1917 |
| War Diary | Dam Strasse Q4c.33 Map Wytchaete | 13/08/1917 | 22/08/1917 |
| War Diary | Ridge Wood | 23/08/1917 | 26/08/1917 |
| War Diary | The Bluff I.34.c.4.1 | 27/08/1917 | 31/08/1917 |

| Type | Description | From | To |
|---|---|---|---|
| War Diary | War Diary of 116 Coy M.G. Corps Sept 1-30 1917 Vol 19 | | |
| Miscellaneous | Operation Orders By Captain At Jackson Commanding 116 MGC. | 17/09/1917 | 17/09/1917 |
| Miscellaneous | E Battery. | | |
| Miscellaneous | E Battery Switch Targets. | | |
| Miscellaneous | E Battery | | |
| Miscellaneous | E Battery Switch Targets. | | |
| War Diary | Battle Wood Sector (Bluff Tunnels). | 01/09/1917 | 07/09/1917 |
| War Diary | Larch Wood 129c 15.85 | 07/09/1917 | 12/09/1917 |
| War Diary | Chippewa Camp | 13/09/1917 | 19/09/1917 |
| War Diary | Larch Wood | 19/09/1917 | 30/09/1917 |
| Heading | War Diary 116 M.G. Coy. Oct 1st-Oct 31st 1917 Vol 20 | | |
| War Diary | Mt. Kokereele | 01/10/1917 | 16/10/1917 |
| War Diary | Coy HQ Canada Tunnels | 17/10/1917 | 18/10/1917 |
| War Diary | Hedge Street Tunnels | 19/10/1917 | 20/10/1917 |
| War Diary | Willebeek Sheet 28 N9d 7.5 | 21/10/1917 | 24/10/1917 |
| War Diary | Hedge St Tunnel | 24/10/1917 | 25/10/1917 |
| Miscellaneous | Firing Report 116 M.G. Coy. 26 Oct 1917 5-4 3a.m to 8-18 a.m. | 26/10/1917 | 26/10/1917 |
| Miscellaneous | Barrage Table "A" Artillery | 26/10/1917 | 26/10/1917 |
| Miscellaneous | Barrage Table "B" Battery | 23/10/1917 | 23/10/1917 |
| Miscellaneous | Barrage Table D Batt | 23/10/1917 | 23/10/1917 |
| War Diary | | 26/10/1917 | 27/10/1917 |
| War Diary | Carnarvon Camp. | 26/10/1917 | 29/10/1917 |
| War Diary | Chippewa Camp. | 29/10/1917 | 31/10/1917 |
| Miscellaneous | H.Q., 7th Division. | 04/11/1917 | 04/11/1917 |
| Heading | War Diary 1st To 30th November 1917 116th Coy M.G. Corps Vol 21 | | |
| War Diary | Chippewa Camp | 01/11/1917 | 04/11/1917 |
| War Diary | Hedge St Tunnel | 05/11/1917 | 06/11/1917 |
| Operation(al) Order(s) | Operation Order No. 5. By Lt. E. ? Commdg 11th Coy M.G. Corps. | 07/11/1917 | 07/11/1917 |
| War Diary | | 07/11/1917 | 13/11/1917 |
| War Diary | Dead Dog Farm. | 14/11/1917 | 25/11/1917 |
| War Diary | Zevecoten | 26/11/1917 | 27/11/1917 |
| War Diary | Rweld. | 27/11/1917 | 30/11/1917 |
| Heading | War Diary Dec 1st To 31st 1917 Vol 22 | | |
| War Diary | Rweld | 01/12/1917 | 10/12/1917 |
| War Diary | Lart | 11/12/1917 | 30/12/1917 |
| War Diary | Siege Camp Elverdinghe Belgium 28 N.W. | 31/12/1917 | 31/12/1917 |
| Heading | 116 M G Coy War Diary Jan 1st-31st 1918 Vol 23 | | |
| War Diary | Siege Camp | 01/01/1918 | 21/01/1918 |
| War Diary | School Camp L 3c Sheet 28 | 22/01/1918 | 26/01/1918 |
| War Diary | Sailly Le Sec (Amiens 1/100,000). | 27/01/1918 | 30/01/1918 |
| War Diary | Heudecourt France 57 SE | 31/01/1918 | 31/01/1918 |
| Heading | War Diary 116 M.G. Coy Feb. 1st-28th 1918 Vol 24 | | |
| War Diary | Heudicourt Ref. Gauche Wood 1/10,000 Adv. Chq. W12b.61.77 | 01/02/1918 | 26/02/1918 |
| War Diary | Line. | 27/02/1918 | 28/02/1918 |
| Heading | 39th Division 116th Infy Bde Lt Trench Mortars Jly-Sep 1916 | | |
| Heading | 116 L.T.M.B. July, August, 8 September 1916 | | |
| Heading | War Diary of 116 Machine Gun By Jan 1st August 1916 To 31st August 1916 Vol 6 | | |

| | | | |
|---|---|---|---|
| Miscellaneous | 116th Light Trench Mortar Battery. | | |
| Heading | 116 Light Trench Mortar Battery Report Of Operations On June 30th | | |
| War Diary | Guinchy | 02/07/1917 | 11/07/1917 |
| War Diary | Ferme De Bois | 21/07/1918 | 21/07/1918 |
| War Diary | 11th R. Suss. R. | 06/07/1918 | 06/07/1918 |
| War Diary | 14th Hants. | 07/07/1918 | 07/07/1918 |
| War Diary | 13th R. Suss. R. | 19/07/1918 | 19/07/1918 |
| War Diary | 12th R. Sun R | 19/07/1918 | 19/07/1918 |
| War Diary | Cuinchy | 10/07/1918 | 13/07/1918 |
| War Diary | Ferme De Bois | 22/07/1918 | 23/07/1918 |
| War Diary | Festubert. | 28/08/1918 | 30/08/1918 |
| Heading | War Diary of 116 Trench Mortar Battery For 1st July To 31st July 1916 Vol I. | | |
| War Diary | Givenchy | 07/08/1916 | 07/08/1916 |
| War Diary | Hamel Section. | 30/08/1916 | 30/08/1916 |
| War Diary | Hamel | 03/09/1916 | 03/09/1916 |
| War Diary | Auchonvil-Lers & Redan Sections | 26/09/1916 | 26/09/1916 |

```
TRAINING CADRE
39TH DIVISION
116TH INFY BDE
```

4TH BN EAST YORKS

AUG-NOV 1918

FROM 50 DIV
150 Bde

Army Form C. 2118.

4 E York Regt

Vol 35

# WAR DIARY
or
## INTELLIGENCE SUMMARY.
(Erase heading not required.)

| Place | Date | Hour | Summary of Events and Information | Remarks and references to Appendices |
|---|---|---|---|---|
| ROUXMESNIL CAMP | Aug 10th | | As training base plus Band. | |
| | 15th | | Strength 8 off. 62 OR | |
| | 15th | | Entrained for ETAPLES transferred to 116th Inf Bde 39th Div together with 4th Yorks, 5th Yorks & 4th S. Staffs. | |
| | 16th | | In camp at CUCQ | |
| | 20th | | | |
| | 21st | | Moved to camp at Sano dunes near Le TOUQUET | |
| | 22nd | | In camp commenced tactical training of officers | |
| | 31st | | at Base Depot at ETAPLES | |
| | | | Strength 4 officers 65 OR. | |

Philips Capt
cmdg 4th act/Yorks R

(6339) Wt. W160/M3016 1,500,000 10/17 McA & W Ltd (E 1898) Forms W3091.    Army Form W.3091.

## Cover for Documents.

### Nature of Enclosures.

CONFIDENTIAL

WAR DIARY.

4TH. BN. EAST

YORKSHIRE REGT.

SEPTEMBER 1918.

### Notes, or Letters written.

VOLUME XIII.

Army Form C. 2118.

# WAR DIARY
## or
## INTELLIGENCE SUMMARY.
*(Erase heading not required.)*

Instructions regarding War Diaries and Intelligence Summaries are contained in F. S. Regs., Part II. and the Staff Manual respectively. Title pages will be prepared in manuscript.

| Place | Date | Hour | Summary of Events and Information | Remarks and references to Appendices |
|---|---|---|---|---|
| Sept | /30 | | Battalion training Cadre in camp near CWCO. Time spent in making camp for No 3 Officers Training School and some training individually. | |
| | | | Strength of Cadre 9 officers 65 OR including Band (which is acting as Camp Band). | |

M.I. Wilkinson Lee
Cmdg 4 East Yorks R.

(6339) Wt. W160/M3016 1,500,000 10/17 McA & W Ltd (E1898) Forms W3091.     Army Form W.3091.

T.C/39

## Cover for Documents.

### Nature of Enclosures.

# CONFIDENTIAL WAR DIARY.

## 4TH. BN. E. YORKSHIRE REGT.

### Notes, or Letters written.

## OCTOBER 1918.

## VOLUME XLIII.

# WAR DIARY
## or
## INTELLIGENCE SUMMARY.
(Erase heading not required.)

Army Form C. 2118.

| Place | Date | Hour | Summary of Events and Information | Remarks and references to Appendices |
|---|---|---|---|---|
| Oct 1/1916 | | | Battalion training in camp near Cucq. | |
| | 11th | | Col. N.T. Wilkinson D.S.O. relinquishes command of Batt & to command 1st Bn. K.O.S.B. | |
| | 16th | | Col. E.W. Montgomery M.C. 1st Norfolk R. assumes acting command of Battn. | |
| | 31. | | Effective strength of Battn. 9 officers 76 O.R. | |

O/Phillips Capt
6/ East Yorks R
Cmdg 4 East Yorks R

4 East York R

Vol 43

**WAR DIARY**
or
**INTELLIGENCE SUMMARY.**
(Erase heading not required.)

| Place | Date | Hour | Summary of Events and Information | Remarks and references to Appendices |
|---|---|---|---|---|
| Nov 1. | | | At Camp near CUCQ Orders received to demobilize Battalion commencing 6th Nov 1916. This was proceeded with personnel being sent to "F" I.B.D. on the 7th inst. All officers being kept quiet to units | |

Lt Col
CmDg 4 East York R

4 E Yrks

**WAR DIARY**
or
**INTELLIGENCE SUMMARY.**
(Erase heading not required.)

Army Form C. 2118.

1/4 BATTN YORKSHIRE REGT
TC/39
VOL 33

38 T
1 sheet

| Place | Date | Hour | Summary of Events and Information | Remarks and references to Appendices |
|---|---|---|---|---|
| ROUXMESNIL | Aug 1 -16 | | Training of N.C.O. & Bn. Coln. Also set subjects such as Drill, Gas, Musketry etc. Bn. Coln. also Radio, Lewis Gun, Officer - Musketry. Cricket matches with 1/5th RFD Acc, & DTMRC all won. Cmft gun & Lewis gun complete at L Camp. Bn returned to ROUXMESNIL 15.8.18. & detrained at STAPLES 16.8.18. & marched to COCQ. | |
| COCQ | Aug 16 -20 | | & pitched camp & a common + training continued at this subjects. | |
| LE TOUQUET | Aug 20 to Aug 31 | | Bn. struck camp at COCQ and moved to new camp sites 2 miles adjacent golf course AE TOUQUET. Walk on camp & drawing horse lines. Training Lewis Gun, Tactical Schemes Bayonet fighting, Musketry, Drill & Signalling. Several football matches with other Coys. of Bn. Reinforcements joined 2/ps C Gooden - Chalmers and 2 other ranks. Strength 1st Aug 1918 - 11 Offs. 1071 OR NCOs. 30 31st 1918 - 15 - 83 - 720. Ration strength at 1st Aug 18 - 19 - 796 - 730. " 31st " - 11 - 76 - 730. | |

M. Leman Lt Col
1/4 Y & L Regt

P.M. 27 1/4 Y&L Regt.

# 4th Bn. Yorkshire Regt. WAR DIARY

## INTELLIGENCE SUMMARY

SEPTEMBER 1918.  Army Form C. 2118.

Vol 39

| Place | Date | Hour | Summary of Events and Information | Remarks and references to Appendices |
|---|---|---|---|---|
| STELLA PLAGE (LE TOUQUET) | Sep 1st to 30th | | Daily working parties supplied to R.E's to assist in construction of Officers Training Depot & Recreation ground. Officers from Base depots taken in Tactical Schemes near Water Tower Etaples. Parades of our own N.C.O's & men chiefly consisted of Communication & Squad Drill, Lewis Gun & map reading classes. Battalion football team played many matches with other units of Brigade, all of which were won. The Camp team also beat the G.H.Q. Lewis Gun School & "F" Infantry Base Depot. Ration Strength 1st Sep. 5 offrs 77 other ranks<br>" " 30th " 7 " 53 " "<br>Effective Strength 1st Sept. 8 offrs 81 other ranks<br>" " 30th " 10 " 81 " "<br>Reinforcements during month 2 officers.<br>Casualties  do.  do.  nil. | |

J Clingi  Capt
Commanding

4TH BATTALION
YORKSHIRE
REGIMENT.
No.
Date 3-10-18

# 4th Bn Yorkshire Regt.
## WAR DIARY
## INTELLIGENCE SUMMARY

Army Form C. 2118.

OCTOBER 1918.

| Place | Date | Hour | Summary of Events and Information | Remarks and references to Appendices |
|---|---|---|---|---|
| STELLA PLAGE (LE TOUQUET) | | | The Bn: Cadre, in Le Gouffre Camp, continued the previous months programme of training and map reading classes. Small working parties supplied to R.E.'s daily to help in construction of No 3. OFFICERS CAMP. All outdoor sports received attention. | |
| | 6th | | BRIGADE SPORTS. The 1st prizes were won by the Bn: for the Mile Race and Obstacle Race. 2nd prizes were secured in the Relay Race, Long Jump and Wrestling on Horseback Cozzies.I. The Bn had the second highest number of points. "all events" the 18th Reinforcement Training Camps. | |
| | 18th | | CAPT: BRADLEY, J.R. Left Bn: to join "No 1. Reinforcement Training Camps." | |
| | 25th | | BRIG: GEN: WYATT. D.S.O. acting on behalf of French Government presented C.Q.M.S Jackson H.J. with CROIX de GUERRE with SILVER STAR. | |
| | 27th | | LT: COL: BARNES. D.S.O. Proceeded to 21st. Division. | |
| | 31st | | LT: COL: KITCHING. D.S.O. Assumed command of Bn: | |

Reinforcements during the month
do             do
Casualties

|  | Officers | Other Ranks |
|---|---|---|
| | 1 | 5 |
| | Nil | 1 (gone in hospital-sickness) |

| | | Officers | Other Ranks |
|---|---|---|---|
| Ration Strength | 1st | 7 | 53. |
| do | 31st | 8. | 62. |
| Effective Strength | 1st | 10. | 81. |
| do | 31st | 9. | 85. |

C.W. Wilson
Lt: Col: Comdg
4th Bn Yorkshire Regt.

Yorks

TRAINING CADRE
39TH DIVISION
116TH INFY BDE

5TH BN YORKSHIRE REGT
AUG - NOV 1918

50 DIV
150 Bde

demobled Nov 1918

5th Bn Yorkshire Regt.

Army Form C. 2118.

# WAR DIARY
## OF
## INTELLIGENCE SUMMARY.
(Erase heading not required.)

for AUGUST 1918.

Volume IV

Vol 46

| Place | Date | Hour | Summary of Events and Information | Remarks and references to Appendices |
|---|---|---|---|---|
| In the Field | August 1st to 14th | | Training of Battalion Training cadre at ROUXMESNIL Camp – near DIEPPE. | |
| do | 15th | | Marched from ROUXMESNIL Camp to the Station & entrained at 10.P.M. Detrained at ETAPLES 1.P.M on the 16th inst. Marched to CUCQ Camp. | |
| do | 16th to 19th | | Training of Battalion training cadre at CUCQ Camp. | |
| do | 20th | | Marched from CUCQ Camp to NEW Camp, near LE TOUQUET Lewis – Gun School. | |
| do | 21st to 31st | | Training of Battalion Training cadre at NEW Camp | |

8/18
31

Dunley Head Lt Col
Comdg 5th Bn Yorkshire Regt.

35.12
1 sheet

5th Bn Yorkshire Regt. Training Cadre

# WAR DIARY
## INTELLIGENCE SUMMARY
for month of SEPTEMBER 1918
Volume V.

Army Form C. 2118.

36.W.
1 sheet

| Place | Date | Hour | Summary of Events and Information | Remarks and references to Appendices |
|---|---|---|---|---|
| In the Field | Sept 1st to 30. | | At STELLA-PLAGE CAMP. Training, Recreation & Working Parties. Tactical Schemes for Officers. | |

Douglas Jones Lt Col
Comdg 5th Bn Yorkshire Regt.

Army Form C. 2118.

5th Bn Yorkshire Regt. Training Cadre.

WAR DIARY
or
INTELLIGENCE SUMMARY.

for month of OCTOBER 1918.

Volume VI.

(Erase heading not required.)

NC 4

| Place | Date | Hour | Summary of Events and Information | Remarks and references to Appendices |
|---|---|---|---|---|
| In the field | Oct 1st to 31st | | At STELLA-PLAGE CAMP. Training, Recreation & Working Parties. Tactical Schemes for Officers. | |

Aylmer Hunt
Lt Col
Comdg 5th Bn Yorkshire Regt.

87.W
where

14

5th Bn Yorkshire Regt Training Camp
for month of
November, 1916.
Volume VII

**WAR DIARY**
or
**INTELLIGENCE SUMMARY.**

Army Form C. 2118.

| Place | Date | Hour | Summary of Events and Information | Remarks and references to Appendices |
|---|---|---|---|---|
| In the field | Nov 1st to 30th 1916 | | At STELLA PLAGE CAMP. Training. Recreation training parties. Tactical Schemes for Officers. Battalion demobilized. | |

Rolfe Ma?
Lt Col
Comdg 5th Bn Yorkshire Regt.

5 Yorks

**TRAINING CADRE**
**39TH DIVISION**
**116TH INFY BDE**

4TH BN STH STAFFS
AUG - NOV 1918

From 25 DIV — 7 BDE

25 DIV 7 BDE OCT 17 to MAY 1918
50 DIV. COMP BDE June July 1918

# WAR DIARY
## INTELLIGENCE SUMMARY

Army Form C. 2118.

| Place | Date | Hour | Summary of Events and Information | Remarks and references to Appendices |
|---|---|---|---|---|
| ROUXMESNIL CAMP DIEPPE | 1-8-18 | | Specialist Training by Personnel of Training Cadre | |
| | 2-8-18 | | " " " " " | |
| | 3-8-18 | | " " " " " | |
| | 4-8-18 | | Divisional church parade at MARTIN EGLISE | |
| | 5-8-18 | | Specialist Training by Personnel of Training Cadre. 2nd Lieut C. BATES D.S.O. M.C. D.C.M proceeded to No 3 I.B.D. ROUEN and is struck off strength | |
| | 6-8-18 | | Specialist Training by Personnel of Training Cadre | |
| | 7-8-18 | | " " " " " | |
| | 8-8-18 | | " " " " " ... 2nd Lieut O.H. MASON M.C. granted leave from 8-8-18 to 22-8-18 | |
| | 9-8-18 | | Specialist Training by Personnel of Training Cadre. 2nd Lieut G.L. BROWN granted leave from 9-8-18 to 23-8-18. Captain A.B. MILLER D.S.O. M.C. proceeded to course of instruction on Tactical Exercises WISQUES. | |
| | 10-8-18 | | Specialist Training by Personnel of Training Cadre. Lt Col R.J. MORRIS D.S.O. acted as Umpire at 50th Divisional Field day. 24 Signallers reported from Cameron etc. | |
| | 11-8-18 | | Specialist Training by Personnel of Training Cadre. The 24 Signallers being surplus to Training Cadre, proceeded to Base Depot. R.E.O | |

Army Form C. 2118.

# WAR DIARY
## or
## INTELLIGENCE SUMMARY.
*(Erase heading not required.)*

Instructions regarding War Diaries and Intelligence Summaries are contained in F. S. Regs., Part II, and the Staff Manual respectively. Title pages will be prepared in manuscript.

| Place | Date | Hour | Summary of Events and Information | Remarks and references to Appendices |
|---|---|---|---|---|
| ROUXMESNIL Camp DIEPPE | 12-8-18 | | Specialist Training. Any personnel of Training Cadre, The 2/4 Seaforths, who reported on 10th inst. proceeded to Base Depot. | |
| " | 13-8-18 | | Moved to WEST end of Camp. Cleaning of equipment. Warning order received re move of Training Cadre and 15th inst. advance parties 14th inst. | |
| " | 14-8-18 | | Advance party consisting of 1 officer (2/Lt W.H.R. LLOYDS) and 2 other ranks proceeded to C.U.C.Q. 5.30 a.m. Lt.Col. MORRIS D.S.O. (commanding) proceeded on leave to U.K. (14 days) | |
| " | 15-8-18 | | Battalion paraded to move 8.35 pm. Train left ROUXMESNIL 10.30 pm. | |
| CUCQ Camp ETAPLES | 16-8-18 | | Arrived ETAPLES 1.30 p.m. and march to CUCQ camp. Time of arrival Camp 3-5 p.m. | |
| " | 17-8-18 | | Commanding officer went to see proposed site for new camp 10 a.m. 9.30 am to 11.30 p.m. Cleaning of equipment de. parlong to Kit Inspection 11.30 a.m. | |
| " | 18-8-18 | | Church Parades. | |
| " | 19-8-18 | | Battalion marched over to parade ground for exercising drill on trench day. | |
| LETOUQUET ETAPLES | 20-8-18 | | Battalion moved over into camps, to new camp one mile away on sand dunes within 1/4 mile of G.H.Q. Lewis Gun School. | |
| " | 21-8-18 | | Infantry Camp. Lt. H.A. HAWKINS M.C. proceeded to 4th Corps School | |

Army Form C. 2118.

# WAR DIARY
## or
## INTELLIGENCE SUMMARY.
*(Erase heading not required.)*

Instructions regarding War Diaries and Intelligence Summaries are contained in F. S. Regs., Part II. and the Staff Manual respectively. Title pages will be prepared in manuscript.

| Place | Date | Hour | Summary of Events and Information | Remarks and references to Appendices |
|---|---|---|---|---|
| LE TOUQUET | 22-8-18 | | Specialist training by personnel of Training Cadre. | |
| " | 23-8-18 | | Work under R.E. Supervision. | |
| " | 24-8-18 | | Specialist training by personnel of Training Cadre. | |
| " | 25-8-18 | | Church parades. Capt. A.B. MILLER D.S.O. M.C. returned from Tactical Schemes Course, WISQUE. | |
| " | 26-8-18 | | Specialist training by personnel of Training Cadre. | |
| " | 27-8-18 | | " " " " " " | |
| " | 28-8-18 | | " " " " " " | |
| " | 29-8-18 | | " " " " " " Captain R.D. OLDHAM, M.C. and Captain A.B. MILLER D.S.O. M.C. went over ground over which a Tactical Scheme by the officers of the Base Depôt is to be carried out on 30-8-18 | |
| " | 30-8-18 | | Specialist training by personnel of Training Cadre. Captain R.D. OLDHAM M.C. acted as instructor to 15 officers from Base Depôt on a Tactical scheme. 2nd Lt. G.L. BROWN returned from leave. | |
| " | 31-8-18 | | Specialist Training by personnel of Training Cadre. Capt. A.B. MILLER DSO M.C. acted as instructor to 15 officers from Base Depôt on Tactical Scheme. Lt.Col. R.J. MORRIS DSO (Commanding) returned from leave to U.K. | |

R.J. Morris
Lt. Col.
Comdg 4th South Staffords. R.

# WAR DIARY
## INTELLIGENCE SUMMARY

Army Form C. 2118.

| Place | Date | Hour | Summary of Events and Information | Remarks and references to Appendices |
|---|---|---|---|---|
| LE TOUQUET | 1-9-18 | | Church Parade. Capt O.H. MASON MC returned from leave | |
| " | 2-9-18 | | Work under R.E. Supervision. Capt R.D. OLDHAM MC acted as instructor for 15 | |
| " | 3-9-18 | | Officers from Base at ETAPLES on tactical scheme. Specialist Training by personnel of Training Cadre. Capt A.B. MILLER DSO MC and 2nd Capt G.H. MASON MC acted as instructors. | |
| " | 4-9-18 | | Specialist Training by personnel of Training Cadre | RDO |
| " | 5-9-18 | | Specialist Training by personnel of Training Cadre. Capt A.B. MILLER DSO MC acted as instructor. | RDO |
| " | 6-9-18 | | Specialist Training by personnel of Training Cadre. Capt. R.D. OLDHAM MC and Capt B.H. MASON MC acted as instructors on tactical scheme | |
| " | 7-9-18 | | Specialist Training by personnel of Training Cadre. A/Col R.T. MORRIS DSO assumed command of 1st Battalion | RDO |
| " | 8-9-18 | | Work under R.E. Supervision. Church Service | RDO |
| " | 9-9-18 | | Work under R.E. Supervision | |
| " | 10-9-18 | | " | |
| " | 11-9-18 | | " | |

Army Form C. 2118.

# WAR DIARY
## or
## INTELLIGENCE SUMMARY.
*(Erase heading not required.)*

Instructions regarding War Diaries and Intelligence Summaries are contained in F. S. Regs., Part II. and the Staff Manual respectively. Title pages will be prepared in manuscript.

| Place | Date | Hour | Summary of Events and Information | Remarks and references to Appendices |
|---|---|---|---|---|
| LE TOUQUET | 12-9-18 | | Work under R.E. Supervision | |
| " | 13-9-18 | | " " " " | |
| " | 14-9-18 | | " " " " | |
| " | 15-9-18 | | Church parade | |
| " | 16-9-18 | | Work under R.E. Supervision | |
| " | 17-9-18 | | " " " " | |
| " | 18-9-18 | | Specialist training by personnel of Training Centre R.S.M. NEALE admitted to Hospital | |
| " | 19-9-18 | | " " " " | |
| " | 20-9-18 | | " " " " | |
| " | 21-9-18 | | " " " " | |
| " | 22-9-18 | | Church parade | |
| " | 23-9-18 | | Working parties | |
| " | 24-9-18 | | Battalion parade | |
| " | 25-9-18 | | Working parties | |
| " | 26-9-18 | | " " | |
| " | 27-9-18 | | C.O.'s inspection at 2 p.m. | |

Army Form C. 2118.

# WAR DIARY
## or
## INTELLIGENCE SUMMARY.
*(Erase heading not required.)*

| Place | Date | Hour | Summary of Events and Information | Remarks and references to Appendices |
|---|---|---|---|---|
| | 28-9-18 | | Work & Indoor. Capt. G.H. MASON M.C. sent to General School at 1st Army School | |
| | 29-9-18 | | Church Service. | |
| | 30-9-18 | | Fatigues etc. | |

J.E. Utter Lt. Col.
Commdg 1st Bn. South Staffordshire Regt.

Army Form C. 2118.

# WAR DIARY
## or
## INTELLIGENCE SUMMARY.
*(Erase heading not required.)*

Vol 8

| Place | Date | Hour | Summary of Events and Information | Remarks and references to Appendices |
|---|---|---|---|---|
| LE TOUQUET | 1-10-18 | | Training Supersonel of Training Cadre. Capt A.B. MILLER D.S.O. M.C. acted as instructor on Tactical Scheme. | |
| " | 2-10-18 | | Working parties. | |
| " | 3-10-18 | | " " Brigade Demonstration Platoon formed. Capt C.E.W. CHARRINGTON M.C. | |
| " | 4-10-18 | | Working parties. Lt Col R.J. MORRIS D.S.O. acted as Director and Capt R.D. OLDHAM M.C. as instructor on tactical scheme carried out by officers of Convalescent Camp. | |
| " | 5-10-18 | | Preliminary heats for Tug of War held. The Battalion team beat the 5th B. York Yeom. | |
| " | 6-10-18 | | Church Services. Finals of Camp sports. | |
| " | 7-10-18 | | Parades. Capt R.D. OLDHAM M.C. acted as instructor on Tactical Scheme. | |
| " | 8-10-18 | | Billets and Kit Inspection. Capt A.B. MILLER D.S.O. M.C. acted as instructor on Tactical scheme. | |
| " | 9-10-18 | | Divisional Commander interviewed Commanding officers. 2/Lt W.W.R. LLOYD M.C. proceeded on leave to ENGLAND | |
| " | 10-10-18 | | Working parties. | |
| " | 11-10-18 | | " " | |
| " | 12-10-18 | | Lt Col R.J. MORRIS D.S.O. assumed duties of Camp Commandant vice Lt Col WILKINSON D.S.O. | |

Army Form C. 2118.

# WAR DIARY
## or
## INTELLIGENCE SUMMARY.
*(Erase heading not required.)*

Instructions regarding War Diaries and Intelligence Summaries are contained in F. S. Regs., Part II. and the Staff Manual respectively. Title pages will be prepared in manuscript.

| Place | Date | Hour | Summary of Events and Information | Remarks and references to Appendices |
|---|---|---|---|---|
| LE TOUQUET | 13-10-18 | | Church Services. | |
| " | 14-10-18 | | Fatigues. | |
| " | 15-10-18 | | Fatigues. | |
| " | 16-10-18 | | " | |
| " | 17-10-18 | | " | |
| " | 18-10-18 | | " | |
| " | 19-10-18 | | Lt.Col. Brown to Course 1st Army Signal School. Church Services. Lt.Col E.W. MONTGOMERIE M.C. took over duties of Camp Commandant. | |
| " | 20-10-18 | | | |
| " | 21-23/10/18 | | Battn Tactical Exercises and Fatigues. Capt H. THOMAS to hospital 21-10-18 | |
| " | 24-10-18 | | Presentation of D.C.M. Ribbons by G.O.C. 39th Division. | |
| " | 25-10-18 | | Capt THOMAS from hospital. | |
| " | 26-31/10/18 | | Fatigues. | |

M.W. Turnis Lt. Col.
Commdg. 4th Bn. S.Staffs. Regt.

4 S Staff R

Army Form C. 2118.

# WAR DIARY
## or
## INTELLIGENCE SUMMARY.
*(Erase heading not required.)*

Instructions regarding War Diaries and Intelligence Summaries are contained in F. S. Regs., Part II. and the Staff Manual respectively. Title pages will be prepared in manuscript.

| Place | Date | Hour | Summary of Events and Information | Remarks and references to Appendices |
|---|---|---|---|---|
| STELLA - PLAGE | 1/4/18 | - | Working Parties - Capt. r. a/Mr R.D. OLDHAM M.C. attached to hapler. | |
| | 2/4/18 | - | do | |
| | 3/4/18 | - | Church services | |
| | 4/4/18 | - | Working Parties - Lt. Col. R.T. INGRAM D.S.O. (Commanding) attend conference at 116th S.R. HQrs. | |
| | 5/4/18 | - | Working Parties - All officers attend lecture on Organization & Training (by Brig. Gen. G.J. Duggan CMG, DSO) at ETAPLES. followed by a demonstration (by 15 Powles MGC) in the handling of the Lewis M.G. | |
| | 6/4/18 | - | Battalion Centre receives orders to demobilize - 19 Officers proceed to Base Depot. | |
| | 7/4/18 8/4/18 | - | 19 other ranks proceed to Base Depot. Remaining Officers & Other ranks proceed to join Nos. 1. 2. & 3 Young Soldiers Battalions. | |

P. 14

M. Ingram Lt Col.
Comp't 4th South Staffords

6th S. Staffs

TRAINING CADRE
 TH DIVISION
 TH INFY BDE
   BDE

 TH BN NTH STAFFS
 AUG-NOV 1918

DEMOBILISED NOV 1918

DIV 176 BDE

To:- Headquarters,
        116th Infantry Brigade.

        Herewith War Diary of this Unit for the
month of September, 1918.

                                    T. Bassett, Capt,
                            Comdg. 5th North Staffs Regt.

Sept. 30th, 1918.

Army Form C. 2118.

# WAR DIARY
## or
## INTELLIGENCE SUMMARY.

(Erase heading not required) 5th North Staffs Reg<sup>t</sup> Training Cadre

August 1918.

| Place | Date | Hour | Summary of Events and Information | Remarks and references to Appendices |
|---|---|---|---|---|
| LA PANNE | 1 | | Recreational Training. | W.R.O. |
| | 2 | | " | |
| | 3 | | " | |
| | 4 | | Sunday:- All Officers + N.C.O. attended lectures at NORDAUSQUE by Lt. Col JAMES R.A.F. "Refinements improving the Lewis gun" | W.R.O. |
| | 5 | | Recreational Training - 2nd Round at Cricket League L. Lucieres 75. 5th N.K. Staffs 69. | W.R.O. |
| | 6 | | " | W.R.O. |
| | 7 | | " | |
| | 8 | | " Range firing at Maf. Ref Sheet 27.A NE FRANCE 1:10000 J28 C. | |
| | 9 | | " | |
| | 10 | | " | |
| | 11 | | Sunday 3 Officers + 12 O.R's attend Special Parade Service at TERDEGHEM. Hm Majesty the King arriving at 11.0 am. | W.R.O. |
| | 12 | | Recreational Training - from the date hereunder 118 Brigade & 119 Brigade at HERBINGHEM. | W.R.O. |
| | 13 | | Proceeded by Motor Route to CUCQ COMMON - billeting the night 13/14 at HERBINGHEM | W.R.O. |
| | 14 | | Continued " " " " " billeting the night 14/15 at SAMER. | W.R.O. |
| CUCQ COMMON | 15 | | Arrived " " " | W.R.O. |
| | 16 | | Recreational Training | W.R.O. |
| | 17 | | " | W.R.O. |
| | 18 | | Sunday. Church Parade. C.of E. Service held in Y.M.C.A. hut. | W.R.O. |
| ETAPLES ADMINISTRATIVE DISTRICT | 19 | | Pitches Camp at ETAPLES. Map Ref Lewis Gun School /10000 MR 25.25 | W.R.O. |
| | 20 | | Improving Camp | W.R.O. |
| | 21 | | Digging drainage to fields adjoining under R.E. | W.R.O. |
| | 22 | | " | W.R.O. |

Army Form C. 2118.

# WAR DIARY
## or
## INTELLIGENCE SUMMARY.

(Erase heading not required.) 5th North Staffs Regt Training Cadre

Instructions regarding War Diaries and Intelligence Summaries are contained in F. S. Regs., Part II. and the Staff Manual respectively. Title pages will be prepared in manuscript.

August 1918

| Place | Date | Hour | Summary of Events and Information | Remarks and references to Appendices |
|---|---|---|---|---|
| ETAPLES A DISTRICT | 23 | | Recreational Training. Bathing parade (Sea) | W.O. |
| " | 24 | | " | W.O. |
| " | 25 | | Sunday. C.of E. Service held in field adjoining Camp. — Battalion on half day for the day. | W.O. |
| " | 26 | | Staining Tests. Bathing parade (Sea) | W.O. |
| " | 27 | | Staining Tests. Parade for Baths at Etaples Gun School. | W.O. |
| " | 28 | | Fatigue duties. | W.O. |
| " | 29 | | Arms drill — Kit inspection — | W.O. |
| " | 30 | | Tactical Schemes — Instruction to officers from Base Depots | W.O. |
| " | 31 | | Tactical schemes Instruction to officers from Base Depots | W.O. |

Sept. 1st 1918.

J.P. Wragg, Lieut-Colonel,
COMMANDING 5th No.H STAFFS REGT

T.C.

Army Form C. 2118.

# WAR DIARY
## or
## INTELLIGENCE SUMMARY.
(Erase heading not required.) 5th Mk Staff Training Cadre.

September 1918.

WR 20

Instructions regarding War Diaries and Intelligence Summaries are contained in F. S. Regs., Part II. and the Staff Manual respectively. Title pages will be prepared in manuscript.

| Place | Date | Hour | Summary of Events and Information | Remarks and references to Appendices |
|---|---|---|---|---|
| ETAPLES ADMINISTRATIVE DISTRICT | 1 | | Sunday. | 6 2 0 |
| | 2 | | Arms drill – Physical & Recreational Exercises | 6 2 0 |
| | 3 | | Arms drill. Physical & Recreational Exercises. 2 Officers instructing Officers from 1.B.D. in Tactical problems. | 6 2 0 |
| | 4 | | Arms drill. Fatigue duties. 2 " " " " " | 6 2 0 |
| | 5 | | Fatigue duties – preparing ground. Erecting Marquee etc. for Brigade Mess. Officers under C.O. training (musketry, field, tactical problems) | 6 2 0 |
| | 6 | | Physical Exercises – Fatigue duties. – 20 Officers instructing Officers from 1.B.D. in Tactical problems. | 6 2 0 |
| | 7 | | Physical Exercises – Fatigue (Bn) Sports – Football match against 1st Yorks (5th Mk Wpn. Cal. 4th Johns 3) | 6 2 0 |
| | 8 | | Sunday. C.of E. Service held in YMCA tent. Adjoining Camp | 6 2 0 |
| | 9 | | Marine men act as working party under R.E.'s. Battalion on Duty for the day. | 6 2 0 |
| | 10 | | Working Party under R.E. – Baths parade leaving Gun School. | 6 2 0 |
| | 11 | | " " " " | 6 2 0 |
| | 12 | | " " " " | 6 2 0 |
| | 13 | | " " " " | 6 2 0 |
| | 14 | | " " " " | 6 2 0 |
| | 15 | | Sunday. C.of E. service held in YMCA tent. | 6 2 0 |
| | 16 | | Working Party under R.E. 116th Brigade Camp v Louen Gun School at football. Result Bde Camp 4 L. S. School 6 2 0 | |

Army Form C. 2118.

# WAR DIARY
## or
## INTELLIGENCE SUMMARY.

(Erase heading not required.) 5th Nth Staffs Training Cadre
September 1918

Instructions regarding War Diaries and Intelligence Summaries are contained in F. S. Regs., Part II. and the Staff Manual respectively. Title pages will be prepared in manuscript.

| Place | Date | Hour | Summary of Events and Information | Remarks and references to Appendices |
|---|---|---|---|---|
| ETAPLES ADMINISTRATIVE DISTRICT. | 17 | | Working Party under R.E. Baths at Keno-Sun School. | WRO |
| | 18 | | Working Party under R.E. Shoot down of Sergeant Moss which officers attended. | WRO |
| | 19 | | Battalion on Duty. – Working Party under R.E. | WRO |
| | 20 | | Working Party under R.E. | WRO |
| | 21 | | Working Party under R.E. | WRO |
| | 22 | | Sunday. C. of E. Service in Y.M.C.A. hut. | WRO |
| | 23 | | Working Party under R.E. | WRO |
| | 24 | | Working Party under R.E. 116th Bde Camps v F. 1.B.D. at football. Result Bde Camps 4 1BD nil | WRO |
| | | | Baths Parade at Keno Sun School. | |
| | 25 | | Working Party under R.E. 116th Bde Camps v G.H.Q. Mec Transport at football. Result head and scene. | WRO |
| | | | Bde Camp Concert held in Y.M.C.A. hut. | WRO |
| | 26 | | Working Party under R.E. | WRO |
| | 27 | | Working Party under R.E. | WRO |
| | 28 | | Fatigue duties in Camp. | WRO |
| | 29 | | Sunday. C.of.E Service in Y.M.C.A hut. Bn on duty for the day. | WRO |
| | 30 | | Fatigue duties in Camp. | WRO |

J. Barrett. Capt.

COMMANDING 5th NORTH STAFFORD REGT

# WAR DIARY
## or
## INTELLIGENCE SUMMARY

(Erase heading not required.)

5th York & Lancs. Regt. Training Cadre

October 1918

No 16

| Place | Date | Hour | Summary of Events and Information | Remarks and references to Appendices |
|---|---|---|---|---|
| Etaples (Reinforcement District) | 1 | | Working Party under R.E. | APP 6 |
| | 2 | | Working Party under R.E. | APP 6 |
| | 3 | | Working Party under R.E. 116 Rev. Bants v. I.B.D. football House, Ban Camp 5th IBDO. | APP 6 |
| | 4 | | Working Party under R.E. Tactical Scheme. Instruction & Officers from Base Depots | APP 6 |
| | 5 | | Working Party on Camp Football ground. Rink for Troops sewn in connection | APP 1 |
| | | | with Winter Sports | APP 1 |
| | 6 | | Divine Service in Y.M.C.A. Base Sports. Battalion on Duty. | APP 2 |
| | 7 | | Tactical Scheme No 2. Instruction to Officers from 57 GC Reinforce. | APP 1 |
| | 8 | | Tactical Scheme No 2 (Divisl) Instruction to Officers from 57 G.C Reinforcements. | APP 1 |
| | | | The Protection throughout convoy & transport from rest. | |
| | 9 | | Working Party on Camp Football ground. Y.O.C. Sports inside Camp. | APP 2 |
| | | | Short Interview & E. Infantry Base Depot. Brigade General of Y.M.C.A. | APP 3 |
| | 10 | | Working Party on Camp Football ground. | APP 6 |
| | 11 | | Working Party under R.E. Tactical Scheme No 3. Instruction to Officers from Base Depot. | APP 6 |
| | 12 | | Working Party under R.E. | APP 6 |
| | 13 | | Divine Service in Y.M.C.A. | APP 6 |
| | 14 | | Working Party under R.E. | APP 6 |
| | 15 | | Baths at Divnl Base School. Instruction to Officers in Tactical Scheme at ETAPLES | APP 0 |

# WAR DIARY
## or
## INTELLIGENCE SUMMARY.

(Erase heading not required.) 5th North Staffs Training Cadre

October 1918

| Place | Date | Hour | Summary of Events and Information | Remarks and references to Appendices |
|---|---|---|---|---|
| ETAPLES ADMINISTRATIVE DISTRICT | 16 | | Instruction to Officers from No. 51 Gen. Hospital in Tactical Scheme. Working parties making R.E.s. | 6x0 |
| | 17 | | " " Battalion on Staffs. | 6x0 |
| | 18 | | Fatigue parties working on Tents (washing & lining with corrugated iron | 6x0 |
| | 19 | | " " | 6x0 |
| | 20 | | C of E Service in Y.M.C.A. hut. | 6x0 |
| | 21 | | Lt Col E.H. Montgomerie M.C. assumed duties of Camp Commandant | 6x0 |
| | 22 | | Instruction by Officers in Tactical Scheme at ETAPLES. Bathing parade at Arena Swim School | 6x0 |
| | 23 | | Battalion on duty. — All rifles inspected by the Camp Armourer Sergt. | 6x0 |
| | 24 | | Distribution of 3 Belgian medals to 116 1st Class details at the Camp by 900 39th Division | 6x0 |
| | 25 | | Instruction by Officers in Tactical Scheme at ETAPLES. Fatigue parties working on tents | 6x0 |
| | 26 | | Fatigues as above | 6x0 |
| | 27 | | Sunday. C of E service in Y.M.C.A. hut. | 6x0 |
| | 28 | | Fatigue parties washing & lining tents with corrugated iron. | 6x0 |
| | 29 | | Battalion on duty. Fatigue party under 936 Area Employment Co. Bath parade at Arena Swim School | 6x0 |
| | 30 | | Instruction by Officers in Tactical Scheme at ETAPLES to Officers from N.Z. depot. | 6x0 |
| | 31 | | Fatigue duties. | 6x0 |

W.R.Allen Capt/A/Lieut.Colonel
COMMANDING 5th NORTH STAFFORD REGT

Army Form C. 2118.

# WAR DIARY
## or
## INTELLIGENCE SUMMARY.
(Erase heading not required.) 5th Nth Staffs Regt Training Centre

November 1918                                                                 982  17

| Place | Date | Hour | Summary of Events and Information | Remarks and references to Appendices |
|---|---|---|---|---|
| ETAPLES | 1 | | Fatigue duties. | GRO |
| ADMINISTRATIVE DISTRICT | 2 | | Fatigue duties. | GRO |
| | 3 | | Sunday. C of E Services in Y.M.C.A hut. | GRO |
| | 4 | | Fatigue duties. | GRO |
| | 5 | | Fatigue duties. Bath at Lewis Gun School. | GRO |
| | 6 | | Battalion Demobilized. Authority O.B. 2257 dated 30/10/18. | GRO |

F. Wragg
LIEUT-COLONEL
COMMANDING 5th NORTH STAFFORD REGT

5. N. Staffs

Ft. M. Stotts
July 1st 16

Answer 116 Batch 71 12-8-16

Army Form C. 2118.

# WAR DIARY
## or
## INTELLIGENCE SUMMARY.
(Erase heading not required.) 5th N. Staff. Regt. Batt. Training Cadre

Volume No 2
June

Instructions regarding War Diaries and Intelligence Summaries are contained in F.S. Regs., Part II. and the Staff Manual respectively. Title pages will be prepared in manuscript.

| Place | Date | Hour | Summary of Events and Information | Remarks and references to Appendices |
|---|---|---|---|---|
| Chargues | 1 | | Instructional Classes continued | France 36A / the own Att |
| " | 2 | | Batt. Training Staff moved by motor bus to Preures (N. of Huesqueliers) where they came under the command of the 49th Brigade, 16th Division, for the purpose of training American Battalions. | Calais 13 / 100,000 Att |
| | 3 | | | France 3D / 25,000 |
| Preures | 3 | | Refresher course for officers & NCOs started under specialist NCOs | ditto |
| " | 4 | | Refresher course continued | ditto |
| " | 5 | | " " " | ditto |
| " | 6 | | " " " | ditto |
| Aix-en-Ergny | 7 | | Batt. Training Staff moved by march route to billets at Aix-en-Ergny. Inspecting billets in neighbouring villages for 318th American Regt. | ditto |
| " | 8 | | " " | ditto |
| " | 9 | | " " | ditto |
| " | 10 | | Batt. Training Staff moved by march route to billets at Bout de Haut (5m. South of Samer) | Calais 13 / 100,000 |
| Bout de Haut | 11 | | Inspecting billets in Rouet for 318th American Regt. | ditto |
| | 12 | | " " Bout de Haut " | ditto |

# WAR DIARY
## or
## INTELLIGENCE SUMMARY.

(Erase heading not required.) 5th N. Staffs Regt. Batt. Training Cadre

Army Form C. 2118.

Vol 17

| Place | Date | Hour | Summary of Events and Information | Remarks and references to Appendices |
|---|---|---|---|---|
| Bout de Haut | 13 | | American Officers & NCOs of 2nd Bn. 318th Regt. instructed in various subjects. Musketry under Capt Wenyn M.C. Lewis Gun under Capt Cotter & 2nd Lieut P.T. + B.F. under Capt Barratt, Bur under Capt Clements, Bombing under 2nd Lyall + Signalling under 2nd Evans. | Calais 13/100,000 |
| | 14 | | do | Ett |
| | 15 | | do | Ett |
| | | | Proceeded to England Instructional Off. strength of Cadre on command of Battalion. | Ett |
| | 16 | | | |
| | 17 | | (Sunday) Instructional classes continued. 16th Division proceeded to England & the Batt. Training Cadre now comes under orders of 103rd Bde. Lt Col. T.H.S. Bromith Capt 2/Lt Wenyn M.C. | Ett |
| | 18 | | 3rd Division. Instructional Classes continued. | Ett |
| | 19 | | do | Ett |
| | 20 | | Regimental School started for officers & NCOs of 318th American Infantry Regt. Bombing: 12 o.R. under Capt a R. Otter, Secretary | Ett |

Army Form C. 2118.

# WAR DIARY
## or
## INTELLIGENCE SUMMARY.
(Erase heading not required.)

Part of 5th Bn. North Staffordshire Regt. Training Cadre   Month June

| Place | Date | Hour | Summary of Events and Information | Remarks and references to Appendices |
|---|---|---|---|---|
| Pont de Nieppe | 20 (cont.) | | 3 Offrs + 12 O.R. under 2 Lt Lyall. Lewis Gun. 24 O.R. under 2 Lt Price. Programme of work attached. | Calais 13 /25,000 |
| " | 21 | | School continued as per programme. | Cal 24 |
| " | 22 | | do | Cal 24 |
| " | 23 | | Sunday | |
| " | 24 | | School continued as per programme. Bombing & Lewis Gun classes end. Scouting & Observation class continued. | Cal 24 |
| " | 25 | | | Cal 24 |
| " | 26 | | New Bombing & Lewis Gun classes arrive. Scouting continued. | Cal 24 |
| " | 27 | | School continued | |
| " | 28 | | do | Cal 24 |
| " | 29 | | do Scouting course ends | 10250 W.O. |
| " | 30 | | 2nd Scouting course commences. Bombing & Lewis Gun classes end. | |
| | | | Sunday. | |

July 1st 1918

J.E. Wray Capt.
Commanding 5th Bn. North Staffs Regt.

**WAR DIARY**
or
**INTELLIGENCE SUMMARY.**
(Erase heading not required.) 5th North Staff Regt Training Cadre

Army Form C. 2118.

July 1918

VOL 18

| Place | Date | Hour | Summary of Events and Information | Remarks and references to Appendices |
|---|---|---|---|---|
| Boitsfort | 1 | | Sending classes continued. Bombing three four classes. 3rd class commenced. Capt Otter Master | 6.10 |
| | 2 | | 117th Brigade for Divis. Rest Camp Scheme. | 6.10 |
| | 3 | | Classes continued at School as per programme | 6.10 |
| | 4 | | All classes terminated (in view of the 80th & 81st A.E.F. leaving the neighborhood) | 6.10 |
| | 5 | | 80th Division A.E.F. Capt Clements received very very from bicycle accident. | 6.10 |
| | 6 | | Medical Inspector at Regimental School Army Order 28/6/18 received awarding M.C. to Capt G.D. Fox | 6.10 |
| | 7 | | Sunday | 6.10 |
| | 8 | | Regimental School groups firing Clement morning. Lecture lewis Jun afternoon | 6.10 |
| | 9 | | " | 6.10 |
| | 10 | | " Capt Clements admitted to Field Ambulance | 6.10 |
| | | | Bout de lent | 6.10 |
| | 11 | | Capt J.B. Hargie M.C. granted permission by Divisional Commander to wear badge of H.M. Master of | 6.10 |
| | | | Foxhounds Kitt is appointment to the Regiment. | 6.10 |
| | 12 | | Medical instructor - Lewis Jun Musketry Map reading | 6.10 |
| | 13 | | " | 6.10 |

# WAR DIARY
## or
## INTELLIGENCE SUMMARY

Army Form C. 2118.

5th N. Staffs Regt Training Cadre

July 1918

| Place | Date | Hour | Summary of Events and Information | Remarks and references to Appendices |
|---|---|---|---|---|
| Bout St Lart | 14 | | Sunday | WRO |
| | 15 | | 117 Brigade Musketry Competition at Bavre - our representatives won 3rd place (Chester teams entered) | WRO |
| | 16 | | Musical instruction transfer Musketry Programme | WRO |
| | 17 | | " | WRO |
| | 18 | | " | WRO |
| | 19 | | " | WRO |
| | 20 | | " Bathing parade at Crecsent | WRO |
| | 21 | | Sunday " | WRO |
| | 22 | | Musical instruction | WRO |
| | 23 | | " | WRO |
| | 24 | | " Capt Clements rejoins from hospital | WRO |
| | 25 | | " hirst at HENNEVEUX the night - (Blaris12 + HAZEBROUCK 5A 1/leave) | WRO |
| | 26 | | The Cadre move by march route to - LA PANNE - (for detail of travel route see Operation Order No. 1 dated 25/7/18) arrive LA PANNE. | WRO |
| | 27 | | Capt Cotton rejoins the unit. | WRO |
| | 28 | | Sunday | WRO |
| | 29 | | The cadre plays cricket against 11th Cheshires at Fuery - the 39th Divisional League Cricket Competition. Result 5 - 77th Staffs qu. 11th Cheshires 7w. | WRO |
| | 30 | | Recreational Training | WRO |
| | 31 | | " | WRO |

August 1st 1918

J.E. Wright, LIEUT-COLONEL.
COMMANDING 5th NORTH STAFFORD REGT

TABLE "A".

## LEWIS GUN COURSE.

**1st DAY.**
- 1st Hour. Lecture.
- 2nd " General Description.
- 3rd " Gas.
- 4th " General Description.
- 5th " Names of Parts.
- 6th " Stripping.

**2nd DAY.**
- 1st " Mechanism.
- 2nd " Names and stripping.
- 3rd " Mechanism.
- 4th " Immediate action.
- 5th " Gas.
- 6th " Immediate action.

**3rd DAY.**
- 1st " Immediate action.
- 2nd " Trench duties.
- 3rd " Mechanism.
- 4th " Gas.
- 5th " Stoppages. Faulty assembly.
- 6th " Care and cleaning.

**4th DAY.**
Miniature Range.
Students not firing to receive instruction in magazine filling, Gas, cleaning and points before and after firing.

===============================================================

TABLE "B."

## SCOUTING and INTELLIGENCE COURSE.

Scouting and Observation as laid down in Appendix III.A. of S.S. 152.

Aeroplane photographs.

Lectures on movements usually seen in the enemy's lines.

Co-operation of Artillery.

Daylight reconnaissance for night marching.

Night marching by compass based on daylight reconnaissance.

Patrolling at night.

TABLE "C."

## BOMBING COURSE.

**1st DAY.**
- 1st Hour.    Lecture - Mills and Egg bombs.
- 2nd "    Throwing.
- 3rd "    Gas.
- 4th "    Drill - formation of bombing squad.
- 5th "    Firing dummy No. 23.
- 6th "    Lecture - 'Hales Rifle Grenade.'

**2nd DAY.**
- 1st Hour.    Gas.
- 2nd "    Fitting Rifle Grenade dischargers.
- 3rd "    Firing dummy No. 35 and 36.
- 4th "    Throwing dummies.
- 5th "    Throwing live Mills.
- 6th "    Lecture and Demonstration "Smoke bombs."

**3rd DAY.**
- 1st Hour.    German grenades (Lecture).
- 2nd "    Firing live No. 35 and 36.
- 3rd "    Firing live No. 23.
- 4th "    Revision.
- 5th "    Gas.
- 6th "    Lecture - Supply and storage of grenades.

**4th DAY.**
- 1st Hour.    Throwing.
- 2nd "    Lecture - Raids.
- 3rd "    Gas.
- 4th "    Throwing and firing tests.
- 5th "    Oral tests.
- 6th "    Lecture - 'Blocking.'

----------oOo----------

5. N. Staffs.

116th Brigade.
39th Division.

Battalion disembarked HAVRE 6.3.16

1/14th BATTALION

HAMPSHIRE REGIMENT

MARCH 1916

Army Form C. 2118

# WAR DIARY
## INTELLIGENCE SUMMARY

(Erase heading not required.)

Instructions regarding War Diaries and Intelligence Summaries are contained in F.S. Regs., Part II. and the Staff Manual respectively. Title Pages will be prepared in manuscript.

14/39th Punj. Regt.  XXXIX 14 H an G
116th Bn. Vol 1 & 2

| Place | Date | Hour | Summary of Events and Information | Remarks and references to Appendices |
|---|---|---|---|---|
| Witley Camp | 5-3-16 | 11.5 p.m. | 1st Trainload 320 men under Capt Finlay leaves for Southampton Docks | |
| " | " | 12.5 p.m. | 2nd " " " " Maj. Gurley " " " | |
| " | " | 1.5 p.m. | 3rd " " " " Col. C.J. Hichie " " " | |
| Southampton Docks | 5-3-16 | 5 p.m. | Transports leave Southampton | |
| Havre | 6-3-16 | 7 a.m. | Disembarkation starts. The whole Battalion reaches camp in | |
| " | " | 6 " | Snow Storm by 3.30 p.m. | |
| Havre | 7-3-16 | 12 noon | 1st Trainload starts for fighting area. | |
| " | " | 5 p.m. | 2nd " " " " | |
| Busnes | 8-3-16 | 3 p.m. | Whole battalion arrives in billets about 17 miles from firing line. Night firing distinctly audible after 7 p.m. All troops comfortably billeted but rather scattered. | |
| Estaires | | | | J.W.Dunlay Capt & Adjt |

# WAR DIARY
## or
## INTELLIGENCE SUMMARY

*(Erase heading not required.)*

Army Form C. 2118

Instructions regarding War Diaries and Intelligence Summaries are contained in F. S. Regs., Part II. and the Staff Manual respectively. Title Pages will be prepared in manuscript.

| Place | Date | Hour | Summary of Events and Information | Remarks and references to Appendices |
|---|---|---|---|---|
| Morbecque | 9-3-16 | 11 a.m. | Three German Taubes flew over the billets, they were pursued by six allied biplanes & made off in a southerly direction. No bombs known to be dropped. | |
| | | 12 noon | Billets inspected by Brigadier. | |
| Morbecque | 10.3.16 | 11 a.m. | Summoned to Bde. HD. Qrts. Orders received to move the following day to Estaires. All preparations completed, & Billetting returns sent in. | |
| Morbecque | 11.3.16 | 8.30 a.m. | Marched to Estaires. Very trying march, men carrying very heavy weights. Reached Estaires about 2.45 p.m. the whole Battalion billetted in one large Brewery store. Orders received from 23rd Bde. as regards dispositions in trenches for the 12th. We are within 6 miles now from firing line. (Bombardment clearly heard all night.) | |
| Estaires | 12.3.16 | 11 a.m. | German Taube brought down & drawn through Streets. | |
| | | 4 p.m. | B & D. Coys starts for trenches, ½ of A & C Coys for reserve posts. | |
| Estaires | 13.3.16 | 10 a.m. | C.O. self, Proctor & R.S.M. make tour of trenches. Rangoon slightly wounded in the head. | |
| | | 11.30 p.m. | Rangoon seriously wounded in Stomach. | |
| Estaires | 14.3.16 | 11 a.m. | Lieut Rangoon died of wounds. C. Coy heavily bombarded, all rations shut burnt but no casualties. Haverstis shelled in the evening. Self & Q.M. has to take shelter for an hour, first casualty in mess, Pte Wills Coy. wounded in Shoulder. | Shirley Capt & Adj |

1875  Wt. W 593/826  1,000,000  4/15  J.B.C. & A.  A.D.S.S./Forms/C. 2118.

# WAR DIARY
## or
## INTELLIGENCE SUMMARY

*(Erase heading not required.)*

Army Form C. 2118

Instructions regarding War Diaries and Intelligence Summaries are contained in F. S. Regs., Part II. and the Staff Manual respectively. Title Pages will be prepared in manuscript.

| Place | Date | Hour | Summary of Events and Information | Remarks and references to Appendices |
|---|---|---|---|---|
| Estaires | 15.3.16 | | Quiet morning. Billets cleaned. 2.30 p.m. Langdon buried near Sailly. | |
| | | 4.30 p.m. | A & C. Coys. move into front line trenches to relieve B. & D. Recvn. information that we shall proceed to Sailly on the 19th | |
| Estaires | 16.3.16 | | Nothing to report. | |
| " | 17.3.16 | | Major Juley & self spent night in front line. Had very narrow escapes from traversing machine guns when returning. | |
| " | 18.3.16 | | Nothing to report. | |
| " | 19.3.16 | 8 a.m. | Move to Bac-St-Maur with B & D. Coys. A & C. Coys. join us same night. | |
| Bac-St-Maur | 20.3.16 | 10.30 a.m. | Orders issued for relief of 11th Sherwood Foresters in Reserve posts at Fleurbaix. Whole Brigade takes over from | |
| | | 6 p.m. | Coys. move down Saturday to posts. | |
| | | | 16th (552.) | |
| | | 8 p.m. | Reliefs reported complete. | |
| Fleurbaix | 21.3.16 | | Nothing to report all day. Boches very quiet. | |
| | 22.3.16 | | Night of 22/23rd Two men of B. Coy wounded when on working party. | |

Shirley Capt & Adjt

Army Form C. 2118

# WAR DIARY
## or
## INTELLIGENCE SUMMARY
*(Erase heading not required.)*

Instructions regarding War Diaries and Intelligence Summaries are contained in F.S. Regs., Part II. and the Staff Manual respectively. Title Pages will be prepared in manuscript.

| Place | Date | Hour | Summary of Events and Information | Remarks and references to Appendices |
|---|---|---|---|---|
| Hustain | 23.3.16 | 6.a.m. | Orders that we shall be relieved by 11th Suffolks that evening, & march to Billets in Estaires | |
| | | 7.30 p.m. | Relief complete. Coys reported all in Billets by 2. a. m. following morning, at villages about 2 miles W. of Estaires. | |
| Estaires ? | 24.3.16 | 6 a.m. | Snow falling, & roads in bad condition | |
| " | 25-3.16 | 3 p.m. | Move to La Gorgue. Very good billets for everybody. | |
| La Gorgue | 26) 27) 28) 3/16 29) 16. 30 31 | | Training carried on. Men got a good bath & change of under clothes. | |
| " | 1-4-16. | 3. p.m. | Move to billets & Cauderac 2 miles N. of Lurville | |
| Cauderac | 3.4.16 | 10 a.m. | Brigade inspected by General taking 11th Corps command. Great praise for the battalion on its turn-out. Lecture given in the afternoon. | |

J.W.Finlay Capt & Adjt

1875   Wt. W593/826   1,000,000   4/15   J.B.C. & A.   A.D.S.S./Forms/C. 2118.

116th Brigade.
39th Division.
-------------

1/14th BATTALION

HAMPSHIRE REGIMENT

APRIL 1 9 1 6

Army Form C. 2118

# WAR DIARY
## or
## INTELLIGENCE SUMMARY

14th Hants

(Erase heading not required.)

| Place | Date | Hour | Summary of Events and Information | Remarks and references to Appendices |
|---|---|---|---|---|
| Cauchecourt | 4.4.16 / 13.4.16 | | Training in billets | |
| " | 14.4.16 | 9.30 am | March to La Panerie. Gen Hornby takes over Command of Brigade vice Gen Watson. | |
| La Panerie | 15.4.16 | 8 am | March into trenches, take over left battalion line Givenchy Section. Relief Complete by 2 p.m. Quiet night, no casualties. 13th Sussex on our right. Batn Hd Qrtrs near Windy Corner. | |
| Givenchy | 16.4.16 | | Enemy shelled Windy Corner for about one hour. Erratic shooting, no casualties. D. Coy got one man killed & 3 wounded by Rifle grenades at about 10.30 p.m. otherwise enemy fairly quiet. Certain amount of aeroplane activity | |
| " | 17.4.16 | | Quiet day. Very little enemy activity at night. Two casualties in D. Coy. | |
| " | 18.4.16 | | Nothing to report. | |
| " | 19.4.16 | | Moves out of front line into Village ruins & relieved by 12th Sussex. Relief complete 5 p.m. Day quiet, nothing to report. | |

Findlay Capt & Adjt

Army Form C. 2118

# WAR DIARY
## or
## INTELLIGENCE SUMMARY
*(Erase heading not required.)*

Instructions regarding War Diaries and Intelligence Summaries are contained in F. S. Regs., Part II. and the Staff Manual respectively. Title Pages will be prepared in manuscript.

| Place | Date | Hour | Summary of Events and Information | Remarks and references to Appendices |
|---|---|---|---|---|
| Qunuchy | 20.4.16 | | Quiet Day. Bad weather. Little activity on either side. Quinnchy Kup shelled. | |
| " " | 21.4.16 | | Quiet Day again. No 15060 Pte W. Cooper recommended for courage & coolness in getting his of a bout dropped among a party of bomb-throwers. (Brigadier-General Hornby states that had the incident occured in action, Pte. Cooper would have been recommended for a decoration. | |
| " " | 22.4.16 | | Nothing to report. Draft of four officers arrive at 7.30 p.m. Moves back to front line, Pulvier 12th Sussex. | |
| Qunuchy | 23.4.16 | | by 11th Sussex. Day exceptionally Quiet. Quiet for us. Our Artillery was active. Lieut. Wilbur who attends yesterday was killed by a fragment of a tram-jar which was one of many sent over in retaliation for action on the part of our Trench Mortar batteries. | |

B W Winlay Capt Adjt

# WAR DIARY or INTELLIGENCE SUMMARY

Army Form C. 2118

(Erase heading not required.)

Instructions regarding War Diaries and Intelligence Summaries are contained in F.S. Regs., Part II. and the Staff Manual respectively. Title Pages will be prepared in manuscript.

| Place | Date | Hour | Summary of Events and Information | Remarks and references to Appendices |
|---|---|---|---|---|
| Givenchy | 24.4.16 <br> 25.4.16 <br> 26.4.16 | | Nothing of particular importance to report. Chief trouble is from Rum jars & rifle grenades, & a few German snipers whose lairs were very difficult to find. The 19th (SWB) on our right carried out a raid on the night of 25th. | |
| " | 27.4.16 | | Relieved by 12th Royal Sussex. Relief completed without casualties. (Battalion proceeds to GORRE as Brigade Reserve. (Gas attack at Annequin). | |
| Gorre. <br> " <br> " | 28. <br> 29. <br> 30. | | Nothing of importance to record. Battalion employed as R.E. working parties. Afternoon of 30th, Draft of 57 men arrive from 16th Battalion. | |

E W Dudley Capt & Adjt
14th Hants

116th Brigade.
39th Division.

---

1/14th BATTALION

HAMPSHIRE REGIMENT

M A Y  1 9 1 6

Army Form C. 2118

14 Hants
Vol 3

D A 9
3rd Echelon

| Place | Date | Hour | | Remarks and references to Appendices |
|---|---|---|---|---|
| Gorre. | 2.5.16 | 2 p.m. | Bn in Billets at Gorre (near Bethune) Arrival of Battalion in 35 army exceptionally civil & [...] inhabitants | XXIX |
| RIEZ DE VIN#AGE | (3.5.16 | | Training carried out by Brig. Gen. A. [...] p.m. River alters Weather remained in its Canal. On the [...] N.C.O's of the [...] by Officers to also on the [...] was carried out | [...] shelled out |
| | 9.5.16. | | Battalion moves at half was [...] | over by us Right Bn. 2 sects |
| | 10.5.16. | | Moves on 4.6 pm guides of 17th Sh. Relief complete [...] No casualties [...] left, & 118th Inf | RT. A long QUAUX & Battalion [...] roads, which train positions [...] about 11 p.m. Sussex on our |

Herriath on you of Capt
B was [illegible] of the
Battalion in 35 army
commenced

G.W. Kerr
Lieut. Col.
Comd. 14th Bn. North Hants
In the field
3/6/16

2.H.
6 sheets

Army Form C. 2118

14 Hants
Vol 3
XXXIX

2.H.
6 sheets

# WAR DIARY
## or
## INTELLIGENCE SUMMARY
(Erase heading not required.)

Instructions regarding War Diaries and Intelligence Summaries are contained in F.S. Regs., Part II. and the Staff Manual respectively. Title Pages will be prepared in manuscript.

| Place | Date | Hour | Summary of Events and Information | Remarks and references to Appendices |
|---|---|---|---|---|
| Gorre. | 2.5.16. | 2 p.m. | Left Billets at Gorre and proceed to Divisional Reserve at Riez-de-Vinage (near Bethune) arriving in billets at about 6.30 p.m. Billets excellent, & inhabitants exceptionally civil & obliging. | |
| RIEZ DE VINAGE. | 3.5.16. | | Training carried out in & around (Billets) in accordance with programme sketched out by Brig. Gen. Jones. Hours. 6.45 to 7.15.; 9 to 12.45.; 2 p.m. to 5 p.m. Recreation. Weather remained very fair. & were were able to enjoy Baths in the Canal. On the 6th, 7th; a Reconnaissance was made by Officers & N.C.O.'s of the "Back defensive Area" - "System of defence." Also on the 8th a Reconnaissance of the new line to be taken over by us was carried out by C.O., 2nd in Command, & Coy Cmdrs. Right Bn. 9.Sisters | |
| | 9.5.16. | | | |
| | 10.5.16. 5/ | | Battalion moves at 1 p.m. to take up new line in FESTUBERT. A long halt was made for tea on the Canal bank at LES. CHOQUAUX & Battalion moves on to 6 p.m. by platoons through GORRE to FESTUBERT cross roads, where guides of 17th Sherwood Foresters met them, & conducted them to their positions. Relief complete at 10.37 p.m. & 17th Sherwood Foresters Clear by about 11 p.m. No casualties during Relief. Evening very quiet. 13th Royal Sussex on our left, & 118th Inf. (Bn. on our right in GIVENCHY. | |

1875  Wt. W503/826  1,000,000  4/15  J.B.C. & A.  A.D.S.S./Forms/C. 2118.

# WAR DIARY
## or
## INTELLIGENCE SUMMARY
*(Erase heading not required.)*

Army Form C. 2118

Instructions regarding War Diaries and Intelligence Summaries are contained in F.S. Regs., Part II. and the Staff Manual respectively. Title Pages will be prepared in manuscript.

| Place | Date | Hour | Summary of Events and Information | Remarks and references to Appendices |
|---|---|---|---|---|
| FESTUBERT O.B.L. | 10.5.16 | | Beautiful weather, O.B.L. in very clean condition. Nothing exceptional to report from the Islands. Work carried on in the O.B.L., and of small improvements and Salvage work. | |
| " | 11.5.16 | | Early in the morning, two men of C. Coy wounded in No 6 Island, too late to be brought down to Dressing Station. Cpl. King crossed in daylight from PRINCES ISLAND & Dressed their wounds & then returned to PRINCES ISLAND. then and Received a report by telephone. This action brought a reconnaissance from Brig. Genl. (see attached memo.) Enemy flew a small drone opposite Princely Keep at about 3 p.m., & subjected the Keep to shelling for about 10 minutes. | [illegible] lost by R.G.C. to be replacing |
| " | 12.5.16 | | Weather still keeps good. Our was killed in No 3 Island by German Sniper. Our aeroplanes very active, & flying very low. It was especially noted that the German anti-aircraft guns were absolutely silent, & gave our the impression of being short of ammunition of that description, in this part of the line. Gas alarm at about 10 p.m. Atmos. was down for about an hour, & alarm was then found to be false. A lot of work was done on the line. | 12695 Pte Critchfield WSG killed |

1875 Wt. W593/326 1,000,000 4/15 J.B.C. & A. A.D.S.S./Forms/C. 2118.

# WAR DIARY or INTELLIGENCE SUMMARY

Army Form C. 2118

| Place | Date | Hour | Summary of Events and Information | Remarks and references to Appendices |
|---|---|---|---|---|
| FESTUBERT | 13.5.16 | | Quiet day. Relieved by 12th Royal Sussex. Relief complete at 10.46 p.m. Battalion moves to Bde. support in Village Line. Battalion sustains no casualties during relief. | |
| VILLAGE LINE | 14.5.16 to 16.5.16 | | Battalion in support. Working parties at work every night. Weather not too-good at night. Nothing of importance to report. Lieut. Marshall reports for duty 15.5.16. | Total 350 men after finding nightly garrisons. |
| " | 17.5.16 | | Fine weather. At about 7.30 p.m. the enemy put one four 5.9. shells presumably at a battery in rear of Batt. H.Q. These were short of our mark sweeping in hitting Battalion Dressing station. Craft of 40 wind arrived about 3.30 p.m. all 60 soldiers 6.30 p.m. commence relief of 12th Royal Sussex in O.B.L. Relief complete by about 11.45 p.m. No casualties. Enemy machine gun & rifle fire very active. | No 12695. Sea. Cpl. Westbrook H W killed |
| FESTUBERT O.B.L. | 18.5.16 | | Weather beautiful. Enemy shelled O.B.L with shrapnel and a few H.E. Two men wounded. No damage to parapet. Small enemy parachute came over the O.B.L, & landed near Village line, but could not be found by us. Remainder of day & night passed without incident. | |

Army Form C. 2118

# WAR DIARY
## or
## INTELLIGENCE SUMMARY
(Erase heading not required.)

Instructions regarding War Diaries and Intelligence Summaries are contained in F. S. Regs., Part II. and the Staff Manual respectively. Title Pages will be prepared in manuscript.

| Place | Date | Hour | Summary of Events and Information | Remarks and references to Appendices |
|---|---|---|---|---|
| O.B.L. FESTUBERT- | 19.5.16 | | Weather continues fine. Enemy Machine guns beginning to be active on the wire, which may be meant to us, being becoming dangerous, but good wiring was done, 194 coils being put out. Nothing unusual to report. | No.14003 Pte. MONGE R. W. Killed. |
| " " | 20.6.16 | | Nothing to report. | No.10638 Pte. LANGRISH H Killed. 20.5.16 |
| " " | 21.5.16 | | Day of relief. Quiet Day. At about 10 p.m. lachrymatory gas was about, emanating from shells on the S. side of LA BASSÉ Canal. No casualties during relief. Relief complete 10.45 p.m. | |
| LE TOURET | 22.5.16 | | Brigade Reserve. Billets good. Battalion finds 1366 men for working parties. No shelling takes place at all. Nothing unusual to report. | |
| | 25.5.16 | | Relieved by 1st Cambridgeshire Territorials 7.30 p.m. | |
| RIEZ de VINAGE | 26.5.16 | | Divisional Reserve. Working party of sixteen Officers and 656 other ranks worked all day on Divisional training ground. Letter No.1195 dated 26/5/16 names 8 Officers "recorded" by B.G.C. as having done valuable patrol work in "no mans land" up to 25th May. Letter No.1191 Sept 26/5/16 - 1903- cold 16 wire cutters this Battalion. 356 Brigade Army order No.1 for relief by 6th Highlanders period of this battalion's first active service action. Put out 594. | |

# WAR DIARY
or
## INTELLIGENCE SUMMARY

(Erase heading not required.)

Army Form C. 2118

| Place | Date | Hour | Summary of Events and Information | Remarks and references to Appendices |
|---|---|---|---|---|
| FESTUBERT | 27/5/16 | | Musketry on MONT BERNICHON range. Names of 3 N.C.O.s and 6 men forwarded to Brigade H.Q. in regard to recommendation for good work on wire. | |
| R. I. E. Zdw. VIMAGE | 28.5.16 | | Battalion leaves billets in the evening to take over the line from 1st MIDDLESEX Reg. at CUINCHY. RIGHT SUB. SEC. One officer & C.S.M. acting C.S.M. were killed in the harbour of the R. Coy. by falling lumps of earth from a mine which was blown by the Germans, in rear of 9 or 9A WHICH CRATER. Relief was completed at 1. a.m. | 2/Lt. Y. L. Ellis No. 5065 C.S.M. J. Graham |
| CUINCHY. RIGHT | 29/6/16 | | The morning passed without disturbance except for a few heavy trench mortar shells being dropped at the R. Coy front. In the afternoon many Trench Mortar shells fell up and caught on our Franklin of the Rt. Coy killing 3 men who were working in the communication trench leading to top head on the rear Lt. of 9A WHICH CRATER. | No.12894 Pte Channing No 2964 Pte Ballen |
| CUINCHY RIGHT | 30.5.16 | | The day passed though quickly till midnight when the British blew a large mine on the front of the left Battalion on our right. No damage was caused on our Battalion front. The Lt. from the Sgt. Guards of the Rt. Coy being blown down. Elf the mine was exploded. Two officers of 9 N.C.O.s were attached from 7th Warwicks to a Coy. for Instruction & Reserve for Instruction. | No.15179 Pte Webber. |
| CUINCHY RIGHT | 31.5.16 | | Nothing of importance occurred through the day. Enemy snipers became rather more active throughout the day. One Lieut was wounded from a sniper in the centre Coy. In the evening about 8.30 p.m. a mine was blown by the Germans in the front of the Lt. Battalion. | No 5110 2nd Lt. Scripture J. |

1875  Wt. W 593/826  1,000,000  4/15  J.B.C. & A.  A.D.S.S./Forms/C. 2118.

116th Brigade.
39th Division.
---------------

1/14th BATTALION

THE HAMPSHIRE REGIMENT

JUNE 1916

Report on Raid 7/8th June attached.

Army Form C. 2118

Instructions regarding War Diaries and Intelligence Summaries are contained in F.S. Regs., Part II. and the Staff Manual respectively. Title Pages will be prepared in manuscript.

| Place | Date | Hour | | Remarks and references to Appendices |
|---|---|---|---|---|
| CUINCHY RIGHT | 1.6.16 | | The morning relieved by the Royal Engineers the 2nd division the strength of Machine Gates 2.N.C.O's 16 me R.E (I 23.d 4 CROSS Roads | machine gunners were wounded, the 12th about 2 a.m. the morning of hospital. the majority of |
| ANNEQUIN NORTH | 2.6.16 | | | NON COMBATANT at tunnelling Company, at 9 men to Hd Qty 11th fold by employee at ANNEQUIN from Shrapnel piece by |
| ANNEQUIN NORTH | 3.6.16 | | One of our airmen on the road to by the R.F.A. which was dug in 16 bombers were it was issued to the afternoon or | A dud shell landed in dug out nearly fused, the dud shell dug up the clay bed a pair of her ————— ornament was played |
| ANNEQUIN NORTH | 4.6.16 | | Bombers. Snipers. 12 a Royal Also along front so a Horn & the G | The Pheasants 5/6 to through the night the Coy A Small turn out N/f. m. |

D.A.G Base

Herewith War Diary for the 14th Battalion The Hampshire Regiment for the month of June 1916.

C. Davenport
14th Bn Hampshire Regt

3-7-16.

Adjutant & 2nd of Regt Hampshire Regt.

14 Hants vol 4

3 H.
15 sheets

# WAR DIARY
## or
## INTELLIGENCE SUMMARY
(Erase heading not required.)

Army Form C. 2118

| Place | Date | Hour | Summary of Events and Information | Remarks and references to Appendices |
|---|---|---|---|---|
| CUINCHY RIGHT | 1.6.16 | | The morning passed quietly. At 12 mid-day the Coldstream Rifley machine Gunners were relieved by the 12th Royal Sussex. At 9.15 p.m. the relief of the Battalion was started, the 12th Royal Sussex coming in as this in. The relief was not complete till about 2 am. The morning of the 2nd. A draft of 26 men, from the 1, 2, 4 & 2 Hants upon Hospital. The majority of the draft being old soldiers. | |
| ANNEQUIN NORTH | 2.6.16 | | Morning Fatigues. 2 N.C.O.S. & 20 men were sent without tools to the 251st Tunneling Company at YOUR RIDDOCH WAY. 2 N.C.O. & 16 men to same Company at Cambrin Support Points. 1 N.C.O. 10 men to Hdqtrs 11th Field Coy. R.E. (T. 23 d. 44) for loading purposes. 1 N.C.O. & 9 men for loading purposes at ANNEQUIN CROSS Roads. Two men were wounded in the village at about 7 p.m. per shrapnel piece of a German A.A. aircraft. | |
| ANNEQUIN NORTH | 3.6.16 | | One of our aircraft was being shelled near the village at 6.30 F.M. A dud shell landed in the road within 100 yds of Bn. Hdqtrs. & did not burst. It was dug out soon after by the I.A. The shell dug out was a 7.7 m.m. No damage was caused. The dud shell which was dug out was not fired at aircraft. Working parties were supplying the day train. 16 bombers went up in reserve to 1 R. Sussex Regt. Every man had a first of bren ???? the afternoon, which A. Coy won. National Anthem was sang. Ol Battalion football tournament was played. | |
| ANNEQUIN NORTH | 4.6.16 | | Bombers, Snipers, Machine Gunners moved up to the line to relieve the Specialists of the 12th Royal Sussex. The enemy bombarded the Right Coy front at intervals through the night. Also along support Trench with Whizz Bangs in rear of the Centre Coy (A Company) was flown & the Left. Direct near to the BRICKSTACKS. They say Germans came about 11 p.m. | |

# WAR DIARY
## or
## INTELLIGENCE SUMMARY

*(Erase heading not required.)*

Army Form C. 2118

| Place | Date | Hour | Summary of Events and Information | Remarks and references to Appendices |
|---|---|---|---|---|
| ANNEQUIN NORTH | 5.6.16 | | Battalion moved up to the line to relieve 12 R. Sussex at 4 p.m. to the 8 CUINCHY RIGHT, Relief. Relief was completed about 6 p.m. G Coy Right front A.Coy. 2/7 R. Warwicks Centre Coy. C. Coy left front. A. Coy in Reserve line. B. Coy in VILLAGE LINE. The remg. Bt. passed quietly. One man of A Coy killed mending the wire in front of TOWER RESERVE TRENCH. | No's 732. Pt. Mason. A. |
| CUINCHY RIGHT | 6.6.16 | | The day passed quietly until about 11 p.m. when the enemy sent a good many Whizz bangs over on the Right Coy & on TOWER RESERVE TRENCH. A few heavy trench mortar shells were dropped on right of Centre Coy front, without doing much damage. Three men killed in the Right Coy front from a whizz bang. Our light trench mortars fired at different times through the night B Coy of 2/7 R Warwicks held Centre Coy front through the night. | No. 5162. Pte. Abbott. G. 15482 Pte Carter. J. 14463. Pte Hoag. J.A. |
| CUINCHY RIGHT | 7.6.16 | | Little activity through the day. The enemy's aerial amount of Rifle Grenades were sent onto our trenches during the night. One officer 2nd Lieut BASTIN wounded. 1 Sergt. killed in the right Coy front at about 11 p.m. from rifle grenades. At 11.45 p.m. a raiding party from our battalion (20 rank & file) Officer left the trenches on the right of the left Battalion. The party left the trenches by HUMPREY'S CRATER. Reaching the Hun Trench on the left of the LA BASSÉE Rd. The enemys wire was broken by a Bangalore Torpedo which was laid by the R.E. under the enemy wire. An explosion of the torpedo between 6 & 7 men of the party rushed into the trench working up towards the LA BASSÉE Rd. & the party bombed for about 9 minutes & came out again. Our Artillery & Trench Mortars kept up a barrage of fire for about 40 minutes. The whole party returned into our trenches, with 3 Sergts wounded & 2 & 1 rivates wounded. Full report attached as appendix one | No. 15554. Sergt Rowbotham |

**Army Form C. 2118**

# WAR DIARY
## or
## INTELLIGENCE SUMMARY
*(Erase heading not required.)*

Instructions regarding War Diaries and Intelligence Summaries are contained in F. S. Regs., Part II. and the Staff Manual respectively. Title Pages will be prepared in manuscript.

| Place | Date | Hour | Summary of Events and Information | Remarks and references to Appendices |
|---|---|---|---|---|
| CUINCHY RIGHT | 8.6.16 | | No activity during the morning. The battalion was relieved at 2 p.m. by the 12th R. Innis. Regt. & withdrew to the VILLAGE LINE. 2 platoons. A Coy & B Coy: C Coy Cambrian Support Post. D.coy. 2 Platoons CUINCHY SUPPORT POINT. 1 Platoon TOURBIERES POST. 1 Platoon to CANTEENS POST. Relief was complete 5 p.m. | |
| CUINCHY VILLAGE LINE | 9.6.16 | | A few 5.9 whizz bangs were sent over during the day. Greatest was close to PONT FIXE. No damage was caused to Bn. H.Q. or the Battalion. The weather enlarged to raining off & on through the day. | |
| CUINCHY VILLAGE LINE | 10.6.16 | | Nothing of importance occurred through the day. C company was relieved at 9 p.m. by the 1st Bn. MIDDLESEX Regt. & D Coy by the same unit. The two Companys arrived back in the Billets in Divisional Reserve at RIEZ du VINAGE. At 3 a.m. the morning of the 11th. O'Claughty & 35 men arrived from the 13 Bn. Hamps. Regt. in the afternoon. Wet weather during the day. A & B Coys were relieved from the VILLAGE LINE at 9 p.m. by the 1st Bn. MIDDLESEX Regt. The two Coys arrived back in Divisional Reserve Billets at RIEZ du VINAGE about 3 a.m. the morning of the 12th. | |
| RIEZ du VINAGE | 11.6.16 | | | |
| RIEZ du VINAGE | 12.6.16 | | Wet weather during the day. One Company reached the baths at LOCON, & the others was unable to get to them, as they closed down. | |
| RIEZ du VINAGE | 13.6.16 | | Wet weather during the morning. Three Officers & 20 Ranks went to the Memorial Service for Lord Kitchener at LOCON in the morning. Major Thomas assumed Command of the battalion during the absence of Lt.Col.Ritchie. | |

**WAR DIARY**
or
**INTELLIGENCE SUMMARY**

(Erase heading not required.)

Army Form C. 2118

Instructions regarding War Diaries and Intelligence Summaries are contained in F. S. Regs., Part II. and the Staff Manual respectively. Title Pages will be prepared in manuscript.

| Place | Date | Hour | Summary of Events and Information | Remarks and references to Appendices |
|---|---|---|---|---|
| RIEZ du VINAGE | 14.6.16 | | The weather still continues to keep wet, throughout the day. Musketry started on the range, two Companys got though before the weather got too bad. Capt. F. L. Shinner assumed Command of the Battalion during Major E.H.P Child Thomas leave of absence. | |
| RIEZ du VINAGE. | 15.6.16 | | The weather changed for the good, musketry continued on the range, much activity amongst the inhabitants of the village celebrating the day. Received orders for the move to go into Bde Reserve, parts of RICHEBOURG. St VAAST. | |
| RICHBOURG St VAAST | 16.6.16 | | Advance party left RIEZ du VINAGE at 9.a.m. arriving here at 12 midday. The Bn. moved up at 11am reaching here at 2 p.m. at 6.45 Relief was complete by 6 p.m. The Bn. relieved the 18th Bn. East Lancashire Fus. No shelling took place during the relief. The billets were good. A draug of 20 men arrived/1.3 Bn. Hamp.A.R. into the afternoon. | |
| RICHEBOURG St VAAST | 17.6.16 | | A quiet night, though till 2.50 am when a gas alarm was spread over a short area. The stand to hour was blown & every one turned out & stood too, ten minutes later the alarm proved to be nothing. The remainder of the day nothing occured. | |

Army Form C. 2118

# WAR DIARY
## or
## INTELLIGENCE SUMMARY
(Erase heading not required.)

Instructions regarding War Diaries and Intelligence Summaries are contained in F. S. Regs., Part II. and the Staff Manual respectively. Title Pages will be prepared in manuscript.

| Place | Date | Hour | Summary of Events and Information | Remarks and references to Appendices |
|---|---|---|---|---|
| RICHBOURG ST VAAST. | 18.6.16 | About 1.30 a.m. | Gas was reported, by the sentry on duty who heard gongs being rung. The Battalion stood to & stood by for gas. By 2. a.m. no more horns or gongs were heard, 4th Battalion stood down. The gas alarm proved to be a false alarm. A new officer reported for duty with the Battalion from ETAPLES. At 11 p.m. A few shells burst on the left which came over during the morning & afternoon. | |
| RICHBOURG ST VAAST | 19.6.16 | | Nothing to report through the day. Bomb stores, in all the posts were made up to a great strength, during the day. Also S.A.A. stores. A very quiet day, & a quiet night, & the weather very cold. | |
| RICHBOURG ST VAAST | 20.6.16 | | No activity through the day. Two posts were slightly shelled during the night of B. Coy. No damage was done. The Company Commanders went up to the front line to reconnoitre the front line, in the morning. | |
| RICHBOURG ST VAAST | 21.6.16 | | No activity through the morning. The Bn received orders to relieve the 13th Bn R. Sussex R.; At 4.30 pm. All specialists & advance party went on immediately. The relief started at 9.30 pm. The last company to go in & other reported relief complete at 11.45 pm. The other 3 Companies were complete before 12 a.m. On shelling took place. N. of WINDY CORNER. 2 at 10 pm. Casualties 5. Casualties to 7th & 13th R. Sussex R. A. C. many of the harm was recorded at WHISKY CORNER going up & to the entrance of WHISKY CORNER Cap. Ot Payre of R. Coy. | |

1875 Wt. W593/826 1,000,000 4/15 J.B.C. & A. A.D.S.S./Forms/C. 2118.

# WAR DIARY
## or
## INTELLIGENCE SUMMARY

Army Form C. 2118

(Erase heading not required.)

| Place | Date | Hour | Summary of Events and Information | Remarks and references to Appendices |
|---|---|---|---|---|
| FERME du BOIS RIGHT SECTION | 22.6.16 | | A good deal of activity on our right (about GIVENCHY) at 2 am, which lasted for about an hour. Some shells fired over and around FACTORY & ROSE POSTS at 2 pm, about a dozen in all 5.9. Lt. Ch. C.T. Hiorns returned from leave & resumed command of the Battalion. FACTORY & ROSE KEEPS were relieved in the evening by the 1/4/1 HERTS. 4 men of D Coy were killed at about 11 pm from a light trench mortar, shell bursting on the dug out. | 16517 QS Tunah D.A. 1582 Lee King R.T. 15584 QS Orwell F. 14038. Q.M. Peake A. |
| FERME du BOIS RIGHT | 23.6.16 | | Between 12.30 am & 11.30 am, the left Coy front & supporting Company were subject to a fairly heavy bombardment, with very little damage to our trenches & none to the men. Our Artillery & light T.M. & mortars retaliated & the Boches shelling in the afternoon on our own craft were very active & the Hun was also active in shelling our aircraft. In the evening about 6 p.m. a very severe thunder storm started & heavy rain which lasted for about an hour. | |
| FERME du BOIS RIGHT | 24.6.16 | | A quiet day, our aircraft being very active during most of the day. The water stores P.A.A. food, & bomb stores were still being made up to a large extent. The water being carried up in 2 gal Petrol tins. The battalion on our left were shelled for a short time in the evening with H.E. & big Bags on PORT ARTHUR POST & then dropped into the front line, or within a 100 yds of it, & also on HUN. Strat. | |

| Place | Date | Hour | Summary of Events and Information | Remarks and references to Appendices |
|---|---|---|---|---|
| FERME du BOIS. RIGHT. | 25.6.16 | | The enemy were unusually quiet, & did not even reply to our own Artillery, which was active through out the day. The Gas in the enemy war 9 hand got in part of our right Coy was kept quiet during the day & night of the 25th by machine & Lewis gun fire. At 4.30 pm balls of fire were suddenly seen to descend from the clouds on to a German Observation Balloon, which rapidly vanished in smoke. The other balloons came down quickly & were along side of at the time. A draught of 30 men & N.C.Os arrived from the 16th Rn. Hamps R. in the evening. | |
| FERME du BOIS. RIGHT. | 26.6.16 | | The enemy shelled our front line slightly & COCKSPUR STREET. A quiet night, & not much work done, except on dug outs. No wire was put out on account of the fire which we kept up through the night. The weather kept wet at different times through the day, & the trenches getting in a bad state. One man was killed in the early morning by a stray shot in the right Coy, from a machine gun. | No. G155 Pte. W.H. Wynne. |
| FERME du BOIS. RIGHT. | 27.6.16 | | The weather still kept bad, raining hard at intervals through the day. The enemy rather more active than day before, shelling our support line & COCKSPUR Street. Causing 4 men wounded. Our artillery active throughout the day, particularly on the front line of the Rock opposite to our right Company. | |

# WAR DIARY
## or
## INTELLIGENCE SUMMARY

Army Form C. 2118

| Place | Date | Hour | Summary of Events and Information | Remarks and references to Appendices |
|---|---|---|---|---|
| FERME du BOIS. RIGHT. | 28.6.16 | | The weather rained hard through the night, causing the trenches to be pretty bad in places. The Boch a little more active with his Artillery, shelling a little in the afternoon to the rear of our Outpost line behind the right Company. By 4 p.m the shelling increased. A good many 4.2 shells came over. At 9.40 p.m. the Battalion was relieved by two Companys of the 12th R Sussex R. On the left of our Battalion front, 1 Support line, & two Companys of the 13th R Sussex R on the right of our Battalion front & Support line. The relief was completed & the whole Bn back in Billets at CROIX. BARBEE. About 4 am on the morning of 29th. | |
| CROIX. BARBEE | 29.6.16 | | Nothing to report through the morning. Our Artillery were very active in the afternoon at 2 p.m to about 4 p.m. The Bn went up to the trenches in Reserve to 124/13 Royal Sussex R at FERME du BOIS. RIGHT. A Coy was the only Company which actually went into the front line & took over the Right Coy front, at the beginning. B.Coy | |

# INTELLIGENCE SUMMARY

*(Erase heading not required.)*

Instructions regarding War Diaries and Intelligence Summaries are contained in F.S. Regs., Part II. and the Staff Manual respectively. Title Pages will be prepared in manuscript.

| Place | Date | Hour | Summary of Events and Information | Remarks and references to Appendices |
|---|---|---|---|---|
| FERME du BOIS. RICHT. | 30.6.16 | | At 2.55am Our artilley commenced an intense Bombardment of the enemy front and trenches on the BOERS HEAD. to B.15am & then lifted onto the enemy support trenches & the attacking units 12&13 & Royal Sussex Regts went over in waves, including Signallers, R.E. & 11th Royal Sussex R. were hidden carrying parties, Stores Blocking parties, this with Bn. Hanqrs. were in advance. On A Coy moved up to the line & took over the right Coy front at 12 mid night the night of 29 & 30th. On B Coy moved up to GUARDS TRENCH RIGHT & BUTE STREET. Our C Coy was in Reserve at RICHBOURG ST VAAST & took over the right Coy front after the attack. Our D Coy was in support by WINDY CORNER, in front of BnHQ in EDWARDS ROAD. & they took over the left Coy front when ordered to by the commanding officer. The attacking units reached the enemy support trench & Signalling was connected up from the enemy front line to our own front line. The enemy retaliation with artillery was so terrific that our attacking units were forced to withdraw under heavy fire & trench to trench from the enemy front line which was wrecked in many places on our B Coy casualties were two officers wounded. Lt. SMKEEN & 2Lt. H.D. SANGSTER. O.R. W90 wounded O.R. 5 killed. D.R. missing 3. 12662. Pte RUDD. H. 14052 Pte AMBLER. 12763 Pte HOARE missing. The artillery quietened by 10am on 30th June. | 12593 Pte CHAMBERS. H 21438 Pte WILTSHIRE J. 12977 Pte MILLS. G. 15050 Pte TAGGUE. 15491 Pte SEAVIERS. |

XIth CORPS.

8th June, 1916.

The O. C. 14th HAMPSHIRE REGT.
----------------------

    I hope you will convey to all ranks in your Battalion my appreciation and congratulations on the successful raid they carried out last night. Of course I am particularly pleased because

Names of Raiding Party 7-6-16
14th Bn. Hampshire Regiment.

| | | |
|---|---|---|
| 14081 | Sgt | Gibbon |
| 12745 | " | Dodd |
| 14308 | L/S | Hatch |
| 20398 | Cpl | Harris |
| 14099 | L/C | Tongue |
| 14463 | Pte | Smith G |
| 12742 | " | Colley |
| 14601 | " | Strange |
| 12804 | " | Potter |
| 12736 | " | Churchman |
| 12719 | " | Barrett |
| 12609 | " | Griffin |
| 14203 | " | Kemp |
| 15060 | " | Cooper |
| 5107 | L/S | Taplin |
| 12908 | Pte | Fairbrother |
| 12762 | Sgt | Ball |
| 15755 | Pte | Smith W |
| 15022 | " | Latter |
| 14021 | " | Fox |
| 13958 | " | Laveridge |

XIth CORPS.
8th June, 1916.

The O. C. 14th HAMPSHIRE REGT.

     I hope you will convey to all ranks in your Battalion my appreciation and congratulations on the successful raid they carried out last night. Of course I am particularly pleased because it is my own Regiment.

     It was quite fit and proper that the Germans should run away when the Hampshire men suddenly turned up in their trenches.

(sd) R. HAKING. Lt. General.
Comdg. XIth Corps.

C.H.532.   REPORT ON RAID ON ENEMY TRENCH at A 22 a 2 2½,
           carried out by 14th Battalion Hampshire Regiment
           on the night of 7th/8th June 1916.

On 31st May 1916 it was decided that a raid should be carried out by the Battalion under my command somewhere along the front held by the battalion between A.21 d 5.0. and A.21 b 8.2. I had then held this part of the line for 3 days and had some knowledge of the front but I consulted Lieutenant GRAHAM R.E. the Mining Officer who confirmed my opinion that only two places in the line offered a fair chance of success to a raiding enterprise owing to craters and that these were opposite A.21 d. 9.8½ and A.21 b 8.2.

That night I sent out reconnoitring patrols on the front of both these points, the northern patrol being under 2/Lieutenant ELLIS whilst the Southern patrol was under Corporal TAPLIN.

From the reports of these patrols and also from personal reconnaissance from O.P's and Fire trench I was enclined to choose the northern area for the enterprise. The Mining Officer had also informed me that an enemy mine might be blown up at any time on the Southern area.

On 2nd June I selected 2/Lieutenant G.M.ASHMORE to carry out the enterprise, visited the line with him and 2 N.C.O's whom he selected and thoroughly reconnoitered, the selected piece of front from the fire trench.

That night he and his two N.C.O's reconnoitered the ground up to the enemy wire. I attach his reconnaissance reports for that night and subsequent nights.

I obtained from Company Commanders the names of their best men for the raid and handed them over to 2/Lieutenant ASHMORE.

On 3rd, Lieutenant BOOTH 12th Battalion Royal Sussex Regt. carried out an excellent reconnaissance of the ground with Lieutenant BALCOMB R.E. whom Captain SIMMS, Commanding 11th Field Company R.E. had placed at my disposal for technical advice as regards destroying the wire entanglement. This reconnaissance was of the greatest use and assured me that the use of the Bangalore Torpedo for breaching the wire was possible.

I decided thereupon to employ this means of surmounting the obstacle and preserving the element of surprise to the last.

2/Lieutenant ASHMORE was not in favour of employing artillery and I was also inclined in this direction. I was inclined to use trench mortars only against the communication and reserve trenches. It was however explained that this use of the Trench Mortars alone would give away their position to too great an extent and finally I arranged Artillery co-operation with Colonel GOUGE, Commanding "A" Group.

Organisation of Raiding party.

It was decided to organise the party as under.
    Commander.     2/Lieutenant G.M.ASHMORE.
    2nd in Command. Sergeant GIBBON.
                     Corporal HATCH.   Bayonet.
                     Private SMITH G. Bomber.

| Left Party. | Right Party. |
|---|---|
| Sergeant BALL. | Sergeant DODD. |
| 7 Men. | 7 Men. |
| 1 Identity Collector. | 1 Identity Collector. |

Covering Party.
    Commander.       2/Lieutenant FAIRLIE-CUNNINGHAM.
                  2 N.C.O's and 12 men.

The raid was then fixed for 7th June.

All the necessary equipment was collected at Battalion Headquarters and personnel of the raiding party brought together. comfortably housed at the same place and extra food and some little luxuries provided for them.

The final arrangements for Artillery, Medium and Light Trench Mortar Co-operation were made on 7 th June and by 3 p.m. everything was complete.

The night was dark. Lieutenant BALCOMB R.E. left Battalion Headquarters with 30 feet of Torpedo at 9-45 p.m. and at 11-30 2/Lieutenant ASHMORE received a report at HUMPHRIES CRATER that the torpedo was ready for firing. On this the raiding party issued from the crater and proceeded quietly to a couple of Shell holes about 20 yards from enemy's wire.

At 11-50 p.m. all being ready, the torpedo was fired by electric contact from the CRATER. The shock was somewhat severe and four or five of the men, more exposed than others were thrown back and did not get forward at once when Lieutenant ASHMORE led his party through the gap. This and the excitement of the moment helped by a shower of bombs from the enemy prevented the previously arranged division of the men into two parties which were intended to enter the trench and bomb outwards. Also both section commanders were wounded on the parapet. The enemy appear to have expected the attack ( they had previously sent a couple of bombs over, directed against the torpedo party). They had Bayonet men in the trenches and bombers behind the parados. They appeared to be in fair strength. After the Bayonet men had fired a few shots point blank. They retired along the trench in both directions but were only followed towards the north by Lieutenant ASHMORE and 6 men who worked along for about 25 yards.

The remainder of our party remained above ground bombing the enemy's bombers who were crawling away across the open to their support trenches.

Lieutenant ASHMORE after being in the trench for about 5 minutes ordered the retirement which was carried out successfully.

80 bombs were thrown by our party who seem certain of having "laid out" four of the enemy.

During the retirement the enemy were plainly seen bombing inwards towards each other during a period of about ten minutes.

It is regretted that no identification was obtained in spite of the fact that two men were detailed for this purpose.

It is the first raid carried out by this Battalion and the novelty and excitement of the operation undoubtably made the men overlook this important point.

Casualties 5 Wounded.

Artillery and Trench Mortars.

Fire was opened on the signal that the torpedo had been exploded. It came at once and was most effective in keeping down hostile rifle and Machine Gun Fire.

Intense fire till 12 midnight, then desultery.

All quiet at 12-30 a.m.

(Signed) C.J.Hickie. Lieut-Colonel
Commanding 14th Battalion The Hampshire Regiment.

8-6-16.

116th Brigade.
39th Division.

----------------

1/14th BATTALION

HAMPSHIRE REGIMENT

JULY 1916

# WAR DIARY or INTELLIGENCE SUMMARY

Army Form C. 2118

| Place | Date | Hour | Summary of Events and Information | Remarks and references to Appendices |
|---|---|---|---|---|
| FERME DU BOIS RICHT. | 1/7/16 | | Our extraordinary quiet day though till the evening when an artillery bombardment took place on the Bluff & our Rt. part. during the day wounded men to the number two were fetched in from NO MANS LAND & daylight by Sergt. GIBBON & Sergt. WILSON & party of the Cents Coy who cuff out & brought back a badly wounded N.C.O. of the 13 Royal Sussex N. in a duckN board, in front of this left Coy. Sergt. LEE & Cpl. MIDLANE the cuft out in daylight & brought back a badly wounded corporal of the 13 Sussex Rt. at 10.15 P.M. the relay was started by the 16th Black Watch with our 2 Battalion. The Battalion was relieved by 2 Bn at 4 P 16 Black in RUES by 4.20 a.m. in LE TOURET. | Operation Order No. 25 attached |
| LE TOURET | 2/7/16 | | The day was spent in cleaning up & punning hits no working parties were out. Our aircraft were very active in the evening. | |
| LE TOURET | 2/7/16 | | About 10 a.m. a Boch aeroplane came over the village later on another Boch aeroplane was sighted in a southern direction. Our aircraft & this failed to bring either machine to the ground. | |
| LE TOURET | 3/7/16 | | Nothing to report till the evening when our C & D Companys went up to the VILLAGE LINE. FESTUBERT in Reserve to the 16th Bn R.B. The 16th R.B. were carrying out a death Company raid from their own front line on the Boch at Mignez Jn. About 8 P.M. in the evening the Germans brought down one of our aeroplanes between the S.R. & the ISLANDS without damage to the pilot - little to the machine | |

Army Form C. 2118

# WAR DIARY
## or
## INTELLIGENCE SUMMARY
*(Erase heading not required.)*

Instructions regarding War Diaries and Intelligence Summaries are contained in F. S. Regs., Part II. and the Staff Manual respectively. Title Pages will be prepared in manuscript.

| Place | Date | Hour | Summary of Events and Information | Remarks and references to Appendices |
|---|---|---|---|---|
| LE TOURET | 4.7.16 | | Nothing of importance though the day, our P.D. Coys were relieved in the evening from the VILLAGE LINE FESTUBERT, & returned to LE TOURET. The weather was wet at intervals throughout the day | |
| LE TOURET | 5.7.16 | | Very quiet day. D & B coys carried out a scheme in the morning. No enemy aircraft came over our lines. Artillery on both sides quiet. | |
| LE TOURET | 6.7.16 | | Companies carried out Musketry practices at HINGES. Enemy shelled the open ground in front of 'B' Coy billet from 10 AM to 10.30 AM but did no damage. Company commanders reconnoitred front line trenches in CUINCHY sector. The Battalion moved to new billets at LE QUESNOY at 11.0 PM, being relieved by 4/5 Black Watch. About 10.15 PM we experienced a little discomfort from enemy lachrymatory shells. | |
| LE QUESNOY | 7.7.16 | | Major E.H. Childe-Thomas left for the 117th Infy Bde Staff. The Battalion relieved the 1st Bn MIDDLESEX Regt about midnight 7/8.7.16. in the CUINCHY LEFT sub-sector. | |

# WAR DIARY or INTELLIGENCE SUMMARY

Army Form C. 2118

| Place | Date | Hour | Summary of Events and Information | Remarks and references to Appendices |
|---|---|---|---|---|
| CUINCHY (LEFT) | 8/7/16 | | A very quiet day until the evening. At 5.55pm. a large mine was blown by our troops N.of the LA BASSÉE Canal, followed by a barrage by our Artillery. At midnight another mine was blown by the Battalion on our Right (11 R. Sussex R.) This was preceded & followed by a short bombardment by our guns & Trench Mortars. The Hun, whether by design or coincidence began to fire actively with T.M's & Rifle Grenades about 10 minutes before ours were intended to begin. Cpl. HARRIS, Bombing NCO of A Coy who worked in the mining by a Rifle Grenade. | |
| CUINCHY (LEFT) | 9/7/16 | | The day was again quiet, but there was a good deal of aeroplane activity. The enemy fired rifle grenades intermittently during the night, causing a few casualties. L/Cpl BOINTON of "C" Coy was killed when out with a wiring party. The enemy exploded a mine just N. of the LA BASSÉE road, but it was short of the enemy's parapet, & was covered by his fire. | |
| CUINCHY (LEFT) | 10/7/16 | | A very quiet day. An order received from the Brigade stating that the trenches would be inspected & cleared between 12th & 17th July. | |
| CUINCHY (LEFT) | 11/7/16 | | A quiet day. The Battalion was relieved by the 12th & 13th R. Sussex Regts. during the day. Battalion Head Quarters were fixed at Maison Rouge & Coys were massed on the whole Brigade front, sending them Railway Post on the right to Quinchy Dugout post on the left. Knoller Colonel for Battalion Headquarters, this afternoon. The enemy shelled Maison Rouge O.P. close by Battalion H.Q. with H.E. & T.G. doing little damage. Sgt. Mawson was wounded by Shell splinters near Battalion H.Q. apart from this the day passed | |
| Maison Rouge | 12/7/16 | | | |

# WAR DIARY or INTELLIGENCE SUMMARY

Army Form C. 2118

(Erase heading not required.)

| Place | Date | Hour | Summary of Events and Information | Remarks and references to Appendices |
|---|---|---|---|---|
| Cuinchy (Left) | 10/7/16 | | The Battalion relieved the 12th & 13th Bns. R. Sussex Rgt. by 8 p.m. The enemy shelled Braddell Posts doing slight damage, but causing no casualties. The enemy blew a mine about 8.50 p.m. just right of our right company. The accompanying barrage blew in the Coy. H.Q. of the right company and about 1/2 to 3/4 of front line parapet. | |
| Cuinchy (Left) | 11/7/16 | | The enemy used throughout the afternoon a very large trench mortar on our front & support lines. The Battalion was relieved by the 2nd Batt. Devonshire Rgt. & went into billets at 3.30 a.m. (12/7/16) by the 2nd Batt. Devonshire Rgt. & went into billets at Gorre. The 11th Batt. R. Sussex Rgt. on our right was relieved by 2nd Scottish Rifles, the 12th Batt. R.S.R. by 93rd Rifle Brigade, & 13th R. Sussex Rgt. by 23rd West Yorks. The 1st Hampshires are now attached to 118th Infy Brigade. The 11th R. Sussex Rgt — to H.Q. 117th Infy. Brigade. | |
| Gorre | 15/7/16 | | The Battalion moved Headquarters from Canal Bank to The Tuning Fork. A, B & C Coys. went into posts in support of Givenchy, D Coy in reserve in the "5". | |
| Gorre | 16/7/16 | | Our artillery bombarded the enemy's line in front of Givenchy with trench mortars for several hours. The enemy replying with 5.9" howitzers & a few 5.9". Nothing further of importance happened. | |
| Gorre | 17/7/16 | | Nothing of importance happened. | |
| Gorre | 18/7/16 | | Our artillery heavily bombarded the enemy's trenches in front of Givenchy. The enemy's retaliation was weak. | |

# WAR DIARY
## or
## INTELLIGENCE SUMMARY
*(Erase heading not required.)*

Army Form C. 2118

Instructions regarding War Diaries and Intelligence Summaries are contained in F. S. Regs., Part II. and the Staff Manual respectively. Title Pages will be prepared in manuscript.

| Place | Date | Hour | Summary of Events and Information | Remarks and references to Appendices |
|---|---|---|---|---|
| Epsec | 19/7/16 | | We made a reconnaissance of the Riere du Bois Section prior to taking over the line on 20 July. Our artillery continued its bombard of the enemy trenches in front of Givenchy, 2 Lieut Forman joined Battalion | |
| Epsec & Riere du Bois | 20/7/16 | | The enemy aircraft was more active than usual. We relieved the 18th Rifle Brigade in the Ferme du Bois Section by 12.30 A.m. 21/7/16. During the night 20/21st the enemy's machine guns were very active. The enemy had a larger number of M.G. in this Sector than he had when this Battalion held the line before. Our front runs from Plum Street (S10 d 2.17½) on the right to the 6th Bn Royal Sussex Bn. on the left to Parm Corner (S05 d 9 6½) Royal Sussex Bn. on our right. | |
| Riere du Bois | 21/7/16 | | The enemy was quiet except the exception of a little shelling on our supplies & communication trenches. During the day our snipers claimed one victim & our artillery caused some damage to enemy's parapet. Our 18 pdrs during the night caused considerable fire on enemy's rear. At 1 - 4.5 pm an our distant troops a searchlight was seen. Red & green rockets went up on our close left. | |
| Riere du Bois | 22/7/16 | | The G.O.C. & G.2 Duncan (General Cuthbert) & the Brigadier visited the Division front. The enemy shelled various parts of the front line & actively kept during the day. Lieut Ashmore of "A" Coy. being wounded. At 6.30 p.m. the enemy fired 3 large Minnies on our left Coy. Front (A Coy) one falling within twenty yards of Sgt Gibbons near causing him shell shock. During the night the Batt. carried out the operations | |

# WAR DIARY or INTELLIGENCE SUMMARY

Army Form C. 2118

| Place | Date | Hour | Summary of Events and Information | Remarks and references to Appendices |
|---|---|---|---|---|
| | 22/7/16 | | on by enemy line. Artillery, L.T.M, Rifle grenades, Lewis guns were employed. V.M.M.G's co-operated with indirect fire on enemy support & communication trenches. Enemy's retaliation caused a few casualties. One of the enemy seen waving a white flag was shot. Four pigeons with men seen to jump on enemy's parapet & from thence flew to the rear of enemy's line. Searchlights were again seen on our front at night. The enemy appeared to direct his artillery fire by night by S.O.S aid of red & green rockets. A unit in mortar Sap (right Coy front) stated that he heard a man crying in enemy trenches also the crash of what. This two or three returned in any way, but the sentry is sure he heard it. | |
| Peronne du Bois | 23/7/16 | | During the day enemy shelled our new parts of our Front Trench for upper N.E. trench (New Street). Receiving attention, in addition to some of our front line. About 9-30 P.M. our Stokes from front 500 rounds on N.E. enemy were first left of our trench making a considerable gap in the wire. The 11th D. Irench M.G. on our extreme left sent a raid & the enemy retaliated on points of our left Coy front causing us many casualties. Our Lewis gun section flying towards the rear of enemy line. Our Lewis gun team one section. The support on Lewis Sup Coy Front up and Lewis team on a - German abaffanj was seen bleed in a few minutes. Our own trench mortars with reply later put in its 10-30 P.M. Scratchley for the following trumps were Town S17 a 9 c. S20 d. (casualties for this day see ref 27/7/16) | |
| Peronne du Bois du Inniseer | 24/7/16 | | The greater part of day was spent in being relieved by the 5th East Surrey Relief complete by 3 am. The Battalion then proceeded to X17 a. 1.3 & bivouaced until 9-30 P.M. they then proceeded to trenches N.E. 2nd Kent. Cunninghams went to Hospital with severe Shellshock. Relief complete 9-30 Am. The afternoon was quiet. | |

# WAR DIARY or INTELLIGENCE SUMMARY

Army Form C. 2118

| Place | Date | Hour | Summary of Events and Information | Remarks and references to Appendices |
|---|---|---|---|---|
| Fatigues Night | 26/7/16 | | A very quiet day. The enemy shelled A.B.1 & Bannter R.S. but did no damage. An old trench in which heliographs were placed on enemy parapet was found to be used by one of the enemy for observing our line. | |
| Fatigues Night | 27/7/16 | | The enemy shelled the village line north & S. from 1.30pm 27/7/16 we carried our fire operation against enemy fire support line. L.T.M. M.Gun, artillery & rifle grenades cooperated during the operation against enemy. Two enemy patrols attempted to get into our line between Prince & No2 Island. Both officers (men) joined Battalion. 2nd Lieut T.A. Slade & Lieut C.L. Peel. 2nd Lieut B.B. Phillips. 2nd Lieut Lyng R.P. Our casualties for 26/7/16 were Sgt Ree Killed. Wounded 14082. Cpl Cameron, 14426 Hepl: Lucy 19709 Pte Rebeck 15197 Pte Went 14405 Pte Danforth 5264 Pte Eatin 1291 Pte Haughton 8939 Pte Jenkins. Officers of On'M Westmorland & Cumberland Yeomanry were attached for instruction. Colonel Riddington Commanding the Yeomanry was slightly wounded. | |
| Fatigues Night | 28/7/16 | | During the day the enemy were very quiet. About 3-30 P.M. shouting was heard on our wire between Prince & No1 Island. Men were sent out & a wounded German prisoner was made. This was the result of the encounter between our patrol & the enemy patrol the previous night. At 9-30 PM on our distant left a very heavy bombardment took place. So on left Island line Coy (?) were relieved by B. Coy of the 12th R.S. Royal Scots up by 1 P.M. The 12th Bn R.S.R. reconnoitred our line prior to a relief which took place 28/7/16. | |
| | 23/7/6 | | Casualties Killed 15262 L/Sgt Barnes 15018 Pte Hayward 15126 Pte Gibbons 8079 Cpl: Rains 13943 Pte Smith 13984 Pte Nancy 15626 Pte Simmons 18170 Pte Walker 10213 Pte Andrews 14425 Pte Jemison. 14611 Pte Inder. Wounded 21619 Pte Maaly 12587 Pte Raynard 13965 Pte Blackman 12673 Sgt Swan 19005 Pte Burchell 14146 Hepl Middle 18916 Pte Gillard 10042 Pte Laiksham 12753 Pte Sorrey 20215 Pte Sheppard 15876 Pte Whitcombe 12853 L/Cpl Smith Brush Pte Cook | |

# WAR DIARY or INTELLIGENCE SUMMARY

Army Form C. 2118

| Place | Date | Hour | Summary of Events and Information | Remarks and references to Appendices |
|---|---|---|---|---|
| Festubert Right. | 28/7/16 | | A very quiet day. During the relief at night our artillery opened fire on the enemy front line. The enemy promptly replied on our front line & communication trenches & although the communication trenches were full of men only one casualty was caused. Relieved by the 12th Bn N Suncashft relief complete 1-30am 29/7/16. C.S.M Tramp was wounded. D.C.M. | |
| Festubert Village line | 29/7/16 | | The following officers joined for duty this day 2nd Lieut Bramwell J.A & 2nd Lt D. Wood, & 2nd Lieut J.S Nordon. Our aeroplanes were active beyond this, nothing of importance happened. | |
| Festubert Village line | 30/7/16 | | The day was quiet except for slight shelling. Rase by our C Coy were arranged to take place were resorted to headqrs 118th Infy Brigade in continuation of my report sent in early this morning dealing with the attempted raid on enemy front line between A3d 52 & 8 A5d 87½. The Raiding Party consisted of 3 officers & 103 other ranks of B Coy. Owing to a mistake on the part of the NCO commanding the Lewis Gun Torpedo Party were not detailed in time & were too late at the sinking place in spite of this time may not have been 2 tomorrow which they got to torpedo from N.E Island into position under the enemy wire the enemy's leaving the island since it have been joined up into 30 lengths before leaving NO MANS' LAND. This caused the lengths kept coming apart in traversing considerable delay & Cpl. Emery R.E who was in charge of the torpedo party went to Lieut Scotic R.E having been relieved of reconnaissance the ground the previous night decided that there was now sufficient time to Exit & lay the torpedo & get back before the bombardment commenced. It appears there are some lengths of torpedo in No Mans Land. | |

1875 Wt. W593/526 1,000,000 4/15 J.B.C. & A. A.D.S.S./Forms/C. 2118.

# WAR DIARY or INTELLIGENCE SUMMARY

Army Form C. 2118

| Place | Date | Hour | Summary of Events and Information | Remarks and references to Appendices |
|---|---|---|---|---|
| Fauquissart Village Line | 30/7/16 | | There are being brought in. Tonight torpedo party also appear to have been held up from 26 mins. by L.G. fire. The raiding party was already wounded at this juncture. The full piece A30 23 to A3d/25 & left it in 3 waves at 50yds distance. They finally went going off at 1.35 A.M. They first met a row of trip wire, then some rather higher entanglement & finally a strong breastwork more or less accurately dropped upon. The whole system of wire entanglements appears to have been 15-16-30yds in depth. (That wire gun space between the 3 wire fences.) This being the case it is most improbable that the Bangalore torpedoes could have done the work even had they been got up to the obstacle in time. Our men when held up by the K.G.'s wire started bombing the enemy trench & threw in 2/2 bombs. They must have been engaged in this for at least 7 mins, mainly, to when the order to withdraw was passed along by 2/Lieut Marshall. The party came back 18th Point of advance dragging the wounded with them. More were collected later amongst them being 2/Lt Lim. Wade who was picked up by C.S.M. Duffin. The casualty list at present stands as follows:- Killed:- 10188 Sgt. Kitching. Wounded:- 2/Lieut J W Wade. 2/Lieut L Meadows 13475 L/Sgt Bennett 14366 L/Cpl. Hawkins 15478 Pte Tainsand. 13910 Pte Furse 14137 Pte Hibbard 17578 Pte Pink. Missing believed killed:- 5104 Pte Reed. Missing:- 12061 L/Sgt Roberts 12884 L/Cpl Blackmore. 13008 Pte Shrubb. 13016 Pte Stocks 15477 Pte Trickett. The men acted with great nerve & did their best to cut up in to & through the last barrier of wire - At 1.50 A.M. L.J. Brown reported to me over the telephone from No.5 Salient that the Germans was on its way back - After which he went to Bde. M.Q. I warned the artillery of this & afterwards the Howitzer fire on Old Main Owner LTM. & rifle grenade batteries fired during the operation. A man at Fauquissart was taken out but did not reach the enemy trenches though the ditches & other obstacles encountered. It stopped 15 seconds it tonight from No Man's Land. |  |

Signed C. J. Hickie Lt Col.
Comdg 1/4 & 5 Leicester R.

# WAR DIARY
## or
## INTELLIGENCE SUMMARY

(Erase heading not required.)

Army Form C. 2118

| Place | Date | Hour | Summary of Events and Information | Remarks and references to Appendices |
|---|---|---|---|---|
| 3rd Sept Authuille Village line | 31/7/16 | | The enemy is found by No. 16. 27/7/16 Inquires a considerable amount of information. The enemy artillery was very active during the night. In addition to the front line communication trenches being shelled a good deal of attention was paid to the village line. "A" Coy Wood 18. The 12th N. Sussex Regt strengthened the salient line & working parties were withdrawn. The trench bombardment during the night lasted about 2 hours. Sharpshooters went out during the night. | |

1/8/16.

J Nevin Lt Col
ind. 14 Bn Hamps R

116th Brigade.
39th Division.

---------------

1/14th BATTALION

THE HAMPSHIRE REGIMENT

AUGUST 1 9 1 6

Instructions regarding War Diaries and Intelligence Summaries are contained in F.S. Regs., Part II. and the Staff Manual respectively. Title Pages will be prepared in manuscript.

# INTELLIGENCE SUMMARY

*(Erase heading not required.)*

| Place | Date | Hour | Summary of Events and Information | Remarks and references to Appendices |
|---|---|---|---|---|
| Vhibet Mays June Les Chognaux | 1/8/16 | | A very quiet day with little relieved by 4th Cambridgeshire being being company left by 10 p.m. The Battalion marched to Les Chognaux | |
| Les Chognaux | 2/8/16 | | Rev'd 2nd Lieut. Davenport met with an accident at the Brigade Bomb School & died shortly after being admitted to hospital. Officers of the 11th 12th 13th Royal Sussex Regt. were also wounded at the Bombardment. The battalion spent the day resting relieving up. Sgt. Seymour was also wounded at the Batt. Bomb School. | |
| Les Chognaux | 3/8/16 | | The battalion rehearsed for the Funeral of 2nd Lieut DAVENPORT in addition Several officers attended the Funeral. Inspection to take place 4/8/16. T.O.C. 39th Division. He to do Officers PLATOON attended. | |
| Les Chognaux | 4/8/16 | | The Battalion was inspected General Cuthbert General Officer Commanding 39th Division. It was a very satisfactory inspection & the battalion attained a great report on clothing, equipment & general turnout. A very quiet day. The battalion went for a route march in the evening. | |
| Les Chognaux | 5/8/16 | | A reconnaissance of the Gommecourt section was carried out prior to taking over the line from 16th Sherwood Foresters. A Parade Service in Commemoration of the Second Anniversary of the commencement of the War was held in the Grande Place Berhure. An address was delivered by General Sir Charles Monro G.C.M.G. K.C.B. The 16th Hants Regt – took part in the ceremony. We relieved the 16th Bn Sherwood Foresters (in Gommeaches, Hebuterne) Relief complete by midnt. | |

# WAR DIARY
## or
## INTELLIGENCE SUMMARY

*(Erase heading not required.)*

Army Form C. 2118

Instructions regarding War Diaries and Intelligence Summaries are contained in F. S. Regs, Part II. and the Staff Manual respectively. Title Pages will be prepared in manuscript.

| Place | Date | Hour | Summary of Events and Information | Remarks and references to Appendices |
|---|---|---|---|---|
| Givenchy (Left S) | 7/8/16 | 6 a.m. | A very quiet morning. Gun artillery fired on enemy front line in rear of certain during the afternoon. Enemy retaliated with minute & intermittent fire of the "Pineapple" numerous on night & centre companies. We fired 175 rifle grenades during the night. He retaliated with some but mostly fell in No Man's Land. | |
| Givenchy (Left S) | 8/8/16 | 6 a.m. | Quiet morning. Gun Heavy T.Ms fired between 4-5 p.m. on NORTHERN craters, also on howitzers. Enemy retaliated with medium T.M. bombs & whiz-bangs on left Coy & artillery on Right Coy. During retaliation one shell on Right Coy dugout wounded 2/Lt CLEMENTS, LEVY, & BAKEWELL + 1 O.R. | |
| Givenchy (Left) | 9/8/16 | 6 a.m. | Enemy howitzer shells destroyed O.P. at LE PLANTIN at 11.30 A.M. — 43 shells were put over. Gun M.T.Ms fired in the morning — no fire shot — The enemy retaliated with 2 Lt minnyers & two whiz-bangs. Gun artillery shelled enemy front line at intervals during the day. Shelling morning & noon. On the night at 6.20 A.M. German & English shells what at start? for Givenchy from across the Sap that — K Sap. Gun men did not answer but immediately bombed them. At 2.30 P.M. hostile airplane flew our lines, but was driven back by one A.A. guns. Same occurred at 7.25 p.m. Camellia on. | |
| Givenchy (Left) | 10/8/16 | 6 a.m. | Very quiet day. Slight T.M. & rifle grenade activity. Little rain but still close. Camellia one. | |
| Givenchy (Left) | 11/8/16 | 6 a.m. | Enemy put with exception of a few aerial torpedoes & rifle grenades — we retaliated with rifle grenades. Relieved by the 2nd Welsh Regt & 23rd Bn. Relief complete by 11.20 P.M. Companies proceeded to Guns via Tommy Fork, where men packs were loaded on motor lorries. By North Bank of Canal to FERME du ROI, where a halt was made & tea & rum were issued. The Battalion moved at 3.30 followed by 1st line transport & baggage wagons on from ambulance in rear, via main BETHUNE - CHOQUES road at V27.c.2.8, D2a 15 ALLOUAGNE, which was reached about 6.15 A.M. | |

# WAR DIARY or INTELLIGENCE SUMMARY

Army Form C. 2118

(Erase heading not required.)

Instructions regarding War Diaries and Intelligence Summaries are contained in F.S. Regs., Part II. and the Staff Manual respectively. Title Pages will be prepared in manuscript.

| Place | Date | Hour | Summary of Events and Information | Remarks and references to Appendices |
|---|---|---|---|---|
| Allouagne | 12/8/16 | 6 a.m. | To billets after foot inspection & breakfast. Men resting all day. | |
| Allouagne | 13/8/16 | midnight | Left at 5.30 a.m. Brigade proceeds from 1.26 n.49. Passed thro' OURTON to BOIS du HAZOIS where we halted from 10 to 5.30 p.m. Divine Church service at 3 p.m. Moved off at 5.30 p.m. with 13th Service Regt - thro' la COMTE HOUVELIN to MAGNICOURT-en-COMTE, with a halt of 20 mins for tea at about Ref very. All in billets by 8 p.m. - daily billets. Bn. H.Q at MONCHY BRETON. | |
| MAGNICOURT-EN-COMTE | 14/8/16 | | Training started. Bn. left at 9 A.M. with Lewis. Platoon + Coy. drill - Bayonet fighting musketry - Swedish drill, etc. Returned to billets at 5 P.M. | |
| MAGNICOURT-EN-COMTE | 15/8/16 | | Training 6.45-7.15 Double. 9-10 march to Training Ground. 10-12 Platoon drill 9-12 midnight. Movement by night, keeping touch. Platoon & Coy. exercises. Afternoon free - divisional band played in village. | |
| MAGNICOURT-EN-COMTE | 16/8/16 | | Training 9.10 march to Training Ground. 10-12 Platoon + Coy. extended order drill. Taking of orders. 2-5 Platoon in attack as a drill + as a scheme. During the afternoon instruction was given to winners on the ground. Bombing Class. | |
| MAGNICOURT-EN-COMTE | 17/8/16 | | Training as before - morning Company in attack (as a drill). Wiring at work 1 to 2 P.M. Company in attack as a scheme in the afternoon. Battalion movements. Heavy shower. Gun Band played in the evening ___ for wood fighting. Returned about 5 P.M. Bt. moved off to Bois du HEROBUS - Draft of 54 men arrived. Coast in 'B' Coy down in the evening. | |
| MAGNICOURT-EN-COMTE | 19/8/16 | | Digging on training area - whole Brigade - Lecture by Major Cafferel on Bayonet fighting Sniper Transport, P.M. Slains + Lewis Gunners shooting in range - had battle put in order | |

# WAR DIARY or INTELLIGENCE SUMMARY

Army Form C. 2118

(Erase heading not required.)

Instructions regarding War Diaries and Intelligence Summaries are contained in F.S. Regs., Part II. and the Staff Manual respectively. Title Pages will be prepared in manuscript.

| Place | Date | Hour | Summary of Events and Information | Remarks and references to Appendices |
|---|---|---|---|---|
| MAGNICOURT-EN-COMTE | 20/5/16 | | Church parade. Demonstration of Flammenwerfer in Training Ground at 10 A.M. Battalion in working clothes. Church service at 5 P.M. | |
| MAGNICOURT-EN-COMTE | 21/5/16 | | Early parade — Running over trenches with 114 Bde in morning. Instruction of specialists etc. in afternoon. Bombing accident — Churning hills 1 O.R. killed, 4 I.O.R. wounded, left accidental. | |
| MAGNICOURT | 22/5/16 | | Parade in trenches with 114 Bde — Btn in training ground all day — attack practice. | |
| " | 23/5/16 | | Divisional Practice on training ground. Twice over again. Holiday in afternoon. | |
| " | 24/5/16 | | Transport left in the morning — going South. Btn moved off at 8.30 — halted for tea — LIGNY-ST-FLOCHEL at 11.10. Entrained + off by 11.30. BOUQUEMAISON via ST POL. at 1.45. Billets at LE SOUICH. | |
| LE SOUICH | 25/5/16 | | Left at 8 a.m. Brigade meeting place LUCHEUX. Through HALLOY — ORVILLE — THIEVRES to BOIS du WARNIMONT at 1.20 P.M. Huts on the ridge. Tedious march — several falling out. | |
| BOIS du WARNIMONT | 26/5/16 | | Cleaning, inspections. Reconnoitre for entire officers + N.C.O.s. Cu party before night, may afternoon. | |
| BOIS du WARNIMONT | 27/5/16 | | Church parade, inspections, etc. Btn moved at 6 P.M, through BERTRANCOURT to work in P.16 d. + h. + k. + t. 13. | |
| P.16 | 28/5/16 | | Patrols for reconnaissance, rumours, sniping etc. Officers patrol at night. 2nd Cd. Hughes left to take new command of 115 B.T.M. Bn. Capt Shannon in command. Operation Orders issued during the evening. Reconnaissance, etc. | |
| P.16 | 29/5/16 | | | |
| P.16 | 30/5/16 | | Heavy rain. Quiet morning. Enemy shelling wood at 3.45 P.M. All out + down the bank. Reluctant upon 5 inch shell shell again. 3 slight casualties. Big small trench systems of front of trench. Shelling again at 10 o'cl. Went back to huts at 11.30. Stand off at 2 o'clock morning. 15 heavy rain | |

**WAR DIARY**
or
**INTELLIGENCE SUMMARY**

Army Form C. 2118

| Place | Date | Hour | Summary of Events and Information | Remarks and references to Appendices |
|---|---|---|---|---|
| P1S. | 31/8/16 | | Shelling started again at 3 A.M., quite heavy for a while. Returned at dawn to tents. Shelled at 10, & again at 1 P.M. Dropping stuff in trenches in the afternoon. | |

E.M. Freeman 6/11
2nd/4th Welsh Regt.

116th Brigade.
39th Division.
---------------

1/14th BATTALION

THE HAMPSHIRE REGIMENT

SEPTEMBER 1 9 1 6

1/6
3d

14 Hampshire
September 1916. Vol 7

6.H.
Hitheat

# WAR DIARY
## or
## INTELLIGENCE SUMMARY
*(Erase heading not required.)*

Army Form C. 2118

| Place | Date | Hour | Summary of Events and Information | Remarks and references to Appendices |
|---|---|---|---|---|
| MAILLY WOOD | Sept 1st | | Quiet day - men resting. Only small parties away working. | |
| " | 2nd | | Final arrangements. Specialist party back to Div. Details under R.S.M. remaining. Bn started off at 4.45 P.M. Via Englebelmer & Route A. Relief complete by midnight. | |
| " | 3rd | | Bn detailed to cooperate in attack of the 116th Bde on enemy trenches between Q.16.b.2.2 and R.12.a.0.4. Assembly complete at 4 a.m. Assault & barrage at 5.10 a.m. "A" Coy on front line right practically no casualties — similarly Red "B" Coy left 2nd line — nearly Red "C" Coy advanced to meet the expected fire & rifle & M.G. fire. Had to retire, heavy casualties. 2 Coys held until 1 P.M. Ordered 11.15 A.M. an order to attack again. This was not necessary. the C.O. CAPT SKINNER was Killed. Enemy casualties heavy, our 18 officers + 400 o.R. (approx). Relieved by the 1/6 Cheshires, completed by Battalion back to same wood - MAILLY - collecting party all night. | |
| MAILLY WOOD | 4th | | Bn re-assembling, good meals & rest. Salvage party all day & collecting wounded & dead at night. Capt Freeman commanding. | |
| " | 5th | | Re-organization. | |
| " | 6th | | Courses of bombs, machine guns, signalling, started. Bn moved at 3.45 P.M. to BERTRANCOURT. Y camp. Good huts. | |
| BERTRANCOURT | 7th | | Courses, parades etc. Two drafts one of 31 & other 297 men - Essex & Suffolks. | |
| " | 8th | | Equipping & inspection. Parades. Slight shelling round room. | |

Army Form C. 2118

# WAR DIARY
## or
## INTELLIGENCE SUMMARY
*(Erase heading not required.)*

Instructions regarding War Diaries and Intelligence Summaries are contained in F. S. Regs, Part II. and the Staff Manual respectively. Title Pages will be prepared in manuscript.

| Place | Date | Hour | Summary of Events and Information | Remarks and references to Appendices |
|---|---|---|---|---|
| BERTRANCOURT | 9th | | Working party of 250 for Signals Instruction. Slight shelling in afternoon. | |
| " | 10th | | Advance party moved off at 7 PM. Bn moved at 11 AM - platoons at 200 yds interval. Via BEAUSSART to MAILLY-MAILLET. Good billets - took over from Oxford + Bucks L.I. Reconnaissance party - officers + N.C.O.s - for AUCHONVILLERS sector. | |
| MAILLY | 11th | | Reconnaissance - specialists parading. Working party of 80 m. Slight shelling. 3 casualties, 2 accidental | |
| " | 12th | | Working parties at 6 am - 320 for duck boarding - 80 at 2.30 for moving Jam cylinders. Quiet. | |
| " | 13th | | Working parties fall kinds. Final reconnaissance - operation orders out. | |
| " | 14th | | Relieved 13th R. SUSSEX Regt in left Sub-Section of AUCHONVILLERS. Relief completed by 8.30 PM. Working parties dusk. Looking. Minor artillery. Mine + raids on left. Preparations for raids, but weather not favourable for its maintenance. few investigations 2 casualties | |
| AUCHONVILLERS | 15th | | Slightly active in the early morning. Minnie active in afternoon. Artillery was cutting 13th Sussex up to raid - couldn't get them over - Strong patrol of ours out. Got mine from South. 3 casualties | |
| " | 16th | | aeroplanes active - enemies + ours. Artillery was cutting. Some about 6 p.m. report that enemy was coming over. Very active - 9th minies + rifle grenades. Gun station + Lewis patrols out + were & casualties. 2 accidental - Cleaning bombs | |
| " | 17th | | Very quiet day - only a few shells + flying about. Bray running. Capt Gunner D.S.O. wounded just before midnight. | |

Army Form C. 2118

# WAR DIARY
## or
## INTELLIGENCE SUMMARY
*(Erase heading not required.)*

Instructions regarding War Diaries and Intelligence Summaries are contained in F.S. Regs., Part II. and the Staff Manual respectively. Title Pages will be prepared in manuscript.

| Place | Date | Hour | Summary of Events and Information | Remarks and references to Appendices |
|---|---|---|---|---|
| AUCHONVILLERS | 18th | | Rain. Reconnaissance of BHn on our left. Trenches in awful state. Patrol around enemy wire. Long working party. | |
| " | 19th | | Minnies very effective on out front line. Watering party. Capt GINNER wounded. | |
| " | 20th | | Rain again – trenches in awful condition. Enemy heavie & minnies busy – then in part of front line & tunnel entrance. Casualties 1 killed 1 wounded. Two officers from the Cambridgeshires. | |
| " | 21st | | Slight rain – quieter day but minnies over. 2 new officers arrived – all with previous experience. Rifle grenades at night. Small patrol out 4 coils of wire put out. Casualties NIL. Major HARMAN assumed command | |
| " | 22nd | | Fairly quiet day & fine. Aeroplanes about. Afternoon activity of the part of the enemy. 6.O.R. wounded. | |
| " | 23rd | | Fine day & fairly quiet. Coy in the left relieved by Reserve Coy. Casualties 1 killed & 1 wounded. | |
| " | 24th | | Misty morning – no wire observation possible early. Very quiet day with exception of our artillery wire cutting – not much damage. Machine Gun played on gap at night & Right supported by Support Coy. Casualties by machinegunfire 1 killed & 8 wounded. | |
| " | 25th | | Misty morning. Qet day. Slight morning activity. Wiring cutting in afternoon. Our artillery very active. Gunners quiet. Preparing for finds attack – dummies, smoke, bells, & red lights. Quiet night. But plenty of work | |

1875 Wt. W593/826 1,000,000 4/15 J.B.C. & A. A.D.S.S./Forms/C.2118.

# WAR DIARY
## or
## INTELLIGENCE SUMMARY

*(Erase heading not required.)*

Army Form C. 2118

Instructions regarding War Diaries and Intelligence Summaries are contained in F. S. Regs., Part II. and the Staff Manual respectively. Title Pages will be prepared in manuscript.

| Place | Date | Hour | Summary of Events and Information | Remarks and references to Appendices |
|---|---|---|---|---|
| Auchonvillers | 26/4 | | Quiet day. Making a feint attack zero 12:55. Artillery bombardment & Machine Guns – Trench Mortars. Smoke bombs, a few bits off but wind in wrong direction. No dummies raised, we no rad. Very lights let off. Retaliation only slight, a few rifle grenades & minenwerfer - 1 killed. Quiet night. Killed 2 + 10RR | |
| " | 27th | | Fairly quiet day - artillery action at intervals. Heavy bombardment down South from 12:30-2:30pm in the evening. B of O 13 OR Casualties NC | |
| " | 28th | | Quiet morning. Artillery active in the afternoon. Heavy bombardment down South & northern South. Quiet night NC Squat. | |
| " | 29th | | Wet - quiet on our front, but heavy rain to our Right & Front usual working. | |
| " | 30th | | Quiet in morning. Gun artillery more active & in the afternoon. Enemy rifle grenades becoming a nuisance - interfering with working parties. Quiet night. Casualties 2 wounded. | |

C.H.Brenner Major
Comdg 14th Hants Regt

A.Q 39 Div.

239/18/G

Conversation of 2nd. Lt. Bartlett, 14th. Bn. Hamp. R.
taken down by Major Lytton at No. C.C.S. GEZAINCOURT, Sept.6th.1916

1. Narrative of what happened during the attack on enemy trenches N. of the river ANCRE on September 3rd. 1916

I was on the extreme left of the Hants attack. I was supposed to go over with the 3rd. wave; but there was confusion at once and the waves immediately got intermingled. Probably we followed our own barrage up a little too closely. I remember coming under M.G. fire immediately we left our own trenches. When I reached the enemy parapet I was hit by shrapnel in the head and for the moment I was stunned and lost consciousness. On coming to, our men were holding the enemy front line. I became unconscious again, and when I again came round the enemy was bombing us from both flanks. We tried to block the trench on either flank and also the communication trenches, - as shown below -

```
L.G.                                        L.G.
  Bombers.                                      
  ⊓⊓    ⎡‾‾‾‾⎤    ⎡‾‾‾‾⎤    ⊓⊓
        |    |____|    |      Bombers.
```

We had two Lewis Guns besides a certain amount of our own and German bombs. Our right flank was secure, but the left flank a bit shaky. We successfully held off the enemy attacks as long as our bombs lasted, and then we went on fighting with L.Gs and rapid fire 2/Lt. Tew fought magnificently, he controlled the fire and used the bombs with the utmost discretion. Furthermore, he shot many of the enemy himself. Also 2nd. Lts. Burn and Ball of the Hants and 2nd. Lt. Tennant of the Rifle Brigade did very well, also a Hants Sergeant and a Sussex Corporal - names unknown.
Finally when our ammunition ran out, the order was given to retire, and then it was a case of "sauve qui peut". If we had had about 100 more bombs we could have hung on indefinitely.
I was sniped just as I got through the German wire, and was hit in the shoulder, I fell into a "Crump" hole and made myself as comfortable as possible. Private Diver of the Hants bound me up, and acted with great courage. I lay there till dusk when another wounded man of the Hants crawled in. I had my ground sheet and an air pillow. It was impossible to get out of the hole at night as the M.G. fire was too intense. About 4 a.m. the morning of the 4th. I tried to crawl out, but was again sniped - shot through the same shoulder. I got into another Crump hole near by and waited with this man all day. At night I again crawled out and succeeded in reaching our parapet without being hit. I believe my companion was again hit on the way back, but I sent the stretcher bearers of the Cheshires after him and they brought him in.
On reaching our lines, I found Padre Thom of the Hants acting with great gallantry bringing in wounded men under fire. The Cheshire stretcher bearers were also magnificient.

2. ENEMY TRENCHES

The enemy trenches were Splendid ~~magnificient~~, much deeper than ours - well revetted with timber - a strong wooden fire step, Good dug-outs under the parapet with steps running down - Practically one to each bay - There were a few enemy dead in the bays, probably all that were in the front line which was very lightly held.

/3. IDENTIFICATION.

2.

3. **IDENTIFICATION.**

The only number that I noticed was a XIX on a dead man's shoulder strap - but even this I cannot swear to. ~~xxxx~~
I did not notice any enemy Officers at all.

4. **ENEMY ARTILLERY.**

I thought their barrage was principally behind our front line - Anyway it did not trouble me much. When we were holding their front line they tried to put a barrage over that; but their shooting was bad, and I don't think we had many casualties from their artillery.

5. **ENEMY SNIPER.**

I can't say whether those who sniped our wounded were the ordinary infantry men, or whether they were special snipers, but I am almost sure that there was an enemy sniper lying up right under our wire and having shots at any of our men moving in No Man's Land.

6. **QUALITY OF ENEMY'S TROOPS.**

I did not think that the enemy were particularly enterprising or dashing - One Mills bomb generally kept them quiet for half an hour or more. With more bombs and reinforcements I am convinced that we could have held their line easily and driven the enemy out.

7. **QUALITY OF OUR TROOPS.**

The men with me were splendid. They were well led by the Officers above-mentioned, and they were cheerful and full of fight. No praise is too much for them. During the whole time I was in the enemy trenches I personally never actually saw a live German as they kept to the trenches and were not in the open.

-------

Note. This is, in substance, what 2/Lt. Bartlett told me in answer to my questions.

Neville Lytton. Maj.

7-9-16.

HQ
39. Div.
The above is forwarded.

M.S. Hornby
Brig.
Comdg. 116 Inf Bde

7/9 1916

116th Brigade.
39th Division.
---------------

1/14th BATTALION

THE HAMPSHIRE REGIMENT

OCTOBER 1 9 1 6

# WAR DIARY or INTELLIGENCE SUMMARY

*(Erase heading not required.)*

Instructions regarding War Diaries and Intelligence Summaries are contained in F. S. Regs., Part II. and the Staff Manual respectively. Title Pages will be prepared in manuscript.

| Place | Date | Hour | Summary of Events and Information | Remarks and references to Appendices |
|---|---|---|---|---|
| AUCHONVILLERS | Oct 1st | | Rather bothered with Rifle Grenades, otherwise intensely quiet. Heavy bombardment down South. Working parties as usual – both R.E. & Bn. arrangements. Reinforcements. | |
| " | 2nd | | Enemy active for an hour in the morning. Ravine on front line. Quiet all afternoon with exception of few minenwerfer & rifle grenades. Very wet. Casualties 4 wounded. | |
| " | 3rd | | Enemy very offensive – throwing in Hunter & North St. by minenwerfer & shells. Rifle grenades becoming a nuisance. Whizz-bangs round HQRS. | |
| " | 4th | | Usual shelling – many minenwerfer notices, tho only few grenades. But certain amount of damage to our trenches. | |
| " | 5th | | Enemy shelling at intervals, also minenwerfer & rifle grenades. Called for retaliation several times. Fairly quiet night. Few gas shells about. 3 new officers arrived. Casualties 1 R, 2 w, + w at duty, 1 shell shock. | |
| " | 6th | | Working Parties cancelled. 12th Sussex reconnoitring. Relieved by them during the afternoon + completed by 5 p.m. C + D Coys to AUCHONVILLERS, A + B to ENGLEBELMER. | |
| ENGLEBELMER | 7th | | 2 officers & 6 NCOs per Coy reconnoitring THIEPVAL SECTION. Two Coys finding fatigue parties in Cleaning up rifles, clothes + equipment. | |
| " | 8th | | No working parties – Coys bathing all afternoon. Very wet day. Another reconnaissance by parties from each Coy. Quiet. | |

# WAR DIARY or INTELLIGENCE SUMMARY

Army Form C. 2118

*(Erase heading not required.)*

Instructions regarding War Diaries and Intelligence Summaries are contained in F.S. Regs., Part II. and the Staff Manual respectively. Title Pages will be prepared in manuscript.

| Place | Date | Hour | Summary of Events and Information | Remarks and references to Appendices |
|---|---|---|---|---|
| ENGLEBELMER | 9th | | Failure, but makers it at work. Coy Comrs on reconnaissance of Y Ravine Sector - prepared to move. | |
| " | 10th | | Guides met at 5 A.M. Relieved 13th R. Sussex Regt. Relief complete by 7.30. M.T.M.s were cutting wire in the afternoon - a certain good amount of damage - small gaps. Enemy artillery active on our trenches. Cas: NIL. | |
| Y. RAVINE | 11th | | Intermittent shelling by enemy artillery - unretaliated. Quiet afternoon. Shelling around Rum shire in evening. H.E. + shrapnel. Casualties 1 K. 2 W. | C. Sm. Gillam |
| " | 12th | | Fairly quiet morning. Gun artillery barrage at 2.5 P.M. Practically no retaliation at all. Enemy quiet. | no bursts |
| " | 13th | | Fairly quiet, with exception of artillery strafe [illegible] | NIL |
| " | 14th | | Slight whiz bang activity otherwise quiet morning. Smoke discharge at 2.46 P.M. - Lewis Gun fire + rifle fire. Artillery bombardment of front + support lines of enemy trenches. Retaliation at 2.50 on front + support trenches normal at 4.15. Quiet evening. | Casualties 1 W. |
| " | 15th | | Whiz - bang activity otherwise quiet morning. Slight artillery activity on our side during the afternoon. M.T.M.s putting over gas shells at midnight. Artillery active at night. | Casualties 4 W. |

1875 Wt. W593/826 1,000,000 4/15 J.B.C. & A. A.D.S.S./Forms/C. 2118.

**Army Form C. 2118**

# WAR DIARY
## or
## INTELLIGENCE SUMMARY
*(Erase heading not required.)*

Instructions regarding War Diaries and Intelligence Summaries are contained in F. S. Regs., Part II. and the Staff Manual respectively. Title Pages will be prepared in manuscript.

| Place | Date | Hour | Summary of Events and Information | Remarks and references to Appendices |
|---|---|---|---|---|
| Y Ravine | 16th | | Relieved by the 63rd Div – Drake Bn. Relief complete by 10.20. Hand not recovered. The night is not fal all. | |
| Englebermer Wood | 17th | | Advance parties off at 9.30 AM. Early dinner & off at 15.12.30. Relieving the 12th R. Sussex Regt. Confusion with guides but all complete by 9.30 p.m with exception of few strong trains. Artillery – enemy very active especially on Front & Support line. Intermittent shelling all night. Wet, heavy rain. The Ravine Killed. | |
| Schwaben Redoubt | 18th | | Heavy shelling all morning. Rations coming up, water etc. Large carrying parties did not turn up. Enemy staffing the day – slightly quieter in early evening. Heavy rain all night. Casualties about 12 k – 30 w. | |
| " | 19th | | Trenches in frightful state – enemy artillery active, 7 T.M. – on our right flank. Continuous all day, heavy barrage about 3 p.m. Runners + men all in. Heavy rain. Casualties 10 k 50 | |
| " | 20th | | Very cold night. Quiet early, but continual rain now started. Heavy about 8.30. The Bn. relieved by the 164 K.R.R. with exception of D Coy – 30 others. Not complete until about 10 p.m. Moved back to Pioneer Road. | |
| " | 21st/ | | Rolled in at 2.30 A.m. Breakfasts at 9. Cleaning up. C.O. with his 2 lt HQRS, DCoy + about 30 men over the top, with several battalions | |

## WAR DIARY or INTELLIGENCE SUMMARY

*(Erase heading not required.)*

Army Form C. 2118

| Place | Date | Hour | Summary of Events and Information | Remarks and references to Appendices |
|---|---|---|---|---|
| Pioneer Road | 21/22 | | All objectives taken. Capt Warren killed 2/Lts Green, Hale, & Bowkett wounded. 9 moved 3 Coys up to Wood Post about 4.30 p.m. in case of Counter Attack. D Coy mixed etc. A number of prisoners taken. We took from R.20 a.5.1 to R.19.2.9.7. | |
| Wood Post | 22 | | Quieter day: relieved by 7th E. Lancs Bouchatte Pioneer Road. All men about done. | |
| " | 23 | | Cleaning up. Moved at 3.30 p.m. to Senlis by Coys. Splendid camp. Cavaillé K.17. W.95. M.32. | |
| Senlis | 24 | | Wet day. Men having baths & none on working parties. | |
| " | 25 | | Preparing to move to Thiepval. Coys moving at noon. Train quite late. All in by 6. Back Coy in good dugouts. Scene of desolation. Early stuff – Boche oven stuff. | |
| THIEPVAL | 26 | | Coys cleaning out – latrines, etc. Slight activity all day. Rain. Trench. | |
| " | 27 | | Guides to meet incoming Bttn. Relieved by 16th Notts & Derby. Relief complete by 4 p.m. Hut on Pioneer Rd Crumpsul – 70 in a hut. Working parties – 160 men – | |
| Pioneer Rd | 28 | | Rest day – rain – Church services. Coys getting fitted | |
| " | 29 | | | |

# WAR DIARY
## or
## INTELLIGENCE SUMMARY

*(Erase heading not required.)*

Instructions regarding War Diaries and Intelligence Summaries are contained in F. S. Regs., Part II. and the Staff Manual respectively. Title Pages will be prepared in manuscript.

| Place | Date | Hour | Summary of Events and Information | Remarks and references to Appendices |
|---|---|---|---|---|
| Pioneer Rd | 30 | | Preparing to move. Offg Coy 1.30 p.m. Relieved 1/1st Cambs in Bde Reserve River Section — at Thiepval. Relief complete by 3.40. Very quiet. | |
| Thiepval | 31. | | Quiet morning. Gun artillery very quiet active during the afternoon. Enemy retaliation at odd intervals. Working party of 360 ntr from 7 p.m. to 10 p.m. on road making under R.E. 1 K. 1 W. | |

A.C. Gammon Lt/Adjt
for
Lt Col.
Comdg 1/4th Herts Regt.

31-10-16

116th Brigade.
39th Division.
-----------------

1/14th BATTALION

THE HAMPSHIRE REGIMENT

NOVEMBER 1 9 1 6

# WAR DIARY
## or
## INTELLIGENCE SUMMARY

*(Erase heading not required.)*

Army Form C. 2118

Instructions regarding War Diaries and Intelligence Summaries are contained in F. S. Regs., Part II. and the Staff Manual respectively. Title Pages will be prepared in manuscript.

| Place | Date | Hour | Summary of Events and Information | Remarks and references to Appendices |
|---|---|---|---|---|
| Thiepval (?) | 1st Aug 1916 | — | Occasional heavy shelling on both sides. Btn was relieved by 11th Lambs, and moved to huts in Pioneer Road AVELUY. | |
| Pioneer Road | 2nd | — | In huts at PIONEER ROAD. During the night about eight, enemy shells dropped near AVELUY ROAD. | |
| Martinsart Wood | 3rd | — | The Battn moved to huts in MARTINSART WOOD. Working parties of all coys unloading trucks at AVELUY SIDING from 8PM till 4PM | |
| Martinsart Wood | 4th | — | Working party detail for 4PM was cancelled. Nothing else of any importance to report. | |
| Point 70 | 5th | — | Btn relieved the 16th R.B. The Regn was shelled rather heavily today. | |
| Lambs | 6th | — | Btn was relieved by 17th K.R.R. Btn arrived at Lambs about 9PM | |
| " | 7th | — | Btn cleaning up and general all work being done. Several aeroplanes were heard about 10PM. | |
| " | 8th | — | Btn working party. All coys provide working parties at 6:30 AM for work on AVELUY SIDING 8AM to 4PM. About 10PM, 16 shells were dropped in district. Only 4 exploded. | |
| " | 9th | — | Usual routine was carried out today. | |
| Point 29 | 10th | — | Btn relieved the 11/5 Black Watch. Subsequent shelling during the night. German artillery fires on their own lines, immediately rockets were fired. Brought — Golden Park. | |
| " | 11th | — | Heavy firing on both sides. Nothing else to report. | |
| " | 12th | — | Btn relieved by 13th Sussex Regt and moved to Thiepval Post. Artillery still active. | |
| Point 65 | 13 | — | Btn moved to Point 65 arrived there about 4PM. Btn moved forward to the attack about 11:30 AM. Btn came not | |
| | | | and moved to Pioneer Road | |
| Pioneer Road | 14th | — | Btn moved from Pioneer Road to Warloy. Route Albert–Hedanit. | |
| Warloy | 15th | — | Btn moved from Warloy to Doullens. Btn on the march all day arrived at Doullens about 5.30PM | |
| Doullens | 16th | — | Usual routine being carried out. | |
| " | 17th | — | Usual routine being carried out. Men issued with underclothes. | |
| Y Camp | 18th | — | Btn entrain at Doullens about 2AM arrived at POPERINGHE about 11AM. March to Y Camp arriving about 12.30PM | |

1875 Wt. W593/826 1,000,000 4/15 J.B.C. & A. A.D.S.S./Forms/C. 2118.

# WAR DIARY
## or
## INTELLIGENCE SUMMARY
*(Erase heading not required.)*

Army Form C. 2118

Instructions regarding War Diaries and Intelligence Summaries are contained in F.S. Regs., Part II. and the Staff Manual respectively. Title Pages will be prepared in manuscript.

| Place | Date | Hour | Summary of Events and Information | Remarks and references to Appendices |
|---|---|---|---|---|
| Y camp | 19th | | Usual Routine. Burial being carried out. | |
| " | 20th | | Usual Routine. Burial being carried out. | |
| " | 21st | | Preparations being made for GOC inspection. | |
| " | 22nd | | GOC's VIII Corps inspected Bn. this morning. Usual working parties RE's. Men played football in the afternoon (afternoon) | |
| " | 23rd | | Usual Routine and working parties. Football was played in the afternoon | |
| " | 24th | | Usual Routine and working parties. | |
| " | 25th | | Bn Route March at 9 a.m. Route taken POPERINGHE, STATION, to YPRES ROAD and back on same route (rain the whole way) | |
| " | 26th | | Usual Routine and working parties. Bn Church parade 11:30 AM. | |
| " | 27th | | Usual Routine and working parties. | |
| " | 28th | | Usual Routine and working parties. Football was played in the afternoon. Signalling scheme most successfully | |
| " | 29th | | Usual Routine and working parties. Signalling scheme cancelled, weather unfavourable. was carried | |
| " | 30th | | Usual Routine and working parties. | |

A.C. Gammon. Lt.
for
Comdg. 14th Hants Regt
Major

1-12-16.

Forwarded with captured maps KLY.

Report of Operations carried out by 14th Hants Regt During period 2.30 a.m. to 10.15 p.m. 13.11.16.

(a) 2.30 a.m. The Battalion less two Coys moved up to assembly positions round point 65 (Schwaben Redoubt Ed.1)

Note. 2 Coys) moved to Dugouts at 15 at 8.45 p.m.

(b) 4. a.m. Movement successfully carried out. The Battalion sustained no casualties.

(c) Zero (5.45 a.m) A. Coy followed up last wave of the 1/1 Herts & occupied the Northern face of the SCHWABEN REDOUBT. A. Coy sustained 8 casualties (wounded only)

(D) Zero + 1 minute Entrance to the Batt. Hd. Qtrs Dug out 30x S.E. of Point 65 was blown in by a shell. No casualties, & damage was soon repaired

(E) 9.15 a.m. Patrol reported that point 63 was still in the hands of the enemy a Platoon was immediately sent out from A. Coy to capture it. This was accomplished no casualties, & a machine gun, machine rifle & 15 prisoners were taken, and a ~~M.G.~~ man of the Cheshires who was a prisoner, was released.

(f) 10.30 a.m. Orders were received to ~~R~~ re-inforce the Cheshires & the Black Watch, a Two Coys to each, & assist in the capture & consolidation of the 3rd objectives of these two units i.e. Q 18. S. 95.30. — Q 24 b.1.1.

(g) 11.5 a.m. Coys. despatched in accordance with (f).

(h) 12. noon All Coys. had reached objective & were consolidating position, but contact had not been made with the Cheshires on the right.

(i) 12.45 p.m. Junction with Cheshires effected.

(j) 1.3 p.m. Orders received to collect Battn. & proceed to THIEPVAL.

(k). 5.40 p.m. All in THIEPVAL.
    (SCHWABEN REDOUBT heavily shelled
    the whole afternoon).

(l) 5.30 p.m. orders received to proceed
    to PIONEER ROAD.

(m) 10.15 p.m. All in PIONEER ROAD.

C.C. Harman Lt Col
~~Capt.~~
Commanding
~~( )~~ 14th Hants.

14.11.16.

116th Brigade.
39th Division.
----------------

1/14th BATTALION

THE HAMPSHIRE REGIMENT

DECEMBER 1 9 1 6

Army Form C. 2118

# WAR DIARY
## or
## INTELLIGENCE SUMMARY
*(Erase heading not required.)*

Instructions regarding War Diaries and Intelligence Summaries are contained in F. S. Regs., Part II. and the Staff Manual respectively. Title Pages will be prepared in manuscript.

| Place | Date | Hour | Summary of Events and Information | Remarks and references to Appendices |
|---|---|---|---|---|
| Y Camp | Dec 1. | | Morning - Route March 9.15 - 1.15, band playing. afternoon games. | |
| POPERINGHE | 2. | | Usual daily routine. Bow respirator drill & test - specialists training. | |
| " | 3. | | Church parade at 11. Corps Comdr present - march past after & camp inspection. Good turnout. | |
| " | 4. | | Daily routine - gas helmets tests & turn out in the enemy. | |
| " | 5. | | Heavy showers. Coys on the Range - rifle - Usual routine. | |
| " | 6. | | Route march - to POPERINGHE - along ABEELE Road - HILHOEK. Passed Army Comdr - General Plumer - | |
| " | 7. | | Reconnoitring party to trenches - Left of Salient -. Usual parades - Coys to range | |
| " | 8. | | Parties for trenches. Coys on range - usual routine work. | |
| " | 9. | | Usual party to trenches. Usual routine - gas tests. | |
| " | 10 | | Voluntary church parades. | |
| " | 11 | | Preparing for move. | |
| " | 12. | | Left at 6.30, marched the 12th R. Sussex. Relief complete at 7 p.m. Canal Bank | |
| Canal Bank | 13 | | Working parties - supplying dugouts. Reconnoissance of front line. | |

1875  Wt. W 593/826  1,000,000  4/15  T R.C.&A.  A.D.S.S./Forms/C. 2118.

# WAR DIARY or INTELLIGENCE SUMMARY

(Erase heading not required.)

Army Form C. 2118

Instructions regarding War Diaries and Intelligence Summaries are contained in F. S. Regs., Part II. and the Staff Manual respectively. Title Pages will be prepared in manuscript.

| Place | Date | Hour | Summary of Events and Information | Remarks and references to Appendices |
|---|---|---|---|---|
| Camp Bank | 14 | | Daily routine – working parties – 100 up at night. | |
| " | 15 | | Daily routine | |
| " | 16 | | Relieved 12 R Sussex in Right Sector – HILLTOP – relief complete by 7.30 p.m. Quiet night. | |
| HILLTOP | 17 | | Day Day. Working parties cleaning & maintenance of trenches. Rickaway & trenches by 15 tanks, although front of front line. | |
| " | 18 | | Daily routine – working parties. Fired 5 yards. Gas shelling 4 p.m. a few | |
| " | 19 | | Dull, miserable weather. Enemy slightly more active | |
| " | 20 | | Wet. Working parties. Enemy up to usual shelling activity | |
| " | 21 | | Very dry, several activity show. Relieved by 12th Sussex. Returned to Camp Bank | |
| " | 22 | | Daily routine – working parties etc. Battalion paraded for BH Chaplain | |
| " | 23 | | Inspected by Br. 2/Lt. RE of Works – turned out in morning. Got up Plant | |
| P. Camp | 24 | | Church parade in battalion. | |
| " | 25 | | Paid. Dinner at Church Army Hut. Xmas dinner for men. | |

# WAR DIARY
or
# INTELLIGENCE SUMMARY

*(Erase heading not required.)*

Instructions regarding War Diaries and Intelligence Summaries are contained in F. S. Regs., Part II. and the Staff Manual respectively. Title Pages will be prepared in manuscript.

| Place | Date | Hour | Summary of Events and Information | Remarks and references to Appendices |
|---|---|---|---|---|
| P Camp | 26 | | Cleaning up camp & making up deficiencies. To Football. Concerts in Sergts Mess. | |
| " | 27 | | Route march through Pyramids about 9 miles. Football in the afternoon | |
| " | 28 | | Remainder of S/gt N. Gd. were constituting — Parade to Race at 10. | |
| " | 29 | | Reconnaissance made on road. | |
| " | 30 | | Training. Service in the afternoon. Relieved 1/7 R.W.F. in Sy trenches. B to BRES/NSH. C. Sector, R.L.I. completed by 7.15 p.m. | |
| Sector | 31 | | On trenches, a great cleaning up. Snipers active, otherwise quiet. | |

J W Finlay Major
Comdg 1/5 Hants Rgt

G.S.O. I
39th Division

Reference Map SCHWABEN REDOUBT 1:5000 Ed I
Report on German line as noticed by me on
13-11-16, STRASBURG line Pt 19 west to PIERRE D
and Old German Front and Support line Pts 47 and 16

I. The trenches were in excellent order very dry and free from mud.

II. Dugouts were roomy, clean and free from mud which would tend to show that the Germans did not move outside their dugouts, this is confirmed by the fact that the prisoners were all very white faced.
Warm felt slippers were also found clean.

III. Equipment well cleaned hung on pegs inside the dugouts, it had not been taken down.
Rifles well cleaned and oiled outside dugouts they had in very few cases except at Pt 63 been fired.

IV. Food. Tinned food of excellent flavour, coffee good food, dark coloured bread good to taste plentiful.

V. Parcels believed the private containing

Confidential

Sir P. B. Hampshire's Pvt.
Vol XI

Diary
for
the month of January 1917

Vol XI

10 H
6...

Army Form C. 2118

# WAR DIARY
## or
## INTELLIGENCE SUMMARY
(Erase heading not required.)

Instructions regarding War Diaries and Intelligence Summaries are contained in F. S. Regs., Part II. and the Staff Manual respectively. Title Pages will be prepared in manuscript.

| Place | Date | Hour | Summary of Events and Information | Remarks and references to Appendices |
|---|---|---|---|---|
| Brewery Sulphide | 1 Jan 1917 | | Slight artillery activity at midnight - otherwise the situation remains peaceful. Weather fine. | |
| do | 2 | | Slight artillery activity in the morning. Various officers reconnoitred the front line, trenches near the Kemp Run, Empress Bombing Posts. A quiet night, and nothing to report. | |
| do | 3 | | Enemy were shelling between the front line & village lines in the morning, but no damage was done. Our Artillery were also active during the day. Bn. relieved the 11th R. Sussex Regt in front line. | |
| Front line Brewery Sector | 4 | | Very quiet. Little activity by either Artillery. We at once commenced sniping, and accounted for two of the enemy. In the evening an attempt was made to put out wire, but moon very bright, and enemy machine guns at once replied. | |
| do | 5 | | Another quiet morning. Slight artillery activity over K.T. No registering, with some success on enemy front line; three more snipers accounted for by us; still too bright for much sniping. | |
| do | 6 | | In the afternoon, enemy for forty minutes heavily shelled the village line - doing some damage to communication trenches and bursting Stokes mortar ammunition. We were slight. Col. Smith R.B. did very good work by causing Bn.s from Run, on hearing the approach of a minenwerfer. We suffered no casualties during this period. | |
| do | 7 | | Bn. relieved by 13th Royal Sussex Regt. and returned to Bees in the support line. One officer for day had to remain in the front line, as for reasons unknown the Bn. had not relieved it; and a relief was thought possible to carry later. | |

# WAR DIARY or INTELLIGENCE SUMMARY

Army Form C. 2118

(Erase heading not required.)

Instructions regarding War Diaries and Intelligence Summaries are contained in F. S. Regs., Part II. and the Staff Manual respectively. Title Pages will be prepared in manuscript.

| Place | Date | Hour | Summary of Events and Information | Remarks and references to Appendices |
|---|---|---|---|---|
| Besingly Support | 8th | | All available men employed on working parties in front & support trenches. Very slight artillery activity; but a good deal of M.G. fire at night. | |
| do | 9th | | All men again on working. enemy artillery very active on the Belgian front. | |
| do | 10th | | Great artillery activity (enemy) on our right (say. (Sussex) front about 11 a.m. About 6 p.m Heavy artillery 4in Q. fire heard, & enemy observed, but no details yet to hand. At 7 p.m the situation became normal. | |
| do | 11th | | Quiet in the day time. About 5 p.m a Battalion on our right in the vicinity of Hooge raided the enemy's trenches. Much artillery and M.G fire was heard and the French sent up several red rockets, evidently calling for a barrage. Everything was again quiet about 7 p.m. | |
| Bessingh Front Line | 12th | | Battalion again relieved the 13th R.W. Surrey in the front line. Relief proved of quality. Nothing to report during the night | |
| do | 13th | | Much work was done pulling up tailing. astillar service etc for inspection by Corps Commdr. that evg thunderstorm from 5 p.m – 9 p.m. the whole Battalion – including all Hqtr Staff was ordered to be out of the front line. however it was found impossible for more than a few men to work at a time. Very quiet all day. | |
| do | 14th | | Work continued. The Royal Sussex parties arrived as it was too wet. At 6 p.m. we were relieved by the 13th R Sussex Regt and returned to Bleuet Farm in support. Only two casualties (wounded) during this tour, while working. | |
| Bleuet Farm | 15th | | Battalion now in support. The Corps Commander arrived at front line at 6.45 a.m. but did not visit the support. Up the evening, 200 men were employed on working parties | |

# WAR DIARY
## or
## INTELLIGENCE SUMMARY

*(Erase heading not required.)*

Army Form C. 2118

Instructions regarding War Diaries and Intelligence Summaries are contained in F. S. Regs., Part II. and the Staff Manual respectively. Title Pages will be prepared in manuscript.

| Place | Date | Hour | Summary of Events and Information | Remarks and references to Appendices |
|---|---|---|---|---|
| BIEUET TARN | Jan 16th | | Battalion relieved at 4.30 p.m by South Wales Borderers, and marched to billets in the Convent at Ypres. Shortly after arrival, a few shells landed in the town, but no damage was done. | |
| Ypres | 17th | | In billets. Two Companies employed on working-parties; remainder employed on returning. Day very quiet. | |
| do | 18th | | Ditto. Quiet - one or two shells in Ypres Square - no casualties - Officers reconnoitred the new line. | |
| do | 19th | | Ditto. Reconnoitring completed. Slight shelling in the afternoon - our guns fairly active. | |
| do | 20th | | Specialist's took over new line at 6 p.m. Battalion relieves 11th Rl Sussex at 8.30 p.m. Relief complete at 8.30 p.m. Quiet night. Wiring | |
| Railway Wood Left Sector | 21 | | Very quiet all day. Working parties on stores, trenches etc. Wiring at night. 1 wounded. | |
| " | 22 | | Fine day, aeroplane activity during the afternoon. Slight shelling, shelling on Right Coy Front - gully trench. Wiring at night, about 105 coils put out. | |
| " | 23 | | Cold. Slight activity - few shells by road near H.Q.R.S. Aeroplanes busy - 3 of ours down. | |
| " | 24 | | Enemy active all day especially on the Right Front. Relieved by 114 R Sussex Regt. Not complete till 11 p.m owing to shelling of YPRES. Coys all in billets by 12.30 A.M. | |

Army Form C. 2118

# WAR DIARY
## or
## INTELLIGENCE SUMMARY
*(Erase heading not required.)*

Instructions regarding War Diaries and Intelligence Summaries are contained in F.S. Regs., Part II. and the Staff Manual respectively. Title Pages will be prepared in manuscript.

| Place | Date | Hour | Summary of Events and Information | Remarks and references to Appendices |
|---|---|---|---|---|
| YPRES | 25 | | Very cold & clear. An enemy raid on 11th R. Sussex - 5 prisoners. Artillery & aeroplane activity all day. False Gas Alarm at 8.15 p.m. | |
| " | 26 | | Daily routine - usual working parties | |
| " | 27 | | Still cold. Artillery active. | |
| " | 28 | | Specialists off at 5.15 A.M. Ypres slightly shelled. Relieved 11th R. Sussex, complete by 8.30 p.m. Very quiet night another dud Boche Trench it out | |
| Railway Wood Left Sector | 29 | | Fine clear day. Heavies registering all day. Enemy retaliated at odd intervals. Cwlts up S.A.A, Smoke Bombs, & Rations | |
| " | 30 | | Wire cleared & bombardment started at 8.45 A.M. - Heavies, 7.18 tons. Heavy retaliation at odd intervals. Practically quiet by 3.30 p.m. except for bursts of fire every few minutes. Two enemy patrols out - enemy Rolling fire. Evening. Cwlts 2 K. 6 w | |
| " | 31 | | Warmer. Artillery active all day. Minenwerfer on the Left Front. Gas, Lewis gun & steam kopfed out. Otherwise fairly quiet. Cwlts 1 k. + 5 w. | |

A.G.Garrigan Lt/Adj
for
Comdg 12th Han Regt

11 H.
Sheet

Confidential
Vol 12

War Diary
for month of February 17
1st B. Hampshire R.

Vol. XII

Army Form C. 2118

# WAR DIARY
## or
## INTELLIGENCE SUMMARY
(Erase heading not required.)

Instructions regarding War Diaries and Intelligence Summaries are contained in F. S. Regs., Part II. and the Staff Manual respectively. Title Pages will be prepared in manuscript.

| Place | Date 1917 | Hour | Summary of Events and Information | Remarks and references to Appendices |
|---|---|---|---|---|
| Railway Wood Left Sector. | Feb. 1 | | S.O.S. up at 5 A.M. on our front. Intense minenwerfer bombardments, also shelling. Bosche on our left driven back. Captain Gollmick got his company up quickly to close support, also when Bosch returned he captured a prisoner in No Mans Land. Capt. Beetham wounded, incls Gilchrist – Doney killed, also 9 O.R. + 14 wounded. Relieved by 11th R. Sussex Regt at night, complete by 9 p.m., to cavalry YPRES |  |
| YPRES | 2 | | Fairly quiet day – cleaning up + working parties. Very cold. |  |
| " | 3 | | Artillery active, on also aeroplanes. Bright day. Two Coys + HQRS left at 9.30 p.m. entrained, about 15 mins train journey. Into "C" Camp. |  |
| "C" Camp | 4 | | Church parade at 11 A.M. in Church Army Hut. Quiet day. Two remaining Coys arrived about midnight. |  |
| " | 5 | | Day spent in cleaning of camp, also clothes, equipment etc. Forming of specialist parties. Football. |  |
| " | 6 | | Battalion parade + then specialists – bombers, Lewis gunners, Rifle grenadiers, snipers + bombers. Football + games in the afternoon. |  |
| " | 7 | | Gas lectures all. for 310 men, + training of specialists. Lewis Gunners firing on the Range all afternoon. |  |

**Army Form C. 2118**

# WAR DIARY
## or
## INTELLIGENCE SUMMARY
*(Erase heading not required.)*

Instructions regarding War Diaries and Intelligence Summaries are contained in F. S. Regs., Part II. and the Staff Manual respectively. Title Pages will be prepared in manuscript.

| Place | Date | Hour | Summary of Events and Information | Remarks and references to Appendices |
|---|---|---|---|---|
| C. Camp | Feb 8th | | Usual Bat'n parade at 9 a.m. from 9.45 a.m - 12.30 m.d training of Lewis Gunners, Bombers, Scouts at 2 p.m a pres received. Inf. reviewed by 10 Co. & 3 Hdqr. Officers. All but lost. At 2.30 p.m Bat'n. inspected by Brig. Genl. No adverse comments. | |
| " | Feb 9th | | Bat'n Route march from 9 a.m - 12.30 m.d. day Bat'n. inspected by Brig. Genl. on return, in afternoon, we were for officers at Penanrough. | |
| " | Feb 10th | | Usual parades & training of Specialists. During day and night reconnaissances of roads in front was made by Sct. Corps. | |
| " | Feb 11th | | Church parade at 10.45 a.m. Bat'n. complimented by Brig. Genl. on their smartness. General holiday for rest of day. | |
| " | 12th | | Usual parades and specialists training. Nearly all of our O/Rs arrived from Frostord. found aeroplanes were not in disuse for day. Lieut Hamly appointed asst. to our commander. | |
| " | 13th | | As for 12th. Lieut. Pochin accidentally wounded by the burst of a rifle grenade whilst believed to be in the afternoon. Two enemy aeroplanes were seen to drop on our lines, one in flames. | |
| " | 14th 15th | | Battalion went on a route march in the morning. | |
| " | 16th | | Taking over. Officers arrived from the 11th Royal Scots Fus. to inspect & more lines etc. relief of Batl'n took place at moon. At 6 M.T. Back Training. | |
| " | | | We left the lines. marched in about 1.30 p.m. The Battalion entrained at 4.30 p.m - being compelled on their orderly to embark. Found Batl'n held at 7 p.m. after a short hectic passage. Little - bottles - billets at various good torch. Very Comfort. | |
| Touvelle | 17th | | Many and in general clean up. Band played in Billage square in the afternoon was greatly appreciated. | |
| " | 18th | | Church parade in the football field. Afterwards Brig. Genl. went round the lines | |

**Army Form C. 2118**

# WAR DIARY
## or
## INTELLIGENCE SUMMARY
*(Erase heading not required.)*

Instructions regarding War Diaries and Intelligence Summaries are contained in F.S. Regs., Part II. and the Staff Manual respectively. Title Pages will be prepared in manuscript.

| Place | Date | Hour | Summary of Events and Information | Remarks and references to Appendices |
|---|---|---|---|---|
| Bollezeele | Feb | | Billets, & enquired himself very satisfied. | |
| " | " | 19 | Morning spent in re-organising platoons on the French system. In the afternoon sports committees elected, & programme of recreation arranged. | |
| " | " | 20 | Orders received to return to the line on Saturday. Reconnoitring parties sent out to OBSERVATORY RIDGE sector. Not formally improved. | |
| " | " | 21 | Reconnoitring continued. Battn. next for 10 mile route march. 3 cases of German measles taken out in 'C' Coy., isolated. | |
| " | " | 22 | Usual training carried out, & reconnoitring continued | |
| " | " | 23 | Usual training of specialists & preparations for move - advance party off early | |
| " | " | 24 | Btn. entrained at 7.30 A.M., & after three hours journey detrained at CHEESE MARKET, POP. Marched to Toronto Camp - went to | |
| Toronto Camp | " | 25 | Church parade - Y.M.C.A. hut. A dinner party off at NOON. Main body 5.15 p.m. Train to YPRES, thence via LILLE GATE. Relieved 112 W. Yorks - not complete until 1 AM. Quiet. | |
| Observatory Ridge | " | 26 | Slight shelling during the day, otherwise quiet. Machine gun firing at night. Few shells around Valley Cottages | |
| " | " | 27 | Patches of smoke to fire remembrance. Exceedingly quiet - few shells. Machine gun fire at night. | |
| " | " | 28 | Misty morning, quiet. Relieved by the 11/R. Sussex Regt. - complete by 10.15 p.m. A steffh on the Right at 9.45, rather warm for a while. Back to YPRES. | |

A.G. Gemmage Lt. Col.
16th Hants Regt.

116/39

12.H.

Confidential

War Diary Vol 13
of
4th Bn. Hants Reg.
for
March 1914.

Army Form C. 2118

# WAR DIARY
## or
## INTELLIGENCE SUMMARY
*(Erase heading not required.)*

Instructions regarding War Diaries and Intelligence Summaries are contained in F.S. Regs, Part II. and the Staff Manual respectively. Title Pages will be prepared in manuscript.

| Place | Date | Hour | Summary of Events and Information | Remarks and references to Appendices |
|---|---|---|---|---|
| BRUSSTRAAT. | 1 March 1917 | | Battalion in Divisional Reserve near Ypres. Between 9am-11am enemy shelled vicinity of Battalion HQ and between 3-5pm the neighbourhood of the Lille Gate was heavily shelled. Throughout the morning at least one hostile observation balloon was up. It probably witnessed an ascent enemy to the presence of our planes as many as eleven in number. | |
| " | 2 March 1917 | | The forenoon was quiet in the vicinity of Batt. HQ, but in the late afternoon the vicinity was shelled with HE and shrapnel (Captain Myhugh). In the evening a great many shells were heard going into Ypres. | |
| " | 3 March 1917 | | Quite until the day was quiet. Draft Battalion went back into rest at TORONTO CAMP [G.16.a 3.7] | |
| TORONTO CAMP [G.16.a 3.7] | 4-9 MARCH 1917 | | Whole Battalion was apparently in rest. The usual Rest Training was carried out. MUSKETRY BAYONET FIGHTING. DRILL. BOX RESPIRATOR DRILL & ROUTE MARCHING | |
| " | 9 MARCH | | Battalion (less one battalion, attached to the grenades) moved up to the OBSERVATORY RIDGE SECTOR [I.24.d] | |
| IN THE LINE. (OBSERVATORY RIDGE) | 10/3/17 9:15pm to 9:15 1917 10/3 1917 | | Battalion in relief the 15th Canadian Regiment. Enemy very quiet. A few rounds were fired at 5.30am in the vicinity of two Turillers (ZILLEBEKE), and in the afternoon a rifle grenades were sent over behind the front line. Our artillery was active between 2-3pm our heavy supported this rifle grenades more went over. Machine Apprise CRAIG BRAWL (Suspected Enemy MGun. Machine others 5 was general except for on front line in the early morning. | |
| " | 10/11 March 1917 | 5pm to 5pm | The night was very quiet and there was no artillery fire on either side. Enemy sent over afew rifle grenades. Our patrols went out on the right and in the centre. Nothing forming was carried on by the front line companies. Bos heard working on angle in enemy line. No report except enemy working party. (working). | |

Army Form C. 2118

# WAR DIARY
## or
## INTELLIGENCE SUMMARY
*(Erase heading not required.)*

Instructions regarding War Diaries and Intelligence Summaries are contained in F.S. Regs., Part II. and the Staff Manual respectively. Title Pages will be prepared in manuscript.

| Place | Date | Hour | Summary of Events and Information | Remarks and references to Appendices |
|---|---|---|---|---|
| IN THE LINE (OBSERVATORY RIDGE) | 10/11 March 17 | 5 pm – 5 pm (cont) | Enemy quiet up to 3 pm when he put over a few "minnies" just behind CROSS TRENCH; and to the right of CRAB CRAWL. Artillery (T.O.V.) was active on HILL 60 TRENCH at 3.30 pm. Our artillery retaliated. Trench mortars and annual activity throughout the early part of the day, and 2 Bombish planes were brought down in aerial encounter, one in the woods at YPRES and the other near RAILWAY WOOD. | |
| " | 11/12 March 17 | 5 pm – 5 pm | Enemy artillery was quiet during the night except for some spasmodic shelling of the duckboards in the vicinity of MAPLE COPSE at about 7 p.m. Enemy machine guns very active between 6–10 pm (11k) on CROSS & VANCOUVER TRENCHES. Some rifle grenades were sent over on HILL 60 STREET. Our artillery, machine guns + T.M.'s were quiet. Patrols went out from all three front line companies. A relief was arranged as very few were very light were sent over and 2 trench mortar bombs behind enemy line at 6.35 pm + 2 am (11K + 10K). All companies trench in front of their line. During the day the enemy was generally quiet except for a few rifle grenades between WINNIPEG & VANCOUVER TRENCHES and other spasmodic shelling of duckboards near MAPLE COPSE and FORT STREET & BORDER LANE. Our artillery fired at intervals on enemy support line, and our heavy trench mortars registered 2 rounds from the right Battalion front. Several trench repairing, cleaning and draining. | |
| " | 12/13 March 17 | 5 pm – 5 pm | Everything was very quiet during the night, but enemy machine guns played on the MAPLE COPSE duckboards between 7–8 pm (12K) and a certain amount of firing took place at 1 am (13K) for about an hour. Apparently there was some alarm on the left (Cheshires) and the Battalion stood to in the front line from a grenade attack. Trench were again beach in rear of enemy line 10.45 pm. 2.20 am + 2.30 am. 3 Enemy were seen in front of CROSS TRENCH near their own trench. Bec refuge to their trench upon a very light going up. During the enemy stay his trench was quiet. Some our 2" T.M. registered (4 rounds) on the left of Battalion front. Trench mortars over 40 minennies (no damage) another artillery shelled with H.A.V. Stopped when our artillery opened. Some rifle grenades in the vicinity of VANCOUVER TRENCH. The enemy was very active in the afternoon in the region of DORMY HOUSE [I. 23 a. 7.4]. His first shot was a burst 24". | |
| " | 13 March 1917 | 5 pm – midnight | The Battalion was relieved in the line by the 11th Royal Sussex Regiment (Relief completed about 10.20 pm). Battalion marched to K. BUND. | |

1875  Wt: W593/826  1,000,000  4/15  J.B.C. & A.  A.D.S.S./Forms/C. 2118.

# WAR DIARY or INTELLIGENCE SUMMARY

Army Form C. 2118

Instructions regarding War Diaries and Intelligence Summaries are contained in F.S. Regs, Part II. and the Staff Manual respectively. Title Pages will be prepared in manuscript.

(Erase heading not required.)

| Place | Date | Hour | Summary of Events and Information | Remarks and references to Appendices |
|---|---|---|---|---|
| BUND [ZILLEBEKE] | 14 March 1917 | 12 midnight – 12 midnight | The Battalion were in support on Ramparts Reserve, and were employed upon the usual working parties. Enemy heavy batteries (5.9s) were very active during the early afternoon near the LILLE GATE especially at point I.14.c.3.8 where a good number of shells dropped or actually into the moat. At 5.30 pm the enemy sent a continuous stream of heavy shells apparently in the neighbourhood of the ASYLUM. These appeared to be all gas shells, but from the fact that there was a little wind blowing and that they were sent over in rapid succession. At 7pm their became apparent that our own artillery replied. | |
| " | 15 March | | Between 11.30 am onwards the enemy reduced the shelling opened on LR.V., with an occasional 4.2. our howitzers covered point was a shelter for about three quarters of an hour and were accurate action on both sides, accompanied by artillery barrages. Throughout the afternoon there was casual activity. The Menin Road with 5.9s & some 4.2 howitzers, in the main activity. At about 6 pm the enemy shelled our WOODCOTE HOUSE [I.20.c.4.2] after the same time after shells burst very high up apparently over colored smoke black & brownish in separate spasmodic. These shells burst with every few explosions an open often low explosion. | |
| " | 16 March | " | Fine clear day, aerial activity. Artillery quiet. enemy shelled the ramparts. Working parties as usual. | |
| " | 17th | " | Specialists up to the line before dawn. Remainder during a rest + general cleaning up. Regts. moved off at 6.15 p.m. Relieved the 11th R.S.R. (relief complete by 9.30 p.m) Quiet night. | |
| IN THE LINE OBSERVATORY RIDGE | 18th | 12 midnight – 5 pm | Very quiet morning. Few dry-bangs on the bakelands during afternoon, also 15 pdrs active on enemy support lines. Two observation balloons up. Signalling seen from Bock balloon. | |
| | 18/19 March 1917 | 5 pm – 5 pm | Snipers active at night. Enemy sent up Very lights all night, many small Lewis fire teamed to our RightFront. Wire put out. Artillery active on both sides. Four round about 4 pr+3 pr put up on Bosche parapet – black bursts. Enemy reported infantry in front line during the morning. | |
| | 19/20 March 1917 | 5 pm – 5 pm | Intermittent artillery fire, otherwise all still quiet all night. Rain, observation poor. Practically quiet. | |

# WAR DIARY or INTELLIGENCE SUMMARY

Army Form C. 2118

| Place | Date | Hour | Summary of Events and Information | Remarks and references to Appendices |
|---|---|---|---|---|
| OBSERVATORY RIDGE | 20/21 March 1917 | 5 p.m. –5 p.m. | Our field guns active. Practically no movement at all. We find several rifle grenades into enemy front line during the evening. Machine guns coming from HILL 60 playing on the front & support lines. Sniping during the night. Various cloud displays over hostile enemy lines – trains slow heard. Specialists of relieving Battn. up before dawn. | |
| " | 21/22 | 5 p.m. –5 p.m. | VALLEY COTTAGES – Batt HQRS shelled from 2 to 2.30 p.m. with 4.2 in. Relief at 11 p.m., not complete till 1.15 p.m. Train from YPRES. Reached TORONTO CAMP at 5 A.M. Cleaning up – no fixed parades. Staff Parade just | |
| " | 22 | midnight before 5 A.M. | | |
| TORONTO CAMP. | 23rd | | Coy parades & specialist Training – 2.00 men to the baths. Parades & specialist training. Col Harman returned with 24 Bt. | |
| " | 24th 27th incl. | | Battalion Specialists moved up to relieve 115 Bde. on the same line as before. Battalion moved up to YPRES by train at 9.45 p.m. relieving Bn. on YSSERS at KRUISSTRAAT and the Bund. Relief complete without casualties by midnight. | |
| KRUISSTRAAT | 29th | Tropl. | Training of Specialists continued. Little shelling. All men employed on working parties up to 3 a.m. | |
| " | 30th | Hospl. | At 9 a.m.–1 p.m. untraped Lewis Gunners and bad shots fired on ranges outside SALLY PORT No1. near LILLE GATE. YPRES shelled intermittently and heavily. Lewis Gunners moved up at 9 p.m. to relieve those of 11 Sussex on the line. Working parties as usual. | |
| " | 31st | Hospl. | Coy parades. A known Battn. up in the afternoon. Relieved 11 R.S.R. in the line – complete by 11.25 p.m. New HQRS in ZILLEBEEKE, old place shelled. VALLEY COTS. Quiet night. | |

A.G. Gammon Lt.
Commdg. for Lt. Col.
16th Hants. Regt.

Confidential

Vol 14

War Diary
of
4th Br Hants Regt.
for
April 1914.

Army Form C. 2118

# WAR DIARY
## or
## INTELLIGENCE SUMMARY
(Erase heading not required.)

Instructions regarding War Diaries and Intelligence Summaries are contained in F. S. Regs., Part II. and the Staff Manual respectively. Title Pages will be prepared in manuscript.

| Place | Date | Hour | Summary of Events and Information | Remarks and references to Appendices |
|---|---|---|---|---|
| IN THE LINE (OBSERVATORY RIDGE.) | 1st April | | Quiet night. Intermittent shelling during the morning. Working party improving HQRS, + erecting baby elephants. Heavier bombardt. enemy trenches from 3 to 5 p.m. Retalitd. on Winnipeg Street, 2 killed + 4 wounded. Demobilisation at CRAB CRAWL Entrance, St Peter Trench, Vince St + Winnipeg St. Very quiet evening | |
| do | 2d | " | Several very bright put ups at night. Another bombardment by our Heavies further on the Right. Quiet, little retaliation. Machine Guns fairly busy at night from left rear – HILL 60 direction. Working Parties busy completing new HQRS. Snow storm at night – dirty night. | |
| do | 3d | | Slight shelling during the morning. Few aeroplanes about, clearing after the snow fall. Working party on filling sandbags, + completing dugouts. Heard into new mess & room. Fairly quiet evening – machine guns a few more than usual. 3 Patrols out, nothing important, 30 coils of wire put out. | |
| do | 4th | | Still morning, dull. Slight shelling on either side, more activity in the afternoon, aeroplanes fairly active. Relieved by the 11th R. Sussex Regt – complete by 11.15 p.m. | |
| BUND | 5th | | Great activity all day – enemy shelld Ramparts YPRES with heavy shells, also Shrapnel Corner. Aeroplanes active. Usual working parties at night. Heavy stuff further South, started at 5.30 p.m. | |

Army Form C. 2118

# WAR DIARY
## or
## INTELLIGENCE SUMMARY
*(Erase heading not required.)*

Instructions regarding War Diaries and Intelligence Summaries are contained in F. S. Regs., Part II. and the Staff Manual respectively. Title Pages will be prepared in manuscript.

| Place | Date | Hour | Summary of Events and Information | Remarks and references to Appendices |
|---|---|---|---|---|
| BUND | 6th April | | Intermittent shelling all day, otherwise quiet. The Battn relieved by the regiments — 11th, 16th, 17th Nth — Derby + 9 York + Lanes. Complete by 12 midnight, to ASYLUM. STA, + back by train. | |
| ERIE CAMP | 7th | | Battn all in by 3.30 A.M. Reveille 8 A.M. Inspection Parades under new organization. Afternoon devoted to games | |
| do | 8th & 9th | | Usual Parades, a few working parties — Disinfecting of men's clothing 260 per day. Wet + windy. | |
| do | 10th & 11th | | Parades as usual, small working parties. Gentlemen from VIMY RIDGES. Advance parties left at 1 pm for the line. Battn left at 8 pm — train to YPRES. Quiet, morning. | |
| OBSERVATORY RIDGE | 12th | | Relief complete by 2.15 P.M — 16th Nth + Derby — Quiet night. Day not clear, little activity. Germans seen wearing gas helmets about 6 pm — Fine clear night — nothing to report | |
| do | 13th | | Fairly clear, quiet all morning, a air-plane activity. A number of enemy + trucks seen about 1200 yds away. Very still night. | |
| do | 14th | | Bright day, artillery fairly active on both sides, otherwise all quiet. A harass parties up at midnight | |

# WAR DIARY or INTELLIGENCE SUMMARY

Army Form C. 2118

Instructions regarding War Diaries and Intelligence Summaries are contained in F.S. Regs., Part II. and the Staff Manual respectively. Title Pages will be prepared in manuscript.

(Erase heading not required.)

| Place | Date | Hour | Summary of Events and Information | Remarks and references to Appendices |
|---|---|---|---|---|
| OBSERVATORY RIDGE | 15th April | | Wet day – fairly quiet. VINCE ST shelled in the afternoon, & also the hinterland near the Aid Post. Relieved by 13th D.L.I. – completed by 1.10 A.M. | |
| ERIE CAMP | 16th | | Batt'n arrived in ERIE CAMP about 4.45 A.M. General cleaning up. Rain all day. | |
| " | 17th | | Wet day – no parades. Advance Party left at NOON for HILL TOP sector. Batt'n left at 8. train to YPRES. (Bowlers on CANAL BANK. Relief completed by 11.30. Quiet. | |
| CANAL BANK | 18 " | | Snowing first - dull day. Reconnaissance of the line by all Coys. Four working parties. Gun artillery firing at intervals. | |
| " | 19 " | | Parades in the morning; Lewis gunners & Bombers training. About 200 men on working parties. Reconnaissance of our own front & the Bde on the left. Weather improving. | |
| " | 20 " | | | |
| " | 21 " | | Usual routine, & working parties. Fine day. | |
| " | 22 " | | | |
| " | 23 " | | Moving Y Sector. Advance parties to relieve 11th R.S.R. Relief completed by 11.25 p.m. | |

# WAR DIARY
## or
## INTELLIGENCE SUMMARY

*(Erase heading not required.)*

Army Form C. 2118

Instructions regarding War Diaries and Intelligence Summaries are contained in F. S. Regs., Part II. and the Staff Manual respectively. Title Pages will be prepared in manuscript.

| Place | Date | Hour | Summary of Events and Information | Remarks and references to Appendices |
|---|---|---|---|---|
| HILL TOP SECTOR | 24th | 6 a.m. | Sort of Galway Reinforcements for the Regiment was ordered to fall on Parade, another draft was ordered. During the morning the Enemy carried out an usual Shelling, bombardment on Bois Pits and GUITHERPE R. At 2.30 p.m. our Artillery and T.M's commenced an actual Shelling along the Front, doing considerable damage to enemy wire. They retaliation was slight, caused no casualties. | |
| | | 9.30 p.m. | Heavy Bosche Artil[lery] was opened about a mile away on our right. Our S.O.S. went up there. The Posts sending up green lights. | |
| | | 10 p.m. | Enemy put barrage along our front line, with heavy's capt. whiltbag, and minnis | |
| | | 10.5 p.m. | Enemy continued his barrage on front line on right, but lifted about 100 yards from Post 9 GUITHERPE Rd to TASTE, forming a box round these posts. He also put a barrage on the village with minnis called the box. | |
| | | 10.10 p.m. | S.O.S. went up from our Pt. 10 Post. Our barrage was prompt and powerful, any attack the Bosch may have contemplated being quelled. The Enemy was observed to clear out of his front line, & round our barrage. Our casualties were only one, slightly wounded. | |
| do | 25th | | A quiet morning – parties of British which had been frozen in, were cleared. Our Artillery & T.M's Shelled our wire cutting, the enemy's retaliation was desultory. Nevertheless being quiet night. Patrols of our N.L.S.H went out to reconnoiter wire, as well as our own. Usual M.G fire. | |
| do | 26th | 2 p.m. | Increasingly quiet as the afternoon wore on. At 2 p.m. Artillery and Trench mortar cutting, with successful results. Enemy retaliation was negligible. From 5 p.m. to dusk both our guns and the Boch's were very active, simply of very R.E.S.'s exchanges on the Line at one time. Quiet night. Artillery wire cutting. Patrols went out but obtained no information. | |
| do | 27th | | Quiet morning. Little activity on part of the enemy. Our Artillery and T.M's cut wire from 2.30 pm to 6.30 pm with good results. Wire interchanges but with large Toms – no damage done. | |
| do | 28th | | Relief was relieved on Hill top Sector, by 1st Batt. Inniskilling. From Yards Reserve Line and marched to Y Camp arriving 4.30 am. | |
| at Y Camp | 29th | | Day spent in checking up. Church Parade formed on afternoon. | |
| do | 30th | | Ordinary daily parades throughout the day. | |
| do | 1st | | Bn. entrained to TOPENSENT and arrived at 10.45 a.m. Arrived ST OMER 3 pm – met by band of 1st Battalion and marched to billets in TRANQUE. Excellent billets. | |
| ARQUES | 2nd | | Bn. paraded 9.30 a.m. and marched via STONFER – ST MARTIN au LAERTE – INCHEQUIRES – to MERINGHEM CROSSROADS – MERINGHEM – returning here and unloading lower ladder which were all very good. | |

W. Lake? Lt Col.
1st Border Regt.

1875  Wt. W593/826  1,000,000  4/15  J.B.C. & A.  A.D.S.S./Forms/C. 2118.

Headquarters
116/ Infy Bde

Herewith War Diary for the
month of May 1917.

[signature] pd.
for [signature]
Lieut Colonel
Commanding 14th Hants Regt.

1-5-17

# WAR DIARY or INTELLIGENCE SUMMARY

Army Form C. 2118

14th Batt'n
Aug 1917
Vol 15

| Place | Date | Hour | Summary of Events and Information | Remarks and references to Appendices |
|---|---|---|---|---|
| MORINGHEM | 1/5/17 | | Bttn left ARQUES at 6 A.M. & marched to Billets in MORINGHEM, Pt. G. DIEQUES. Men marched well. 70th Rest of day spent in settling in & cleaning up. Glorious weather. | |
| do | 2/5/17 | | Bttn left Billets 7:30 A.M. & carried out Platoon Training for the Attack till NOON. Rest of the day was spent on the Range at CORMETTE. Each Coy went round till 9 P.M. | |
| do | 3 | | A Batt'n attack scheme carried out, finished by 4 P.M. | |
| do | 4 | | Platoon Training in the morning, & on the Range rest of day. Inspection by Surgeon General | |
| do | 5 | | Training in the Attack — during afternoon on many men on parade held Pack Drill | |
| do | 6 | | Church Parade 10 A.M. Remainder of the day holiday. | |
| do | 7 | | Coy training, Platoons & Coys in the Attack. | |
| do | 8 | | Brigade Field Day. Left at 7 A.M. Attack on CORMETTE from BOUDINGHEM. Bn in general reserve. Remainder of Brigade. Back at 6 P.M. | |
| do | 9 | | Training by Coys until 1 P.M. Regimental Sports in the afternoon, went off well. | |
| do | 10 | | Jumping for Batt'n Platoons — two Coys the morning, two in afternoon. Very hot. | |
| do | 11 | | Brigade Field Day. Bttn in reserve all the morning, & held up final assault later in the afternoon. Company & Platoon football match. | |
| do | 12 | | Training apart when Coy manoeuvres — afternoon off — sports at 112th R Sussex Regt. Good sport. Most of the officers & men. Very hot. | |
| do | 13 | | Church parade at 10 A.M. on Transport Field. Inspection of the Bttn afterwards, went off well | |

# WAR DIARY
or
## INTELLIGENCE SUMMARY
*(Erase heading not required.)*

Army Form C. 2118

Instructions regarding War Diaries and Intelligence Summaries are contained in F. S. Regs., Part II. and the Staff Manual respectively. Title Pages will be prepared in manuscript.

| Place | Date | Hour | Summary of Events and Information | Remarks and references to Appendices |
|---|---|---|---|---|
| MORINGHEM | 14/5/17 | | Inspection of the Bn. by Brigadier General Hanby. Spent the morning after the Battalion left the Bn — No 1. | |
| ARQUES | 15/5/17 | | The Bn left at 8 AM — arrived at ARQUES at 10 AM — men marched well. Resting during the afternoon. Calm. | |
| ARNEKE | 16" | | Left at 9.15 AM. arrived at 11 AM — went to ARNEKE, good billets. Rain. | |
| WORMHOUDT | 17" | | Left 11.6 AM. Brigade marched heavy rain — all in billets by 11.45 AM — afternoon spent cleaning up. | |
| do | 18" | | Field day training and preparing for Bde Sports. Bde Sports at 1.45 pm. Bde did afternoon very first class. 5 pts out of 100 — 13th second with 19 | |
| do | 19" | | Cleaning of kit & Wars rifles & transport. Training as best as possible on roads etc — muskettry rpt. Football final for last place No I won 4 - nil. | |
| do | 20" | | Bde checked. Marched to the town to BULFORD. Very hot day. | |
| do | 21 | | Fatigue Coy. to the Baths at HERZEELE, 520 men bathed. Sports & games in the afternoon. Heavy thunderstorm about 5 o'clock of the Salient. | |
| do | 22 | | Wet morning. Usual parades. | |

# WAR DIARY or INTELLIGENCE SUMMARY

Army Form C. 2118

| Place | Date | Hour | Summary of Events and Information | Remarks and references to Appendices |
|---|---|---|---|---|
| WORMHOUDT | 23-5-17 | | A Coy inspected by the Brig Gen Comdg. Bombers party told by the B.B.O. Remainder usual parades. | |
| do | 24 | | Inspection of B & C Coys by the C.O. Lewis Gun Limbers to Bde for inspection. | |
| do | 25 | | Patrols at the lines & reconnaissance by lorry. Usual training. Sports at Bde. | |
| do | 26 | | Inspection of D Coy by C.O. Sports at Bde. | |
| do | 27 | | Packing up. Transport off at 1.8 am. The Bn relieved the 1/1st Kent Regt in the new NIEUTJE entrenchment. Relief completed at 11.30 am 28/5/17. 'D' Coy and 2 platoons of 'C' Coy remained behind at 'D' Camp | |
| NIEUTJE SECTOR | 28 | | Fairly quiet. Enemy shelled NIEUTJE DUGOUT about 8pm with 5.9's (70 rds). 10 casualties. | |
| do | 29 | | Fairly quiet. Shelling & sniping a feeling in retaliation for our bombardment. 3 men wounded. | |
| do | 30 | | Quiet. From 6pm to 6.10 enemy were forced in neighbourhood of ST JEAN. Afternoon quiet. | |
| do | 31 | | During morning a few shells were fired in neighbourhood of ST JEAN. Afternoon quiet. Bn relieved at 12.30am by 1/7 & 1/8 Devons. No casualties. | |

J. A. [signature]
Lt. Col.
Comdg. 7 Bat.

Original

14 Hampshire Regt  
Vol 16

Army Form C. 2118.

# WAR DIARY
## or
## INTELLIGENCE SUMMARY.
(Erase heading not required.)

Instructions regarding War Diaries and Intelligence Summaries are contained in F.S. Regs., Part II. and the Staff Manual respectively. Title pages will be prepared in manuscript.

| Place | Date | Hour | Summary of Events and Information | Remarks and references to Appendices |
|---|---|---|---|---|
| WFNTZE | Augt/June | | Relieved by 11th Middx Regt. (11/11/16 do) proceeded to Left Reserve Sector in CANAL BANK, taking over from 11th Middx Regt. C & D Camp reorganised from 3rd Coy. | |
| COCONUT GROVE | 1/6/17 | | All Coys in various working parties by day & night: TRENCH ST retained for R.E./purposes | |
|  | 2/6/17 | | B. & D Coys HERNIBY TRENCH & Communication Trench Torpedo 177 & 6 casualties – 2 off wounded. C R – JACOBS ROAD/VINSCONT, LANCASHIRE | |
|  | 3/6/17 | | Dug in holes communication trenches in C HILL 2 1 killed & 4 wounded. | |
|  | 4/6/17 | | Dug Dug-outs BUGGLES TRENCH hole of 3.6" deep under upright posts | |
| HILL TOP | 5/6/17 | | Relieved 11th R. Sussex Regt. on Left Sub-Sector of HILL TOP Sector 1 OR wounded (accidental) | |
|  | 6/6/17 | | Reconnaissance made by Coys. 1, 2, 3 of approaches to first line of posts from POST 11 to POST 16. | |
|  | 7/6/17 | | Coys as on 6th but shooting from left of Sector TURCO & HILL TOP | |
|  |  | | Patrol sent to Juttern Bow reported Bosch line uncommonly quiet at 3.10 a.m. In accordance with orders for 2nd Army parole side of YPRES SALIENT many vehicles noted & houses on Juttern Hill damaged. Patrol met no enemy at shelled – 1 OR wounded. Mud areas actually on our front all thru mud of an unusual | |
|  | 8/6/17 | | Lines shelled at our rear many shorts to summit shelling of TURCO & some at OBSERVATORY HILL | |
|  | 9/6/17 | | Wet, uncertain lighting, one aircraft hostile near us, 2 OR killed 2 wounded. | |
|  | 10/6/17 | | Relieved by 11th Royal Sussex Regt. returned to Reserve LEFT Subsector CANAL BANK | |
| CANAL BANK | 11/6/17 | | Digging by the different parties on Line of posts from Post 11 to 16 | 37H |
|  | 12/6/17 | | | 15H |
|  | 13/6/17 | | Digging & carrying & pushing water on connection with work on line 11 to 15 11-16 | 2 Weeks |
|  | 14/6/17 | | Company training | |
|  | 15/6/17 | | Relieved by 15th Notts & Derbys. & moved to "C" Camp | |

Army Form C. 2118.

# WAR DIARY
## or
## INTELLIGENCE SUMMARY.
*(Erase heading not required.)*

Instructions regarding War Diaries and Intelligence Summaries are contained in F. S. Regs., Part II. and the Staff Manual respectively. Title pages will be prepared in manuscript.

Original

| Place | Date | Hour | Summary of Events and Information | Remarks and references to Appendices |
|---|---|---|---|---|
| "C" Camp | 16th–19th June | | Working parties at ASC Lorry Parks – Training of Lewis gunners Bombers & Rifle Grenadiers + Scouts | |
| | 20th | | Battalion marched & Camped at 11 am & entrained for at POPERINGHE & arrived for | |
| | | | HOUlle around a little 7pm | |
| HOULLE | 22,23rd | | Continued training & of Lewis gunners Bombers & Rifle Bombers - also new Short enfield Rifle | |
| | | | (Musketry) ranges used by Bn | |
| | 24th | | Church Parade 10.45 am | |
| | 25th | | Musketry & Lewis Gun Range | |
| | 26th | | The Platoon, Company & Battalion in the attack. | |
| | 27th | | " | |
| | 28th | | Training in Billets. Lecture by Corps Commander. | |
| | 29th | | " | |
| | 30th | | Digging Trenches. | |

E. C. Hannen Lt. Col.
Comdg 14 & Hampshire Regt.

Original
11/9/14 9th North'd Rept C.2118
Army Form C.2118

# WAR DIARY
or
## INTELLIGENCE SUMMARY.
(Erase heading not required.)

Vol 17

16/H
3 sheet

| Place | Date | Hour | Summary of Events and Information | Remarks and references to Appendices |
|---|---|---|---|---|
| Hotton | July 1st | | Church Parade & Baths | |
| | 2nd | | Dug practice trenches | |
| | 3rd | | Fired on Rifle & Bombing ranges | |
| | 4th | | Training under Company arrangements & reconnoitring of practice trenches | |
| | 5th | | Full reconnaissance of practice trenches by all ranks | |
| | 6th | | | |
| | 7th | | Bn practice attack over practice trenches | |
| | 8th | | Church Parade. Officers revolver shooting. Lewis gunners fired L.G. test. | |
| | 9th | | Brigade Practice attack over Practice trenches | |
| | 10th | | Bn attack over practice trenches & further practice trench dug | |
| | 11th | | Battalion, Brigade Practice Attack & consolidation by Bullino a 3.9.7 | |
| | 12th | | Tommy Cooker Cooking arrangements. 4.25 & 12.25 am. Batt. marched 11.35 to Beauval & | |
| | 12th | | Forts & Trenches | |
| | 13th | | Battalion in Beauval district - Attack on Tambour Duclos. | |
| | 14th | | Attack on Durien, & Practice Attack over Practice Trenches 2 am 7½ | |
| | 15th | | Church Parade 10.30 am | |

# WAR DIARY
## or
## INTELLIGENCE SUMMARY.
(Erase heading not required.)

Army Form C. 2118.

| Place | Date | Hour | Summary of Events and Information | Remarks and references to Appendices |
|---|---|---|---|---|
| Devonport | 16 | | A.8 of 2nd Bn. Royal Dublin Fusiliers disembarked at Mudros for Hospitals | |
| "V" Camp | 17 | | Battalion moved to Camp at 10.45 a.m. | |
| " | 18 | | Training in Camp from 8.30 to 12.30 p.m. School-hours 2 to 5. | |
| " | 19 | | Training under Coy arrangements. As on 17th | |
| " | 20 | | Training as on 18th. A by-no-parade party dug a Practice Assault Trench from 2.30 to 3.30 p.m. | |
| " | 21 | | Training as on 19th | |
| " | 22 | | Training as on 20th | |
| " | | | Battalion marched out of Camp at 6.30 a.m. and proceeded to "O" Camp arriving 9 a.m. A, B & D Coys. sent out on working parties to Canal Bank leaving "C" Camp at 5 p.m. and returning at 3.30 a.m. | |
| "O" Camp | 23 | | Training under Company arrangements, 100 men of "C" Coy and 20 of Hd. Qrs. with 3 Officers on working party for T.H.B. at 9 p.m. returning at 4 a.m. | |
| " | 24 | | Training under Company arrangements. Working party 100 O/R, 2 men & R.E. Hd. Est. | |
| " | 25 | | Training under Company arrangements from 9 a.m. to 12.30 p.m. | |
| " | 26 | | Training under Company arrangements | |
| " | 27 | | Training under Company arrangements | |

# WAR DIARY
## or
## INTELLIGENCE SUMMARY.
*(Erase heading not required.)*

Army Form C. 2118.

| Place | Date | Hour | Summary of Events and Information | Remarks and references to Appendices |
|---|---|---|---|---|
| O Camp | 28 | | Training. Mob. Coy. arranged. from 9 am to 12.30 pm. | |
| | 29 | | Moved to CANAL BANK 9 pm | |
| CANAL BANK | 30 | | Moved into Assembly positions in & behind BILGE TRENCH. 13th R Sx Regt on Right 11th | |
| | | | SHERWOOD FORESTERS on Left. 11th R Sx Regt in front | |
| HILL TOP SECTOR | 31 | | ZERO 3.50 AM advanced from assembly positions passed through 11th R.Sx Regt on BLUE LINE, attacked | |
| | | | and consolidated, BLACK & DOTTED BLACK LINES at FALKENHYN REDOUBT. From there | |
| | | | advanced onto ALBERTA & DOTTED GREEN LINE on EAST of STEENBEEK which were | |
| | | | captured & here passed the 118 K. Intr to pass through to ultimate SOLID GREEN LINE. Coys Self | |
| | | | STEENBEEK retired with 118 K. into on right 31st Sep/1st Aug. 17 machine Guns (undmg) about 200 prisoners. | |
| | | | (captured 2 Field Guns & one 4.5" How.) | |
| | | | Casualties: 2/Lt D.G.W. HEWITT. 2/Lt J.K. FALCONER. Wounded:- 2/Lt N.F. TYLER. 2/Lt B.M. PEET. Lt C. CHEVALLIER. Capt | |
| | | | A.O. GAMMAN. M.C. 2/Lt COLLIS (sligly wounded). O.R. KILLED 17. R(ight) wounded 156 missing 42. | |

C.B. Harrison Lt Col

Comdg. 14th Bn Hampshire Regt.

# WAR DIARY or INTELLIGENCE SUMMARY

Army Form C. 2118.

116/39
14 Bn. Hampshire Regt.

| Place | Date | Hour | Summary of Events and Information | Remarks and references to Appendices |
|---|---|---|---|---|
| | 1/8/17 | | Line of Steenbeek received | |
| | 2nd | Noon | Casualties O.R. - 3 Killed, 1 died of wounds, 22 Wounded, 1 Missing | |
| | | | Troops on Steenbeek withdrawn 150 Yds. from MN to 1 AM to allow of bombardment. No reception. | |
| | | | St Julien. Relieved by 11th Royal Sussex Regt. in Front-line and occupied dotted blue line | |
| | | | in support. Casualties - Killed, 15 Wounded, 1 Missing | |
| Canal Bank | 3rd | | Batt. returned to Canal Bank 5 a.m. | |
| | 4th | | Batt. entrained at YPRES detrained at POPERINGHE and marched to School Camp. | |
| School Camp | 5th | | Inspection and making up of deficiencies. Voluntary Church Parade | |
| | 6th | | Training under Company arrangements. Reorganisation of Companies | |
| | 7th | | Training under Company arrangement from 9 a.m. to 12.30 p.m. | |
| | 8th | | Batt. marched out of School Camp and entrained at Hopoutre Siding for Caestre at 8 a.m. Detrained at Caestre at 10 a.m. and proceeded by motor bus to Meteren to billets. | |
| Meteren | 9th | | Inspection by Divisional Commander at 10 a.m. | |
| | 10th | | Inspection by Second Army Commander at 10.15 a.m. | |
| | 11th | | Training under C in C arrangements also training of Lewis gunners & Bombers 9 to 12.30 p.m. | R.R.B.E.H. Commdg 14th Bn. Hampshire |
| | 12th | | Left Meteren and proceeded to Hele Mes to Ridgewood Camp | 17th |
| Ridgewood | 13th | | Bn. marched out of Ridgewood at 8 p.m. and relieved 12th R.W. Kent Regt. in left sub-section C & B Coys. - Front line, B Coy. at WHITE CHATEAU and OAK RESERVE | |
| HOLLEBEKE | | | | |

Army Form C. 2118.

# WAR DIARY
## or
## INTELLIGENCE SUMMARY.
(Erase heading not required.)

14th Hampshire R.

| Place | Date | Hour | Summary of Events and Information | Remarks and references to Appendices |
|---|---|---|---|---|
| | Aug. 1917. | | | |
| HOLLEBEKE | 14th | | A Coy in OPTIC and NEW TRENCH. | |
| | 15th | | A Quiet day. Front line and WHITE CHATEAU received some shelling. 9 O.R. wounded | |
| " | | | Wiring of Front and Support-line. Considerable bombardment of front-line during night. | |
| | 16th | | B Coy. provided working party. Our mule track moving up to front-line | |
| | | | Barrage by our Artillery in conjunction with operation further North at 4.45 a.m. on 16th | |
| | | | until 5.45 a.m. Enemy retaliated. 4 O.R. Killed, 1 died of wounds, 28 wounded | |
| SPOIL BANK | 17th | | Relieved by 11th R. Sussex Regt. and moved into Reserve at SPOIL BANK. 2 O.R. Killed, 2 wounded | |
| | 18th | | Improvements of Reserve trenches (OAK TRENCH and OAK SUPPORT). Working party in 4 wounded | |
| " | | | Continuation of mule track to HOLLEBEKE | |
| " | 19th | | 4 O.R. Wounded. | |
| " | 20th | | Coys. R.E. and 11th R. Sussex Regt. 1 O.R. Wounded | |
| " | 21st | | Relieved 11th R. Sussex Regt. in Left Subsector HOLLEBEKE | |
| HOLLEBEKE | 22nd | | Covering party for working party of 11th R. Sussex Regt. in front line. 1.5 R Wounded | |
| " | 23rd | | Relieved by 17th K.R. Rifles and returned to RIDGEWOOD CAMP | |
| RIDGEWOOD | 24th | | Training of Specialists - Reorganisation and Re-equipment | |
| " | 25th | | | |
| " | 26th | | | |

Commanding 14th Hampshire R.

Army Form C. 2118.

# WAR DIARY
## or
## INTELLIGENCE SUMMARY.
(Erase heading not required.)

14th Hampshire R.

| Place | Date | Hour | Summary of Events and Information | Remarks and references to Appendices |
|---|---|---|---|---|
| | 1917 Aug. | | | |
| RIDGEWOOD | 27 | | Left RIDGEWOOD and relieved 1/1 Herts R.in Reserve for KLEIN ZILLEBEKE Sector at GORDON LANE, SPOIL BANK, BLUFFS and CONVENT LANE. | |
| GORDON LANE | 28 | | Carrying R.E. material to front line. | |
| | 29 | | ditto | |
| | 30 | | ditto | |
| | 31 | | Relieved 11 R. Sussex R. in Right subsector of KLEIN ZILLEBEKE Sector. | |

P.H. Ell—
Comdg 14th Hampshire R.

Original

39 Div
14 Hampshire
Vol 19

18H
+ March

**WAR DIARY**
or
**INTELLIGENCE SUMMARY**
Army Form C. 2118.

| Place | Date 1917 Sept | Hour | Summary of Events and Information | Remarks and references to Appendices |
|---|---|---|---|---|
| WHEN ZILLEBEKE | 1st | | Usual activity of our artillery. Enemy artillery very quiet. Some shells of Buffs during afternoon. | |
| | 2nd | | Relieved by 11th R Warwick Regt and returned to RIDGEWOOD CAMP. | |
| RIDGEWOOD | 3rd | | Inspection and reorganisation. | |
| | 4th | | Batt. marched out of RIDGEWOOD at 2.30 p.m. and proceeded by march route to CHIPPEWA CAMP. | |
| CHIPPEWA CAMP | 5th | | Training of Specialists and Coys carried out under Coy. arrangements. | |
| | 6th | | do | |
| | 7th | | do | |
| | 8th | | Marched out of CHIPPEWA CAMP and relieved 11th Highd Regt in Brigade Support in SHREWSBURY FOREST section. Both H.Q. in LARCH WOOD TUNNELS. | |
| LARCH WOOD AREA | 9th | | Carrying parties for 225 Field Coy. R.E. to Front-line. | |
| | 10th | | Carrying parties for 225 and 227 Field Coy. R.E. to Front-line Casualties 2 O.R. | |
| | 11th | | to Casualties 2 O.R. | |
| CHIPPEWA CAMP | 12th | | Relieved by 16 Bn Rifle Brigade and returned to CHIPPEWA CAMP. Casualties 1 O.R. | |
| | 13th | | Inspections and reorganisation under Coy. arrangements. | |
| | 14th | | Marched out of CHIPPEWA and bivouacked at COTTAGE CAMP near RIDGEWOOD | |

# WAR DIARY
## or
## INTELLIGENCE SUMMARY.
*(Erase heading not required.)*

Army Form C. 2118.

| Place | Date | Hour | Summary of Events and Information | Remarks and references to Appendices |
|---|---|---|---|---|
| COTTAGE CAMP | 1917 Sept 14 | | Left bivouac and relieved 17th R.B. R.R. in left sub-section of SHREWSBURY FOREST sector. C Coy in front line, D Coy in support, A & B in Bn. Reserve at CANADA TUNNELS. Casualties 10 OR wounded | |
| SHREWSBURY FOREST | 15 | | Barrage by our Arty on enemy front lines and on 3rd objective front at 6:15 am Very little retaliation by enemy. Reserve Coys in Canopy trenches + work party of 30 OR for 227 Hanoverian Coy. Casualties 3 OR killed, 5 OR wounded. | |
| " | 16 | | 10 Oz of rum issued. Some gas shells over during the night. Casualties 3 OR killed, 6 OR wounded. | |
| " | 17 | | Relieved by 10th Queens R.W. Surrey Regt. 8 posts on right, 2½ KRR, 2 pts to relieve him. 3 posts on left. Manstadt AB Coys marched to bivouacs at COTTAGE CAMP. A and B/C Coys (in support) | |
| | | | to SPOIL BANK | |
| COTTAGE CAMP | 18 | | B & C Coys joined remainder A B at COTTAGE CAMP. Bath marched out 7.30 a.m. and proceeded to CURRAGH CAMP in to bath. | |
| CURRAGH CAMP | 19 | | Provided water Coy + squadron to Infantrie. Holiday A.M. | |
| " | 20 | | Bath marched to COTTAGE CAMP to be in reserve during relation in SHREWSBURY FOREST sector | |
| COTTAGE CAMP | 21 | | Sorting of kits and bivouacs | |
| " | 22 | | Bath moved up to SHREWSBURY FOREST and relieved 15th HANTS and 11th QUEENS in line. A Coy front line, 2 Platoons of B Coy Armagh in support, D Coy Hanna Suffolk, C Coy Reserve. Casualties 3 OR wounded and Lieutenant B Coy and C Coy Reserve | |

# WAR DIARY
## or
## INTELLIGENCE SUMMARY.

*(Erase heading not required.)*

Army Form C. 2118.

| Place | Date | Hour | Summary of Events and Information | Remarks and references to Appendices |
|---|---|---|---|---|
| SHREWSBURY FOREST | 23 | | Heavy Shelly by Enemy during early morning intermittent Shelly during day. Casualties | 2/Lt A.R. Clarke wounded 6 killed 22 wounded |
| " | 24 | | Relieved during night of 23/24 by 12th R. Sussex Rgt in front line and Suffolks and 11th Sussex in Reserve. Two coys of each Battn. Casualties. | 2/Lt F.W. Charlton wounded |
| COTTAGE CAMP | 25 | | Returned to "COTTAGE CAMP" (Nght) for M.G. & Musketry at HEDGE ST TUNNELS & Arms Stamping & General Camp fatigue | |
| " | | | Battn. moved out of camp at 11. SHREWSBURY FOREST Scale and took up arsenals front in front of 11th B. R. Sussex Rgt. | |
| SHREWSBURY FOREST | 26 | | Latter attacked at 5.30 a.m 1st Objective my TOWER HAMLETS and 2nd Objective my TOWER TRENCH. Heavy casualties though M.G. fire. My lines were reached and held and consolidation carried out on own side of TOWER TRENCH. | |
| | | | Other Units. Major S.H. Smith advd of attack, killed. Capt T.C Micholls Lieut-Bainbridge 2/Lieut R.G. Wilson wounded. 2/Lieut H. Songster 2/Lieut L.W. Batt 2/Lieut Beavers 2/Lieut Thomas. O/R ranks 41 killed 113 wounded. Heavy shelly and sniping | |
| | 27 | | Very quiet morning. Shelly very heavy during afternoon which developed at night. Casualties O.R 5 killed 10 wounded. Relieved by 13th R. Fusiliers & 5 Sussex. Now 13 K.R.R. in Support line. | |

Army Form C. 2118.

# WAR DIARY
## or
## INTELLIGENCE SUMMARY.
*(Erase heading not required.)*

Instructions regarding War Diaries and Intelligence Summaries are contained in F. S. Regs., Part II. and the Staff Manual respectively. Title pages will be prepared in manuscript.

| Place | Date | Hour | Summary of Events and Information | Remarks and references to Appendices |
|---|---|---|---|---|
| HOUTHULST FOREST | JANUARY 28 | | Coys. relieved the both movements of Avers at BUS HOUSE and Emerged at MOUNT CORNER KEEP (RIFLE) | |
| MOAT | 29 | | Camp at MOUNT CORNER KEEP (RIFLE) | |
| CORNER | 30 | | Supervision and Instruction work Lewis rangework | |
| KEEP | 31 | | ditto | |

S. H. Allen Major
Comdg. 1/4th Hampshire R.

Original
116/39
14 Hants Sy
Army Form C. 2118.

# WAR DIARY
or
## INTELLIGENCE SUMMARY.
*(Erase heading not required.)*

20

| Place | Date | Hour | Summary of Events and Information | Remarks and references to Appendices |
|---|---|---|---|---|
| MOUNT KOKEREZ (PIECE 15) | Oct 1st | | Onwards shell under Enemy aeroplanes. About 9pm enemy aircraft over Mudros several bombs on the Camp. Casualties 10 Killed 1 Died of Wounds 14 Wounded | Nil |
| | 2nd | | [illegible] ... Enemy ... 2.30pm Inspection of Battalion | Nil |
| | | | 12 Battalion Honours [illegible] by [illegible] 1.29 Divisional General also [illegible] returns | Nil |
| | 3rd | | A divine service was on 9.15. | Nil |
| | 4th | | Company wore B.D. Parade | Nil |
| | 5th | | Company Training | Nil |
| | 6th | | do | Nil |
| | 7th | | do | Nil |
| | 8th | | Church Parade 9.15 a.m | Nil |
| | 9th | | Battalion out on maneuvers 10 am [illegible] of [illegible] to the [illegible] about 3pm Lytype | Nil |
| | 10th | | 6.15am & 12.15pm inspection. 9 AM thanks. 12M HQ & I trains 4 [illegible] 2 Lytype B.T. Bath Mess | Nil |
| | 11th | | 8.30am [illegible] of the Brition [illegible] Honour 12.45pm march morning 4A | Nil 19H |
| | 12th | | 8.30am & 12.30pm [illegible] [illegible] by D.C [illegible] 5pm Entertainment of Preceded | 3 weeks |
| | 13th | | 6.30am & 12.30pm Battn Bath Parade Morning 2 Lytype Lytype Shereddy | Nil |
| | | | [illegible] Doubt Trying Afternoon Auction Bt |

# WAR DIARY
## or
## INTELLIGENCE SUMMARY.
(Erase heading not required.)

Army Form C. 2118.

| Place | Date | Hour | Summary of Events and Information | Remarks and references to Appendices |
|---|---|---|---|---|
| MOUNT KOKEREEL (R.13.c.B.5) | 14 | | Reconnaissance of TOWER HAMLETS sector. Company training. | MAC |
| TOWER HAMLETS | 15 | | Most ordinary hr. KOKEREEL and proceeded to BUS HOUSE. Detachment was however to 4th MIDDLESEX & 8 LINCOLNS | MAC |
| " | 16 | | Got in touch with battalions on right and left. (3 Coys on Working Party) | MAC |
| " | 17 | | Part relieved by 13th R. SUSSEX in morning, and went into Brigade Reserve | MAC |
| " | 18 | | Enemy barraged our lines and communication during the day. | MAC |
| " | 19 | | Heavy barrage by own artillery before dawn. Enemy replied. Relieved by 1st Notts & Derbys. after relief, battalion found relief in no front line | MAC |
| " | 20 | | and then proceeded to VYVER BEEK CAMP, N.9.b. | MAC |
| " | 21 | | Cleaning up of camp, equipment etc. | MAC |
| " | 22 | | Remade in morning. Cleaning up. Examination of Companies. Draft of 107 O.R. arrived | MAC |
| " | 22 | | Physical Drill. Bayonet fighting. Platoon Drill and training of specialists. Baths | MAC |
| " | 23 | | Baths. Battalion in working party changing cable in TOWER HAMLETS sector | MAC |
| " | | | Battalion moved to CARNARVON CAMP | MAC |
| CARNARVON CAMP M.16.c.9.3 | 24 | | Reorganisation. Cleaning up of camp | MAC |

V. Farber Lt Col
Commanding 14th Hants Regt

Original  
11/39/14 Hawk. Bn  
VOL 21

Army Form C. 2118.

# WAR DIARY
## or
## INTELLIGENCE SUMMARY.
*(Erase heading not required.)*

| Place | Date | Hour | Summary of Events and Information | Remarks and references to Appendices |
|---|---|---|---|---|
| BRIELEN CAMP | Nov 1917 1 | | B. & C Companies route marching morning. Afternoon recreational | |
| — | 2 | | Drill. "D" Company practised raid on elephant — 1/2 day & night. | |
| — | 2 | | Company arranged. All Companies practised raid. | |
| — | 3 | | Battalion proceeded to Canada Tunnels & Hedge Street Tunnels and relieved 6th Cheshires in Reserve | |
| CANADA TUNNELS | 4 | | Working parties for R.E.s etc. | |
| — | 5 | | "D" Coy moved up to Front Line on the nights of 4/5 and attacked Pill Boxes to their front. Objective was not reached owing to wire defences, bad nature of the ground and intense hostile machine gun fire from both objective and LEWIS HOUSE on right flank. They were also heavily shelled with gas shells. Two attempts were made. Casualties G.C Enterprise [Capt. G.M. Finlay] killed. Other Ranks 5 killed 9 wounded | |
| — | 6 | | Working parties for R.E.s etc | |
| LINE | 7 | | Proceeded to front line & took over from the 13th R Sussex Rgt on the left sector, astride MENIN Rd. B & A Coys front line C & D Coys in support. | 20 H/2 |
| — | 8 | | Casualties front line before day dawn due to bombardment of LEWIS Ho. & Pill Boxes at — | |

**Army Form C. 2118.**

# WAR DIARY
## or
## INTELLIGENCE SUMMARY.
*(Erase heading not required.)*

Instructions regarding War Diaries and Intelligence Summaries are contained in F. S. Regs., Part II. and the Staff Manual respectively. Title pages will be prepared in manuscript.

| Place | Date | Hour | Summary of Events and Information | Remarks and references to Appendices |
|---|---|---|---|---|
| LINE | | | J24 & S.8. by Howitzers etc. Front line reoccupied at dusk. Battn relieved by | |
| | | | 17th Sherwood Foresters & proceeded to BEGGARS REST Camp. "25" men sent | |
| | | | 2/Pr TOWER attempted to reach the Pill Boxes at J21 & 9.8. but were unsuccessful | |
| CHIPPEWA CAMP | 8 | | Battn proceeded to CHIPPEWA Camp. | |
| | 10 | | Refitting & reorganising of Coy | |
| | 11 | | | |
| RIDGEWOOD HUTTED CAMP | 12 | | Moved out to RIDGEWOOD HUTTED CAMP | |
| HEDGE ST. | 13 | | Taken over from 14th to 117 Bde. and Hedge St Tunnels & 177th Sherwoods in CASCADE St. 3 Coys | |
| | | | occupy HEDGE ST. 6 Coy in Support to 12th R Sussex in Reply Trench ad TOWER HAMLETS | |
| | 14/15/16 | | Carrying & working parties for R.E. material & front line; Coy in front line entering | |
| | | | support line. ½ Coy digging C.T. to night front at EVE Farm. ½ Coy working under Tunnellers | |
| | 6/7 | | relieved 13th R Sussex Regt in front line. A,B & D Coys in front line. C in Support. | |
| Front line | 17-19 | | Work of digging and deepening drawing & rewetting front line & saltern egate a.C.T between | |
| | 20/21 | | Relieved by 12th R Sussex Regt & took up quarters in HEDGE St in Battn Support. C coy remain | |
| | | | ing in close support to front line Bn. C coy working on C.T. to night front line | |
| | 22/24 | | 3 Coys working on C.T. to front line. Digging of trench practically completed & 140' revetted | |

# WAR DIARY
## or
## INTELLIGENCE SUMMARY.
*(Erase heading not required.)*

Army Form C. 2118.

| Place | Date | Hour | Summary of Events and Information | Remarks and references to Appendices |
|---|---|---|---|---|
| CARNARVON CAMP M1069.S. | 25. | | Company Training | WHC |
| " | 26 | " | " | WHC |
| " | 27 | " | All Officers attended a demonstration in the construction of shell holes. | WHC |
| CHIPPEWA CAMP | 28 | | Church Parade Service. Moved to Chippewa Camp. | WHC |
| " | 29 | | Company Training. Preparation for construction of mud model. "A" Company | WHC |
| " | 30 | | practical consolidation of shell holes. "B" Company practical consolidation of shell holes | WHC |
| " | 31 | | Company Training "C" Company practical consolidation of shell holes | WHC |

J Allen Lt Col
Commanding
14 Bn Hants R.

# WAR DIARY
## or
## INTELLIGENCE SUMMARY.
*(Erase heading not required.)*

Army Form C. 2118.

| Place | Date | Hour | Summary of Events and Information | Remarks and references to Appendices |
|---|---|---|---|---|
| Line | 25/7 | | Relieved 12th R. Sus. Regt. in line, dispositions as arg. 16/17. First night patrols sent out. Hincombrals of trouble, enemy dugouts at J.27c.3.8.; BERRY COTTS (CAMP FARM), which had been landed by "tanks" during day. It was found that there was good wire still in front of these points & that they were also strongly held, & could not be demolished. | |
| | 26/27 | | Relieved by 19th Manchesters & proceeded by light railway from TRANSPORT FARM to OUDERDOM for CHIPPEWA CAMP. | |
| | 27 | | Went by train to GODEWAERSVELDE & thence by march route to WINNEZEELE Area. | |
| | 28 | | Proceeded by train from GODEWAERSVELDE to WIZERNE & for march on ACQUIN to rejoin Bde. | |
| | 30-3 | | Working on relaying & making of wooden roads forward. Day at R.R.'s entrainment of NORTHERN SPOR, & entrain to training to St. Julien. | |

4/9/17

O.C. Duncan Capt
2 i/c O.C. 6th Rayal
4 Hants

Original

14 Hampshire Rgt
Army Form C. 2118.

# WAR DIARY
## or
## INTELLIGENCE SUMMARY.
December 1917
(Erase heading not required.)

Vol 22

| Place | Date | Hour | Summary of Events and Information | Remarks and references to Appendices |
|---|---|---|---|---|
| WEILTJE YPRES | 1917 Dec.1 | | Working parties during morning. Proceeded by march route to Canal Bank near YPRES. Working parties all day. | |
| " | 2 | | Working parties all day. | |
| " | 3 | | Working parties to HELL FIRE SIDING & intensive railway junction. Blois Wood. | |
| " | 4 | | Moved to POTIZE Chateau. Relieved 4/6th BAVARIA HOUSE. | |
| " | 5 | | Batt. in reserve. Parties doing work for tunnel. | |
| " | 6 | | | |
| " | 7 | | | |
| " | 8 | | Entrained at ASYLUM STATION, YPRES, detraining at GODEWAERSVELDE and proceeded | |
| WINNIZEELE area | 9 | | by march route to WINNIZEELE area. Athlete. | |
| " | | | 4 Officers rejoined. 4 Officers & party went to PASSENDHELE area. | |
| " | | | Battalion resting. | |
| " | 10 | | at WINNIZEELE | |
| " | | | Batt. proceeded by march route to GODEWAERSVELDE and entrained for LUMBRES | |
| " | | | arriving there & billetted at BAYENGHEM. | |
| BAYENGHEM | 11 | | Inspection of kit by Commander. | 21 H |
| " | 12 | | Training with Company from 9 am to 4pm. 2 A/ship Recruits Joinedbvn | |
| " | 13 | | Trg. inclu. Bath & C. drill from 9 am to 4pm. 2 A/ship Recruits Joined | |

# WAR DIARY or INTELLIGENCE SUMMARY

Army Form C. 2118.

*(Erase heading not required.)*

Instructions regarding War Diaries and Intelligence Summaries are contained in F. S. Regs., Part II. and the Staff Manual respectively. Title pages will be prepared in manuscript.

| Place | Date | Hour | Summary of Events and Information | Remarks and references to Appendices |
|---|---|---|---|---|
| BAYENGHEM | 1917 Dec 14 | | Troops laid down. Brigade programme of work includes musketry/muskelies on X Ranges. 2nd & 4th Reorderational training. | |
| " | 15 | | Church Parade at 10 a.m. | |
| " | 16 | | Battn. marching to X ranges at practised firing from kits. Preceded training afternoon | |
| " | 17 | | Battn. examined after Inspection by Brigadier General Cunnock. | |
| " | 18 | | Musketry and Coy. Troops on Short Ranges | do |
| " | 19 | | Battn. examined and in attack practices. | do |
| " | 20 | | Musketry and Coy. Troops on Short ranges | do |
| " | 21 | | Musketry and Coy. Troops on Short ranges. | do |
| " | 22 | | Church Parade at 11 a.m. | |
| " | 23 | | Batt. asked Short ranges for musketry. Platoon and Squadron field hockey drill (physical) | |
| " | 24 | | Xmas Day. Church Parade at 10 a.m. | |
| " | 25 | | Inspection of Coy. in Billets during morning. Football match — Officers v Sergeants. | |
| " | 26 | | Orderly room Officers won 4-2. | |
| " | 27 | | Cleaning up. Relief by 5ths between BAYENGHEM and LUMBRES. "C" Coy. to be Adv. Div. | |
| " | | | Coy. billets — on march 2nd. | |

# WAR DIARY
## or
## INTELLIGENCE SUMMARY.
*(Erase heading not required.)*

Army Form C. 2118.

| Place | Date | Hour | Summary of Events and Information | Remarks and references to Appendices |
|---|---|---|---|---|
| BAYENGHEM | 4/7/28 | | L.H.B. MYENGHEM by march route and preceded by QUESQUES Relief in billets of 16th SHERWOOD FORESTERS. Roads my bad, my snow. | |
| QUESQUES | 29 | | Relieved by march route 11th BAYEN & HEM ammy 12 noon. | |
| BAYENGHEM | 29 30 | | Left BAYEN & HEM and proceeded by march route to WIZERNES Aerodrome. ELVERDINGHE and thence by march route to DAMBRE CAMP arriving at 1 p.m. | |
| DAMBRE CAMP | 31 | | R.A.F. Archies out general clean up | |

F. H. Symons  
Major  
Commanding 14th Bn Hampshire Regt

14 Hampshire Army Form C. 2118.

# WAR DIARY
## or
## INTELLIGENCE SUMMARY. January 1918.

(Erase heading not required.)

Vol 23

| Place | Date | Hour | Summary of Events and Information | Remarks and references to Appendices |
|---|---|---|---|---|
| DAMBRE CAMP | 1 | 9-1 | Specialist training. Remainder of Coys. under coy arrangements. | |
| | | 2-4 | Recreational Training | |
| " | 2 | 9-1 | Training of Specialists. Remainder of Coy under Coy arrangements | |
| | | 2-4 | Recreational Training | |
| " | 3 | 9-10 | Physical Training and Bayonet Fighting. 10-1 p.m. Training of Specialists. | |
| | | | Afternoon recreational training. | |
| " | 4 | | As on 3rd. | |
| " | 5 | | On morning of 3rd and 4th Batt. marched by Coy. to throw box respirators | |
| | | | tested at Bras Chambre at 137 R Sussex Camp | |
| " | 6 | 10 am | Church Parade in Church Army hut. Battn in afternoon | |
| " | 7 | 2 pm | Bn. marched out of DAMBRE CAMP and relieved 1/1 CAMBS at CANAL BANK | |
| | | | in Brigade support | |
| CANAL BANK | 8 | | All Coys on various working parties by day and night. | 22 H. 3 Neet |
| " | 9 | | ditto Casualties E Coy 2/Lieut S.R. Gough wounded 2 O.R killed 5 wounded | |
| " | 10 | | ditto | |
| " | 11 | | All Coys on working parties by day and night | |

**Army Form C. 2118**

# WAR DIARY or INTELLIGENCE SUMMARY

*(Erase heading not required.)*

Instructions regarding War Diaries and Intelligence Summaries are contained in F.S. Regs., Part II. and the Staff Manual respectively. Title Pages will be prepared in manuscript.

| Place | Date | Hour | Summary of Events and Information | Remarks and references to Appendices |
|---|---|---|---|---|
| CANAL BANK | 12th | | Whole Bn. on working parties by day at night. | |
| " | 13th | | do | |
| " | 14th | | do | |
| " | 15th | | Bn. left CANAL BANK at 8 p.m. being relieved by 16th R. Sherwood Foresters. Casualties A Coy - 3 O.R. wounded. A.B.& D Coys. to camp at HILL TOP FARM and C Coy to STEENBECK defences relieving 4/5th Black Watch at each place. | |
| HILL TOP FARM. | 16th | | C Coy. pushed 2 Platoons for working party at CORNER COT ad 1 Platoon for working party front at KRONPRINZ FARM. Rest of Bn. improving camp. As on 16th. A Coy. also found 1 Off, 50 O.R. working party at Divn. Hd. Qrs. at CANAL BANK. | |
| " | 17th | | | |
| " | 18th | 4 p.m. | Battn. marched out of HILL TOP FARM and relieved 11th R.R. Service Batt. in Left Front Section WESTROOSEBEKE. A Coy. on right, B Coy on left, D Coy. in Support at BURNS HOUSE and C Coy in Reserve at WINCHESTER HOUSE. Bn. Hd. Qrs. at HUBNER FARM. Casualties Nil | |
| WESTROOSEBEKE (Left Section) | 19th | | Enemy very quiet. Some shelling during day and night around WINCHESTER HOUSE and HUBNER FARM. Casualties Nil. | |
| " | 20th | | Heavy shelling took place on our night front about 8.50 a.m. and was replied to by an S.O.S. barrage by our guns. A Coy. relieved in centre by D Coy. on night front and went into Support. B Coy. was relieved by C Coy. in left front and went into reserve. Casualties Nil | |
| " | 21st | 7.30 a.m. | Relieved by 16th Highland Infantry and entrained at WIELTJE debussing at RAILHOEK and marched to SCHOOL CAMP. Casualties Nil | |

**Army Form C. 2118**

# WAR DIARY
## or
## INTELLIGENCE SUMMARY
*(Erase heading not required.)*

| Place | Date | Hour | Summary of Events and Information | Remarks and references to Appendices |
|---|---|---|---|---|
| SCHOOL CAMP | 22 | | Inspection and Cleaning of Equipment. | |
| " | 23 | | Fitting of New Clothing and Training under Coy. arrangements. | |
| " | 24 | | Training under Coy. arrangements. Baths at TUNNELER'S CAMP. | |
| " | 25 | | do | |
| " | 26 | | Training under Coy. arrangements. | |
| " | 27 | | Batt. marched out of SCHOOL CAMP at 1.45 a.m. and marched to PROVEN to entrain. Left PROVEN at 4.15 a.m. and detrained at MERRICOURT L'ABBÉ at 3.30 p.m. and marched to billets at SAILLY-LE-SEC. | |
| SAILLY-LE-SEC | 28 | | Ablutions and Training under Coy. arrangements from 9 a.m. ≠ 12.30 p.m. | |
| " | 29 | | Training under Coy. arrangements. | |
| " | 30 | | Batt. paraded at 3 a.m. and marched to CORBIE to entrain. Left CORBIE at 8 a.m. and detrained at PERONNE at 11 a.m. and marched to Camp at HAUT ALLAINES. | |
| HAUT ALLAINES | 31 | | Training under Coy. arrangements. Wall aft test against aircraft bombing. | |

K. Watson
Major
Commdg. 14 Hampshire Regt.

14 Hampshire Regt
Vol 24

**WAR DIARY**
or
**INTELLIGENCE SUMMARY.**
(Erase heading not required.)

Army Form C. 2118.

February 1918

| Place | Date 1918 | Hour | Summary of Events and Information | Remarks and references to Appendices |
|---|---|---|---|---|
| HAUT ALLAINES | 1 | | Bn. paraded at 1.45 p.m. and marched to station in light marching at Sq. I.12.a (Sheet 62c) detraining at HEUDICOURT and proceeded to relieve 9th Scottish Rifles (Cameronians) in Corps Subsection of 59 Div: Front. A Coy. right front. B Coy. left front. C Coy. Support and D Coy. Reserve.  Casualties Nil | |
| GAUCHE WOOD | 2 | | Improvements to front line parts and QUENTIN REDOUBT. Casualties Nil | |
| " | 3 | | Relieved in line by 11th R. Sussex Regt. and moved into support with A Coy. and Bn. Hd. Qrs. with 2 Platoons B Coy at REVELON FARM, 2 Platoons B Coy at CHAPEL HILL, C Coy at Sunk Road (W.6.B.6.9.) D Coy. at W.4.d (R.d M.d GAUCHE Wood Special Sheet 1/10,000)  Casualties Nil | |
| REVELON FARM | 4 | | Improving trenches and salvage work. A & C Coys. on working parties at QUENTIN REDOUBT at night. Casualties Nil | |
| " | 5 | | Working parties (B&C Coys) at QUENTIN REDOUBT at night. Casualties Nil | |
| " | 6 | | 5 Officers 100 O.R. attached to 11th R. Hants. Regt. A & B Coys. working parties at night. 2 Platoon of B Coy. at REVELON FARM replaced D Coy. at W.4.d. C Coy. improved by day and worked at night. | |
| " | 7 | | Several salvage work by day and C Coy. improved by day, working party at night. AA.B. working party at night. | 23 H 3 sheets |
| " | 8 | | myM on QUENTIN REDOUBT and SOMME TRENCH. C Coy improved and strengthened trenches at W.6.d.6.0. B Coy working party at night on QUENTIN REDOUBT. Casualties 1 OR wounded | |

Army Form C. 2118.

# WAR DIARY
## or
## INTELLIGENCE SUMMARY. February 1918.
(Erase heading not required.)

Instructions regarding War Diaries and Intelligence Summaries are contained in F. S. Regs., Part II. and the Staff Manual respectively. Title pages will be prepared in manuscript.

| Place | Date 1918 | Hour | Summary of Events and Information | Remarks and references to Appendices |
|---|---|---|---|---|
| REVELON FARM | 9 | | A & D 2 Platoons of B Cy. at W yd relieved by 11th R Sussex Rgt. C Cy. relieved by 13th R Sussex Rgt. | |
| | | | Remaining Bttn. moved into billets at HEUDICOURT | |
| HEUDICOURT | 10 | | 2 Platoons of B Cy. at CHAPEL HILL relieved by 16th R Brigade. Accompanied by CHAPEL HILL BC | |
| | | | Inspection of arms and general cleanup. A and C Cys. working parties & front line at night. | |
| | | | Training under Cy. arrangements during morning. B & C Cy. working parties at QUENTIN REDOUT C.T. | |
| " | 11 | | at 2 p.m. A Cy. working party at trenches outside CHAPEL HILL | |
| | 12 | | Training under Cy. arrangements during morning. Working parties as in past. A Cy. Tramway billets. | |
| | | | at CHAPEL HILL, B Cy. chipping track, found from QUENTIN REDOUT to residences, C Cy. billets | |
| | | | at GAUCHE C.T. Gun.... 4 wounded. | |
| | 13 | | Training under Cy. arrangements during morning. Working parties as before at night. A Cy. as on 12th, | |
| | | | B Cy. Carry R.E. Stores from REVELON FARM to QUENTIN REDOUBT. C Cy. as on 12th | |
| | 14 | | Training under Cy. arrangements during morning. Work. Ye. Parties at night. A Cy. digging out trench | |
| | | | from B Cy.'s HQ to [?] outwards from trenches to QUENTIN C.T. In front of this. C Cy. at tramway from | |
| | | | trenches to QUENTIN C.T. at front line | |
| | 15 | | Training during morning parties by arrangement. One [?] of WILLIETS from 3.30 p.m. | |
| | 16 | | A Bttn.d Coys. cookers. 1 Arranging Lewis Guns & POS. F. to QUENTIN REDOUT from 9 ... to 2 p.m. | |

**Army Form C. 2118.**

# WAR DIARY
## or
## INTELLIGENCE SUMMARY.
*(Erase heading not required.)*

February 1918.

Instructions regarding War Diaries and Intelligence Summaries are contained in F. S. Regs., Part II. and the Staff Manual respectively. Title pages will be prepared in manuscript.

| Place | Date | Hour | Summary of Events and Information | Remarks and references to Appendices |
|---|---|---|---|---|
| HEBUTERNE | 16 | 4 p.m. | Relief in and farewell speech by Maj. Gen. Cayley of 39. Division. | |
| | | | Band played a sacred hymn at SOREL-LE-GRAND about the same time. | |
| | 17 | | Killed 5 horses 7 men wounded. | |
| | | | Transferred by carrying party during morning. All Coys carts brought at night. | |
| | 18 | | Rested. 1 O.R. wounded. Casualties 7 | |
| | 19 | | Training under by parties -- C. during morning. All Regimental Stores handed in to Bde. | |
| | 20 | | Battn marched out of HAUDICOURT at 9am & proceeded by march route | |
| | 21 | | 4th C.C. of HADT ALLAINES. | |
| MŒUVRES | 21 | | Training under by parties C. during morning | |
| | 22 | | ditto | |
| | 23 | / | Battn. disbanded. Arrive A. A.B. Coys. of 17th Entrenching Battn. | |

R.W. Brennan M. Ch.
Commandg. 14 Hampshire R[egt]

# 39TH DIVISION

## 116TH MACHINE GUN COY.
## MAR 1916-FEB 1918

116th Brigade.
39th Division.

---

Disembarked FRANCE 16.5.16.

116th BRIGADE MACHINE GUN COMPANY

MARCH TO JULY 1 9 1 6

Attached:-

Report on Operations 29/30 June.

# WAR DIARY or INTELLIGENCE SUMMARY

Army Form C. 2118

| Place | Date | Hour | Summary of Events and Information | Remarks and references to Appendices |
|---|---|---|---|---|
| Grantham | 1.3.16 | | The 116th Machine Gun Company was formed in B. Lines, Belton Park, Grantham on March 1st 1916. The nucleus being three Officers & 33 men. The first O.C. was Captain Herbert Smith of the R.W.F. on his appointment shortly afterwards to the Instructional Staff of the M.G.C. he was succeeded by Lieut. G.R. Henniker-Gotley of the 9th North Stafford Regt. under whose command the Company was brought up to War Strength & having completed its training, embarked for France on 16th May. 1916. & at once proceeded up country to join the 116th Infantry Brigade then in the trenches at Festubert. Officers & men went into the trenches for instruction for 24 hrs each. | |
| Festubert | | | | |
| Cuinchy | 28.5.16 | 6 a.m. | The company moved at 2 hrs. notice & entered the trenches at Cuinchy, taking over from 98.M.G.Coy. Twelve guns went in & four guns kept in Reserve at Beuvry, which were moved up to Annequin the next day. | |
| | 30.5.16 | | Indirect fire was directed on to enemy's roads &c. where he was reported to be bringing his transport. This was continued every night. Generally three guns being used each night. | |

G. R. Henniker-Gotley Capt.
O.C. 116. M.G.Coy.

Army Form C. 2118

# WAR DIARY
## INTELLIGENCE SUMMARY
(Erase heading not required.)

Instructions regarding War Diaries and Intelligence
Summaries are contained in F. S. Regs., Part II.
and the Staff Manual respectively. Title Pages
will be prepared in manuscript.

| Place | Date | Hour | Summary of Events and Information | Remarks and references to Appendices |
|---|---|---|---|---|
| Ferme du Bois. | 30.6.16 | | The Company suffered severely, losing four killed & fifteen wounded, 2/Lt. Dowdy being amongst the latter. Every gun was very gallantly under very trying circumstances. 2/Lt. Pearson was out in No man's land for 6 hours with his gun mounted in a shell hole, to repel any counter attack that might have been attempted & by the enemy he got his gun in safely with the help of Cpl. Bird. & also a severely wounded man. The following were commended for gallant conduct & devotion to duty. 2/Lt. A.J. Pearson, Cpl. 14958 Cpl. Bird. 28049. Lee. Cpl. McLean & Pte. Catt of the 11th Royal Sussex Regt. who were attached to the company for carrying ammunition. | |
| | 1.7.16 | | The company was relieved on the 1st July by 118 M.G. Coy. | |
| | 3.7.16 | | On the 3rd July the Brigade including the company was inspected & congratulated by the G.O.C. of the 39th Division. & by the Corps Commander of the XI Corps. | |
| | 5.7.16 | | 28049. Lee. Cpl. McLean was awarded the Military Medal for gallantry in action & devotion to duty at Richebourg on the morning of June 30th | G.R. Henniker-Sotherton Capt.<br>O.C. 116. M.G. Coy |

## INTELLIGENCE SUMMARY

*(Erase heading not required.)*

Instructions regarding War Diaries and Intelligence Summaries are contained in F.S. Regs., Part II. and the Staff Manual respectively. Title Pages will be prepared in manuscript.

| Place | Date | Hour | Summary of Events and Information | Remarks and references to Appendices |
|---|---|---|---|---|
| Beuvry | 6.7.16 | | On the night of the 6th: the Company moved to Beuvry; & relieved 98.M.G. Coy. in the Auchy section on the night of the 7th/8th. Fourteen guns were put in the Support & Reserve lines. | |
| Auchy | 7.7.16 | | The Company co-operated with the battalions in raids, & demonstrations on the enemy's lines, by the use of indirect fire. | |
| Lacouture | 13.7.16 | | The Company was relieved by the 23rd M.G. Coy. on the night of 13th/14th June, & moved to Gillets in Lacouture. | |
| Ferme du Bois | 19.7.16 | | The Company relieved 117. M.G. Coy in the Ferme du Bois Section during the afternoon of the 19th June & were in turn relieved by 92 and 94 M.G. Coys on Monday 23rd June, after the relief they moved down to the featubert section & relieved 118. M.G. Coy. during the night of the 23rd/24th June. Six guns being placed in the O.B.L. & 6 in the Village line. | |
| Featubert | 23.7.16 | | 2/Lt. A.J. Reeves was awarded the military cross for gallantry in action & devotion to duty, at Richebourg on the morning of June 30th. | |
| Bethune | 1.8.16 | | The Company was relieved by 118. M.G. Coy. & moved into Billets in Bethune. | |
| | 2.8.16 | | Lieut. W.H. Penn left the company, to take command of 93. M.G. Coy. | |

G.V. Henniker-Gotley. Capt.
O.C. 116. M.G. Coy.

Army Form C. 2118.

# WAR DIARY
## or
## INTELLIGENCE SUMMARY.
*(Erase heading not required.)*

| Place | Date | Hour | Summary of Events and Information | Remarks and references to Appendices |
|---|---|---|---|---|
| | | | It decided to wait for direct targets as points of our troops not accurately known. | |
| | | 11.20 AM | OC 18 MGC (OC ESnap Barrage guns) sent word for guns to cover from ST JULIEN CHURCH to ALBERTA. | |
| | | 8.30 - 9 | Our Artillery put up heavy barrage. | |
| | | | Total Casualties on 13.12.17 | |
| | | | 1 Off killed (Lt Hobson) 1 Off wounded (Lt Brown) | |
| | | | O.R.s killed 4 — O.R.s wounded 19 | |
| | | | O.R.s missing 4. | |

A.T. Jackson, Captain,
O.C. 116 M.G. Coy

## Secret

### Operation Report.

### 116. M.G. Coy

To Headquarters
116th Infantry Brigade.

From O.C. 116. M.G. Coy.

Report of operations of the 116th Infantry Brigade Machine Gun Coy during the night of 29th–30th June.

A gun in Lansdowne Keep fired indirect fire from 9 p.m. till 2. a.m. on enemy communication trenches in rear of position to be attacked. Four guns in our front line trenches played on the enemy wire from dusk till 3. a.m & guns on each flank fired on the enemy's front line & supports while the attack was launched & also covered the retirement.

The Gun teams for Strong Points A and B were at their allotted place of assembly

"Pict Hall" at the obtained time, also the teams for B2, C and D were at Bott Street

b time.
The teams moved forward at the Stafford time. A team under the immediate command of 2/Lt. G.O. Brady, went over with the fourth throw, & succeeded in reaching the attained place, but there eventually contained in nature through sights of outposts. B. 2. C (team did not go over). B. 2. C. + D arrived almost simultaneously at the front line, + C. + D. went over. C got in within 15 yds. of the German wire, when they remained till a short half fire, was the infantry should attack again, + so supported them. + also it didn't any could attack that night.

be attempted by the enemy.
I should like to mention
the way that all the men
stuck to their guns; every
gun being brought back &
under very trying circumstances,
especially C team which
remained out in No mans land
till 8.45. a.m. under heavy
fire most of the time; the
2/Lt. A.J. Pearson who was in
charge then crawled back to
our line & found a sally point;
he then returned to his gun
& got it safely in & with the
help of Pte. Catt. 11th Royal
Sussex Regt attached to
us for carrying ammunition,
brought in his servant
who was very severly wounded
& unable to move they took it
in turns to carry him on their
backs, whilst crawling, &
eventually got him in, with

the Canadians at Courc. House who went out to holf them
His poch from in fear + a quarter. They had to find
the ditches in front of our own wire. I personally saw the
above getting out, + am forwarding 2/Lt Pearson's +
Pte Cull Thomas with a recommendation to awards.

The wire in front of Stony Point
(1) was not cut at all, nor does it
for some distance to the right.

One very important lesson can
I think be learnt from the operations
+ that is that

Guns should not be sent forward
till the intensity or family established
in the new line, as the rifles become
casualties before they reach their
objective.   G.D'A.Henniker Maj G.O.C.
                                    O.C 116 In.f.g Bde

116th Brigade.
39th Division.
-----------

116th BRIGADE MACHINE GUN COMPANY

V    AUGUST 1 9 1 6 ::

# WAR DIARY
## or
## INTELLIGENCE SUMMARY
*(Erase heading not required.)*

Instructions regarding War Diaries and Intelligence Summaries are contained in F. S. Regs., Part II. and the Staff Manual respectively. Title Pages will be prepared in manuscript.

| Place | Date | Hour | Summary of Events and Information | Remarks and references to Appendices |
|---|---|---|---|---|
| Gertebert Bethune | Aug.1 | | On Tuesday Aug.1st the Company was relieved in the Festubert Section by 118 M.G.Coy. & went into rest billets in Bethune where it remained till Sunday | |
| Givenchy Gorre | "6 | | Aug.6th when it took over the Givenchy section from 118.M.G.Coy. No.1 remained in reserve at Gorre. Headquarters were at Pont Fixe. | |
| | "6 | | On Aug.2nd Lieut. Jem left the Coy. to take command of 93.M.G.Coy. 2/Lt.2. | |
| | "2 | | Brampton becoming 2nd in command. | |
| Allonagne | 11. | | On Friday Aug.11th 21.M.G.Coy. (Major Bidder) relieved the Coy. who went back to Gorre & the left the same night marching to Allonagne, the next day marched to | |
| Cauchy à la tour | 12 | | Cauchy à la tour, on the 13th the Coy marched with the Brigade to Roeux | |
| Roeux | 13 | | where it remained till the 23rd where it put in much useful work, | |
| | 23 | | both as a Company & with the Brigade. On the 23rd the Coy marched with the Brigade to Serbicourt & moved on the next morning to Ivergny where it | |
| Ivergny | | | stayed the night, next day marching on the to the Bois de Warnimont, where | |
| Warnimont | 25-27 | | it remained from the 25th - 27th Whilst the Officers + N.C.O's of the Company | |
| Ancre. | 27. | | went over the AUCHONVILLERS section north of the river ANCRE. | |
| | -Sept. 2nd | | On the 27th the Coy moved to Mailly - Maillet woods where it remained till Saturday Sept. 2nd. | |

G.R. Henniker-Gotley. Capt.
O.C. 116. M.G.Coy.

Army Form C. 2118.

# WAR DIARY
# INTELLIGENCE SUMMARY

*(Erase heading not required.)*

Instructions regarding War Diaries and Intelligence Summaries are contained in F.S. Regs., Part II. and the Staff Manual respectively. Title Pages will be prepared in manuscript.

| Place | Date | Hour | Summary of Events and Information | Remarks and references to Appendices |
|---|---|---|---|---|
| Festubert | Aug.1 | | On Tuesday Aug.1st the Company was relieved in the Festubert section by 118. M.G.Coy & went into rest billets in BETHUNE where it remained till Sunday | |
| Bethune | Aug.1 | | | |
| GIVENCHY, GORRE. | Aug.6. | | Aug. 6th when it took over the GIVENCHY section from 117.M.G.Coy. No.1. Section remainder in reserve at GORRE. Headquarters were at PONT FIXE. No.2. Section had it's guns in | |
| " | " | | On Aug. 2nd Lieut. Gunn left the Company to take command of 93.M.G.Coy. 2/Lt. M. Brampton becoming 2nd in command. | |
| | ..2.. | | On Friday Aug. 11th 21.M.G.Coy. (Major Bidder) relieved the Coy, who went back to | |
| ALLOUAGNE | 11 | | GORRE, & left the same night, marching to ALLOUAGNE & the next day | |
| Cauchy a la Tour | ..12 | | marched on to Cauchy a la Tour, on the 13th the Coy marched with the Brigade | |
| Rocourt | ..13 | | to ROCOURT, where it remained till the 23rd where it hut in much useful | |
| | ..23 | | work, both as a Company and with the Brigade. On the 23rd the Coy marched with the Brigade to SERICOURT & moved on the next morning to IVERGNY where | |
| IVERGNY. | | | it stayed the night, next day marching on to the Bois de WARNIMONT | |
| Warnimont | 25-27 | | where it remained from the 25th - 27th whilst the officers & N.C.O's of the Company went over the AUCHONVILLERS section north of the river ANCRE. | |
| ANCRE. | 27. -Sept.2nd | | On the 27th the Coy moved to MAILLY-MAILLET woods where it remained till Saturday Sept.2nd | |

J.R. Henniker-[Hetty] Capt. O.C. 116. M.G. Coy.

2449 Wt. W14957/M90 750,000 1/16 J.B.C. & A. Forms/C.2118/12.

116th Brigade.
39th Division.
------------

116th BRIGADE MACHINE GUN COMPANY

SEPTEMBER 1 9 1 6

# WAR DIARY
## INTELLIGENCE SUMMARY
*(Erase heading not required.)*

| Place | Date | Hour | Summary of Events and Information | Remarks and references to Appendices |
|---|---|---|---|---|
| MAILLY-MAILLETWOOD | Sept 2nd | | Whilst the Company was encamped under canvas in MAILLY-MAILLET Wood, the wood was on several occasions heavily shelled, during which three drivers were wounded, & two gunners received shell shock. In addition to this five officers chargers were killed, & 7 mules killed | |
| LOUVENCOORT, | | | & missing; in consequence of this the transport moved back to LOUVENCOURT. | |
| LE HAMEL. | | | On Saturday afternoon Sept. 2nd the Company went into the line at LE HAMEL, taking over from 118. M.G. Coy. No.1. Section going in with the 11th Sussex & No.2. Section with the 14th Hants, No.3 & 4 Sections taking up positions along PROSPECT ROW. | |
| ANCRE | 3rd | 5.10 a.m. | At Zero (5.10.a.m.) On Sept. 3rd the attack was launched on the enemy's trenches immediately north of the River ANCRE. The battle lasted till 5.h.m. by which time most of our troops had regained our trenches, being unable to hold the captured positions. The Company lost heavily, the total casualties amounting to 38. Many of whom were reported missing amongst them being the two Section Officers 2/Lt. H.V. HIGGINS & 2/Lt. G. R. GREENE. | |

# WAR DIARY
## INTELLIGENCE SUMMARY
*(Erase heading not required.)*

Instructions regarding War Diaries and Intelligence Summaries are contained in F. S. Regs., Part II. and the Staff Manual respectively. Title Pages will be prepared in manuscript.

| Place | Date | Hour | Summary of Events and Information | Remarks and references to Appendices |
|---|---|---|---|---|
| | | | three guns were lost out of No.2. Section. One gun was blown up in the German front line, & the other two penetrated to the German third line with 2/Lt. Greene in command, & neither the teams or guns returning. It is supposed that they were cut off. | |
| | | 7.10.A.m | The guns of No.1. Section did some excellent work, jamming the German second line, three of the guns were mounted & successfully repelled several counter-attacks, finally withdrawing at 7.10.A.m. after being in the enemy trenches for 14. hrs. under Pte. Worthington & Humphries, greatly assisted by Pte. Boulter & Rainer. | |
| Englebelmer. | | 8.30./.m. | The company was relieved the same night by 118. M.G. Coy & went back to billets in ENGLEBELMER & remained there till Sept. 6th when | |
| Betrancourt. | 6.9.16 | | they moved back to huts at BETRANCOURT till Sunday Sept. 10th when | |
| Beaumont-Hamel. | 10.9.16 | | they relieved 145. M.G. Coy in the BEAUMONT-HAMEL sector, Headquarters were at No.10. (Gillet MAILLY-MAILLET. with Nos 1 & 2 Section out, & No.4 on the right & No.3. on the left. On the 19th Sept. the brigade extended its front, & took over from the 5th Brigade; the Company took over 5 positions from 5. M.G. Coy, & they left two teams in | |

# WAR DIARY
## INTELLIGENCE SUMMARY
*(Erase heading not required.)*

| Place | Date | Hour | Summary of Events and Information | Remarks and references to Appendices |
|---|---|---|---|---|
| | 26th | | During the day of the 26th & night of the 26th/27th all guns were taken into the line, & continuous direct & indirect fire was brought to bear by twenty guns on BEAUMONT-HAMEL, Y Ravine, & trenches & communication trenches in rear, in conjunction with a feint attack which the brigade was making. Lt. Ridler joined the coy for duty on Sept. 8th; 2/Lt. Hutson & 2/Lt. Traylen on Sept. 9th; 2/Lt. Stuart on Sept. 20th; 2/Lt. Brown on Sept. 21st. | |
| | 28. | | From 1. p.m. throughout the afternoon of the 28th & during the night of the 28th/29th, five guns were firing on the enemy support & communication trenches on BEAUCOURT HILL, in conjunction with the attack on THIEPVAL. | |

G. H. Flennihen = F/Stry. Capt.
O.C. 116. M.G. Coy.

116th Brigade.
39th Division.

116th BRIGADE MACHINE GUN COMPANY

OCTOBER 1 9 1 6 :::::

# INTELLIGENCE SUMMARY

*(Erase heading not required.)*

| Place | Date | Hour | Summary of Events and Information | Remarks and references to Appendices |
|---|---|---|---|---|
| MAILLY-MAILLET. ENGLEBELMER. AUCHONVILLERS | 3rd 6th | | On Oct. 3rd the Division was transferred from the 5th Corps to the 2nd Corps, & the Company had therefore to vacate their billets, & put up for the night at ENGLEBELMER. the next day it moved to AUCHONVILLERS, where it stayed till the 7th, when the Brigade staff further extended its front, taking altogether from WATLING STREET to the river ANCRE, the gun positions being as follows, 2 guns in JACOBS LADDER, 1 in SHOOTERS HILL, 1 in CARNELER, in BOND STREET, 1 in FORT ANLEY, 1 in FETHARD STREET, 1 in HAYMARKET, in ESSEX ST. 1 in SEAFORTH TRENCH, 1 in the BOWERY, 1 in 6th AVENUE, 1 in 4th AVENUE, & 1 off KING ST. Company H.Q. was at FORT PROWSE. On the 17th & the Company moved to the South of the river, & took over the SCHWABEN REDOUBT from 118th M.G. Coy & BAINBRIDGE TRENCH from 75th M.G. Coy. | |
| SCHWABEN REDOUBT. | 17th —23rd | | At 5 a.m. on the 21st the enemy made a determined & strong attack on the SCHWABEN REDOUBT, but was finally beaten off, leaving 79 prisoners in our hands, during this attack 2/Lt. Traylen & Cpl. Kirkwood behaved with great personal courage, & amongst them prisoners was Lieut. Bahr; Cpl. Kirkwood amongst them being a bomber, & a flammenwerfer, the remainder of both 2/Lt. Traylen & 2/Lt. Platts' teams showed great courage & resource, & received their swords. | |

# INTELLIGENCE SUMMARY

*(Erase heading not required.)*

| Place | Date | Hour | Summary of Events and Information | Remarks and references to Appendices |
|---|---|---|---|---|
| STUFF TRENCH | 21st | | At 12.6. p.m. the Brigade attacked STUFF TRENCH, 8 guns going over the top with the attacking troops. The attack was everywhere successful, but altogether during the operations, the Company lost 2/Lt. Hutar shot through the left eye, whilst very gallantly leading his men, +17. Other ranks. On the 22nd the guns in STUFF TRENCH were relieved by | |
| AVELUY WOOD JACOBS LADDER. MARTINSART. | 22nd | | 34. M.G. Coy, & those in the SCHWABEN REDOUBT were relieved by 147. M.G. Coy on the 23rd. The Company moving back to tents in AVELUY WOOD, on the 26th 8 guns went in again to JACOBS LADDER, & the Coy moved to MARTINSART for 2 nights, & then went in with the remaining eight teams to the RIVER SECTOR. | |
| RIVER SECTOR. AUTHUILLE | | | the 29th & going in again on the 30th. Coy H.Q. was at in AUTHUILLE, on Oct. 4th Lee. Cpl. Humphries & Lee. Cpl. Worthington were granted the D.C.M. for gallant conduct during the operations of Sept. 3rd on BEAUCOURT. On Oct. 29th Lieut. Gibbon reported for duty with the Coy, & on the 31st Lieut. Hoben also reported. A draft of 17 O.R's. reported for duty on the 29th. | |

A.H. Hemming Capt

116th Brigade
39th Division.
---------------

116th BRIGADE MACHINE GUN COMPANY

NOVEMBER 1 9 1 6

# WAR DIARY
## or
## INTELLIGENCE SUMMARY

Army Form C. 2118.

| Place | Date | Hour | Summary of Events and Information | Remarks and references to Appendices |
|---|---|---|---|---|
| AUTHUILE | 1916 Nov. 14th | | Coy. H.Q. at AUTHUILE, in the RIVER SECTION (ANCRE) on this date we had eight guns in the line. Two guns at front 86, one at GORDON CASTLE, one at front 16 and four guns in the SCHWABEN REDOUBT. The remaining eight guns of the Coy. were on the other side of the river (i.e. N. side of the ANCRE) in the MESNIL SECTION. These guns were in position along JACOB'S LADDER, they were laid on NO MAN'S LAND in front of the SCHWABEN REDOUBT and opened fire on prearranged S.O.S. went up; there main object being to provide a barrage by enfilading NO MAN'S LAND. Till Nov. 13th these gun teams of these eight guns were employed in building light rail emplacements, actually ten more were constructed. These emplacements were carefully sighted, during frosts etc. laid out on four definite barrage lines on which the guns would fire on 'Z' day so as to offer covering fire to troops attacking from the SCHWABEN down to the ANCRE in the direction of St. PIERRE DIVION. Two or three of these guns were employed on sending certain areas during the night. Reports were received forth as the result of aerial and direct observation that the enemy had taped certain sketches of ground opposite the SCHWABEN. The direct reaching fire during the night by the above mentioned guns appeared to be very successful; if it did not altogether stop work, it certainly greatly hindered it. In the RIVER SECTION eight guns were attached to the Coy. from 118 M.G. Coy., these were in position two at Coy. H.Q.(AUTHUILE), two at GORDON CASTLE, 3 in the TUNNELS and 1 at the MILL (an emplacement on the river). | |

Army Form C. 2118.

# WAR DIARY
## INTELLIGENCE SUMMARY
*(Erase heading not required.)*

Instructions regarding War Diaries and Intelligence Summaries are contained in F. S. Regs., Part II. and the Staff Manual respectively. Title Pages will be prepared in manuscript.

| Place | Date 1916 | Hour | Summary of Events and Information | Remarks and references to Appendices |
|---|---|---|---|---|
| MARTINSART | Nov. 2 | | In the morning 118 M.G. Coy. relieved our eight guns in the RIVER SECTION and took over the Coy. H.Q. from us at AUTHUILE. Coy. H.Q. and three eight teams moved into billets at MARTINSART. The relief of the guns in the SCHWABEN was never easy, it had to be carried out practically across the open, and of a relief was spotted by enemy (as generally did happen), he at once commenced shelling with 77cm. and 4.2 and 5.9. Added to this the exceedingly bad condition of the ground added to the difficulties. | |
| do. | Nov. 3-4 | | At MARTINSART, men were bathed and got their clothes dry. Guns were thoroughly overhauled. Eight guns arrived in at JACOB'S LADDER. | |
| AUTHUILE | Nov. 5 | | Coy. H.Q. moved to AUTHUILE, and took over from 117 M.G. Coy. in the RIVER SECTION. The two sections (eight teams) relieved two sections of 117 Coy.; four guns in the SCHWABEN, two in the TUNNELS and two at Coy. H.Q. & two sections of 117 M.G. Coy. remained in position and were attached to us. They were located at GORDON CASTLE three, at the MILL one, two at pt. 86 and one at pt. 16 and one in one of the three TUNNELS. | |
| MARTINSART | Nov. 6 | | In the early afternoon our two sections in the RIVER SECTION were relieved by 117 M.G. Coy, the relieved sections and Coy. H.Q. moved back again to MARTINSART. | |
| do | Nov. 7-9 | | At MARTINSART, the time was spent in resting the men, and cleaning up generally. | |

Army Form C. 2118.

# WAR DIARY
## INTELLIGENCE SUMMARY

(Erase heading not required.)

| Place | Date 1916 | Hour | Summary of Events and Information | Remarks and references to Appendices |
|---|---|---|---|---|
| AUTHUILE | Nov. 10 | | Two sections of 118 M.G. Coy. in the RIVER SECTION, at the SCHWABEN (4 guns), point 86 (2 guns), & point 16 (4 guns), & point in GORDON CASTLE & look over the RIVER SECTION. 118 Coy. left eight guns in position which were attached to us. They were at GORDON CASTLE (2 guns) one at the MILL three in the TUNNELS and two at Coy. H.Q. During the night orders were received that the eight guns attached to us from 118 Coy. were to be relieved by 8 guns of 117 Coy., and that these eight relieving guns of 117 were to be in position in the right and centre of the RIVER SECTION. | |
| do. | Nov. 11 | | To obtain this it was necessary to issue orders for a double relief. When the two sections of 118 Coy. were out of the line the position was our Coy. had 3 guns in the TUNNELS, one at the MILL, 2 at Coy. H.Q., 2 at GORDON CASTLE, there was one section of No. 117 in the SCHWABEN, one gun at GORDON CASTLE, 2 guns at point 86, and 1 gun at point 16. | |
| MESNIL (JACOBS LADDER) | Nov. 12 | | Our eight guns in the RIVER SECTION were relieved by 118 Coy., and we moved into the star side of the river (N. side) and joined our other 8 guns which had been in # JACOBS LADDER. These eight guns moved into positions which had been previously made, sighted with away guns etc. The whole 16 guns of the Coy. were in position by 4 p.m. On this day ready to supply the barrage (or evening fire) for an attack to be launched on St. PIERRE DIVION and the HANSA LINE | |
| do. | Nov. 13 | | This 2' day, Zero was at 5.30 a.m., we opened fire (rapid) with all 16 guns on our front franage line and then gradually traversed to the left till we were firing in the direction and into St. PIERRE DIVION. At zero + 20 we ceased firing. During the whole time and the | |

# WAR DIARY or INTELLIGENCE SUMMARY

Army Form C. 2118.

| Place | Date 1916 | Hour | Summary of Events and Information | Remarks and references to Appendices |
|---|---|---|---|---|
| | | | the whole day, a thick mist prevailed, so we had to rely entirely on our right lines and enemy posts for fixing. We had particular attention to preventing our comms. of fire coming across to the N. bank of the river as here we should have been shutting the R.N.D. i.e. we made our front at Grandcourt St. PIERRE DIVION. The attack our division took part proved eminently successful, their objectives being gained and held. That evening we received orders to move out of JACOB'S LADDER, so all 16 guns were taken out and we returned to MARTINSART. | |
| MARTINSART | Nov. 14 | | At 11 a.m. we received orders to move, we left MARTINSART at 2 p.m. to pass the starting point 2.30 (PIONEER ROAD junction with road leading S. from LANCASHIRE DUMP). We arrived at WARLOY at 6 p.m., we were taken to our billets by a billeting party which had preceded us. During the night a hostile aeroplane dropped some bombs and fired V.B.s at Machine Gun. | |
| WARLOY | Nov. 15 | | So left WARLOY at 9 a.m. in the morning & marched to FRESCHVILLERS. Our billets were situated at the last mentioned place and AUTHIELLE (about DOULLENS) | |
| FRESCHVILLERS | Nov. 17 | | We stayed here till the 17th, when the Coy. was split up into four section, each section with its transport was attached to a battalion in the Brigade. The sections marched into DOULLENS and entrained there in four different trains. The first left in the afternoon, and the last one late at night. | |

Army Form C. 2118.

## WAR DIARY

## INTELLIGENCE SUMMARY

*(Erase heading not required.)*

Instructions regarding War Diaries and Intelligence Summaries are contained in F. S. Regs., Part II. and the Staff Manual respectively. Title Pages will be prepared in manuscript.

| Place | Date | Hour | Summary of Events and Information | Remarks and references to Appendices |
|---|---|---|---|---|
| ST. JAN-TER-BEZEN (Y Camp) | Nov. 18 | | We detrained at varying hours during the late hours of the 17th and early hours of the 18th at HOPOUTRE (outside POPERINGHE) and marched to 'Y' camp nts hutments which we shared with the 14th Bath. Hampshire Regt. and the 116th Trench Mortar Battery. | |
| do | Nov. 19-22 | | Time was spent in getting the men cleaned, their equipment etc. cleaned up. | |
| do | 23 | | The Corps Commander inspected the Coy. | |
| do | 24-30 | | Training and Rest. | |

J.R.G. Potter
2nd Lt.
M.G. Coy.
711

116th Brigade.
39th Division
------------

116th BRIGADE MACHINE GUN COMPANY

DECEMBER 1 9 1 6

# Summary of Events and Information

## of

## 116th Coy., Machine Gun Corps

## 1st Dec. — 31st December 1916.

and the Staff Manual respectively. Title Pages
will be prepared in manuscript.

INTELLIGENCE SUMMARY

*(Erase heading not required.)*

| Place | Date | Hour | Summary of Events and Information | Remarks and references to Appendices |
|---|---|---|---|---|
| 'Y' CAMP near POPERINGHE | 1916 Dec. 1-10 | | Training during this period was continued, shortages as far as possible were made up. 'Y' Camp was shared with 116th Light Trench Mortar Battery and the 14th Bn. Hampshire Regt. | POP. |
| Do. | 11th | 1.30 p.m. | The Coy. left 'Y' Camp and marched to the VLAMERTINGHE Cross Roads at 4.30 p.m. On arrival at 5.30 p.m. at C.30 a H.5. they were met by guides of 115 M.G. Coy, when we relieved in the Right Sector, 13 guns were placed in the line, and 3 were held in Reserve to the CANAL BANK. Coy HQ. at C.19 e 25.60. The relief with 115. M.G. Coy was complete by 9 p.m. | Map. Belgium 28 N W |
| CANAL BANK C.19c 25.60 | 13-14 | | Between the hours of 8 p.m. and 11 p.m. the guns of THREAD NEEDLE ST. (C.27 b 05.70) fired at the area around C.10 c 0.3½. | POP. Map 28 N.W. |
| | 15-16 | | From 10 p.m. to 2.30 a.m. Guns at C.30c 6.7½ fired at Target C.8a 7.8½ Ammunition expended 15,000 Rounds. | |
| | 17-18 | | From 10 p.m. to K.4.45 a.m. 2000 rounds were fired from a night firing position at C.20c 6.7½ at Targets C.8a 7.8½ to C.2c 8.5.8. Rapid fire was a gun case was most essential to keep these latter positions as a surprise in the event Battle positions they were walled, and hence could only be approached by night of attack. Most of the positions were placed to cover gaps in our front system of trenches. | St. Julien 28 N.W. |
| | 18-19 | | 9 New cases guns were placed. from 7 p.m. to 11 p.m. The Gun at C.20c 6.7½ fired at the area C.8a 7.8½ to C.2c 8.5.8 (2000 Rounds) at 8.55 p.m. (I.R.) there was a gas alarm, which proved to be false. All box respirators were found to be adjusted quickly and without difficulty. | Map 28 N.W. POP. |

2449 Wt. W14957/M90 750,000 1/16 J.B.C. & A. Forms/C.2118/12.

(Erase heading not required.)

| Place | Date | Hour | Summary of Events and Information | Remarks and references to Appendices |
|---|---|---|---|---|
| CANAL BANK C19c 28.60 | 1916 Dec. 19-20 | | From 2a.m. to 4.30 a.m. (19th) 1500 rounds were fired at area C.18d.7.8½ to C.20.c.8½ & from a gun at C.20.c.6.7½. | MAP |
| " | 20-21 | | From 7p.m. to 10 p.m. 2000 rounds were fired as above. About 11.40 p.m. enemy shelled area of HILLTOP (C.21d) with shrapnel and H.E. (20th) | MAP |
| " | 21-22 | | From 10 p.m. to 12 midnight (21st) 1250 rounds were fired at area C.18.d.7.8½ to C.20.c.8½ from a gun at C.20.c.6.7½. Also from 7p.m. to 11 p.m. 1750 Rounds were fired at C.9.d.15.05 to C.9.b.55.05 from a gun at C.27.d.15.85. | MAP ST JULIEN 28 N.W. |
| " | 22-23 | | From 7 p.m. to 6.30 a.m. (22nd) 2000 Rounds were fired at once C.8&7.K.2 C.2c.5.5 from a gun at C.20.c.6.7½. | MAP |
| | 23 | 5 p.m. | We were relieved by 118 M.G. Coy. Relief was reported complete by 10.45 p.m. Each section in relief proceeded to "S" Camp on the POPERINGHE – ELVERDINGHE ROAD (A.23.c.4.8) (Asp. Belgium 28 N.W.) which was taken over from 113 M.G Coy. | MAP |
| "S" CAMP nr POPERINGHE ELVERDINGHE ROAD (A.23.c.4.8.) | 24 | | In the gazette dated 22nd inst. Sec.Lieuts. J.R.A. PLATTS, G.L. HIGGINBOTTOM, J.P. TRAYLEN S.W. BROWN, W.O. STOTT were promoted to the rank of "Temp. Lieuts." A.S Coy dated 1st inst. Lieut. L.W. EVANS (115 M.G Coy) was appointed 2nd in Command of the Coy | MAP |

Sgd. T.E.J. FITZ GERALD 2nd in Command of the Coy (late 113 M.G. Coy.) Lieut. L.W. EVANS (115 M.G Coy) was appointed 2nd in Command of the Coy

2449 Wt. W14957/M90 750,000 1/16 J.B.C. & A. Forms/C.2118/12.

| Place | Date | Hour | Summary of Events and Information | Remarks and references to Appendices |
|---|---|---|---|---|
| B. Camp on POPERINGHE - ELVERDINGHE ROAD | 1916 Dec 24 cont | | The day was spent in cleaning up. | POP. |
| | 25-30 | | Time was spent in training & fatigues. Fatigues were provided for building horse-standings. On the 28th and 29th respectively 3 Officers went up to the left sector (BOESINGHE) heavily wooded by the French) to accommodate same. Orders were issued for the relief of 115 M.G.Coy to be complete by 12 noon on the 30th inst. As the relief would have been being carried out by Coy guns, tripods and a certain no. of belt boxes were left in charge of 115 M.G.Coy and placed in position on the night of the 29th, these were left in charge of MAP. | M.W. MAP 28 N.W. |
| B13 C.5.6. & ELVERDINGHE - POPERINGHE RD | 30-31 | 9.30 a.m | At 9.32 a.m on the 30th the relief of #115 M.G.Coy commenced, it was affected & completed by 1 p.m. 2 guns were placed in the "A" line (front line), 4 in the "B" line and 2 in the "X" or Reserve line, and it is the "D" line, a accommon of Strong points (one at SALVATION CORNER and (YPRES), 2 at WAGNER FARM, at the WINDMILL, REIGESBURG CHATEAU, and one at in line beyond at Coy A.Q. on the ELVERDINGHE - POPERINGHE ROAD. | MAP 51 N.W. MAP 28 N.W. |
| | 31st | | No firing was done. Nothing to report. | |

J.R.Q. Parker Lieut
1/16 Coy M.G.C

Vol XI

16 Coy M.G. Corps
War Diary
to end of January 1917
Vol XI

Army Form C. 2118.

# WAR DIARY
## or
## INTELLIGENCE SUMMARY

*(Erase heading not required.)*

Confidential

116 Company
M.G. Corps.

Jan 1st — 31st 1917

Army Form C. 2118.

# WAR DIARY
## or
## INTELLIGENCE SUMMARY

(Erase heading not required.)

Instructions regarding War Diaries and Intelligence Summaries are contained in F. S. Regs., Part II. and the Staff Manual respectively. Title Pages will be prepared in manuscript.

| Place | Date | Hour | Summary of Events and Information | Remarks and references to Appendices |
|---|---|---|---|---|
| 13 f. 2. 80 | 1/1/17 | Noon | Firing during night 31 Dec / 1st Jan Nil. Casualties - Nil | |
| BOESINGHE SECTOR | | 4 AM | Very quiet on front. | |
| | | 11 AM | About 100 heavy shells dropped on WOESTEN-ELVERDINGHE Rd. | |
| | | 2 PM | Enemy T.M. very active - damaged gap in which Vickers gun is placed A3 B.12.b.40.40. | |
| | | 5 PM | Evening - Casualties nil | |
| | | 4 PM | Quiet on front - Intersection relief carried out | |
| | 2/1/17 | | Firing nil - casualties nil | |
| | 3/1/17 | 1.45 PM | Enemy very active on BOESINGHE VILLAGE & BELGIAN front. On front line T. Mortared - M.G. Sap B.12.b.40.40 Bournin & Gun Ret turned - Vickers team charged Lewis Gun — Gun (Vickers) carried. Vickers gun temporarily withdrawn & teeth in readiness for use with light howitzer from parapet. Firing nil - casualties nil. Continued Hostile artillery activity in BOESINGHE AREA. | |
| | 4/1/17 | | Firing Nil - casualties nil | |
| | 5/1/17 | 4 PM | E. activity on BOESINGHE CHURCH. Intersection relief carried out — 1st stage. | |

**Army Form C. 2118.**

Instructions regarding War Diaries and Intelligence Summaries are contained in F. S. Regs., Part II. and the Staff Manual respectively. Title Pages will be prepared in manuscript.

# WAR DIARY
## or
## INTELLIGENCE SUMMARY
*(Erase heading not required.)*

| Place | Date | Hour | Summary of Events and Information | Remarks and references to Appendices |
|---|---|---|---|---|
|  | 6/1/17 |  | Army reveille nil. Intersection relief (commenced last night) completed - Napoleonry Gunn's change. | |

Guns :   MAP Ref :   Section H.Q.   Officer
A3       B12.b.40.40
A4       B12.a.95.80     } BOESINGHE     } Lt. Traylen
S3       B12.d.05.95     } B12.a.10.70
S4       B12.a.70.30

S5       B12.a.45.55
S6       B6.c.18.00                      } 2Lt. Gibbon

X1       B11.d.90.00
X3       B11.d.10.80                     } B17.d.40.90  } Lt. Holzon

X4       B11.a.85.15
X5       B11.a.76.40                     }              } 2/Lt Mitchell

B23. Central
WAGRAM FM.
REIGERSBURG CHAT.  H6.c.4.MNMMM.MM6.a.90
WINDMILL                       H6.a.60.90     } H6.a.60.90  } 2/Lt Redding
SALVATION CORNER               I.1.c.90.90

Temporary M.G. position near Rd. Salt down in...

2449  Wt. W14957/M90  750,000  1/16  J.B.C. & A.  Forms/C.2118/12.

# WAR DIARY or INTELLIGENCE SUMMARY

Army Form C. 2118.

| Place | Date | Hour | Summary of Events and Information | Remarks and references to Appendices |
|---|---|---|---|---|
| | 7/1/17 | | Mass for R.B's 10.45 AM. C.A. Hut. Intense Hostile shelling of BOESINGE. Aerial activity – 2 British planes engaged two enemy planes & drove them off. Jimmy McE – casualties NIL | hurt |
| | 8/1/17 | | Quiet – nothing – no casualties at night – our communications shelled & communic. at intervals | MsR |
| | 9/1/17 | | Cope M.G.O. watch the line. Intercoln relief carried out. Rey. Sgt. repaired LMT loopholes not completed. Quiet day. Casualties nil – Enemy nil | |
| | 10/1/17 | 6.30 AM | Two Officers & two P's reconnoitred Rly WOOD sector at present held by 1/164 M.G. Coy. Gun positions at A3 & 55 buried by hostile "Minnies." Casualty – one wounded in head at S5. Ennis sent up from X' line to replace & twopon Coy. HQ to X' line. | |
| | | 9 AM to 10 AM | BOESINGE shelled with HV. YPRES bombarded during the day | |

Army Form C. 2118.

# WAR DIARY
## or
## INTELLIGENCE SUMMARY

*(Erase heading not required.)*

Instructions regarding War Diaries and Intelligence Summaries are contained in F. S. Regs., Part II. and the Staff Manual respectively. Title Pages will be prepared in manuscript.

| Place | Date | Hour | Summary of Events and Information | Remarks and references to Appendices |
|---|---|---|---|---|
| 10/1/17 | | | Army NIL | |
| | | | Guns at S.5 & A.3 received & mounted at night in temporary emplacement. | |
| | 11.1.17 | 7 AM | Army previous night NIL. | |
| | | 1 PM | Casualties NIL. | |
| | 12.1.17 | | Reconnaissance of RAILWAY WOOD SECTOR by two officers | hut |
| | | | Snowing all day & heavy mist | |
| | | | Army fire - casualties nil | |
| | | 9.10 PM | S.O.S. went up on our right & stand to ordered | |
| | | 10.15 PM | Stand down resumed | |
| | | | Emplacement at Bn. a 4.2.5. completed. | hut |
| | 13/1/17 | 4 AM | Interstream relief carried out. | |
| | | | Casualties & firing N.L. | |
| | | | Trenches very wet owing to heavy rain previous night. | hut |
| | | | Heavy mist | |
| | 14/1/17 | | Army & casualties NIL | hut |
| | | 9.15 AM | L.M.V. on BOESINGHE | |
| | 15/1/17 | 7 AM | The Corps Commander inspected the BOESINGHE. | |
| | | 8 AM | " " visited A4 position | |
| | | 10 AM | " " the's line positions & questioned the team thoroughly at S.5 | hut |
| | | 11 AM | Also had them to mount gun in the trench. | |
| | | -12 noon | Enemy artillery active. | hut |

2449 Wt. W14957/M90 750,000 1/16 J.B.C. & A. Forms/C.2118/12.

# WAR DIARY
## or
## INTELLIGENCE SUMMARY

Army Form C. 2118.

| Place | Date | Hour | Summary of Events and Information | Remarks and references to Appendices |
|---|---|---|---|---|
| | 15/1/17 | | Army & casualties nil | nil |
| | 16/1/17 | 3.30 PM | Relief by 115 M.G. Coy commenced in the following positions A3, A4, S3, S4, S5, S6, X1, X3, X4, X5. | |
| | | 4.15 PM | Relief of WAGRAM Fm. REIGERSBURG CHATEAU, WINDMILL by 196 M.G. Coy commenced. | |
| | | 6.45 PM | Relief complete. | |
| | | 7.30 PM | Company moved to 'C' camp for night. To huts left by 117 Bde. A30.d 0.8 (Belgium 28NW2) | |
| | | 11.30 PM | 2 coys from L. hrs arrived in camp. Transport went to 'S' Camp for night. Snowing. | |
| | 17/1/17 | 10 AM | Cleaning & packing of limbers. | |
| | | 1 PM | | |
| | | 12 noon | Officers I No.1 left for RAILWAY WOOD Sector to take over. | |
| | | 3 PM | Coy with Transport left 'C' camp for École YPRES via VLAMERTINGHE. | |
| | | 6.30 PM | Relief commenced. | |
| | | 9.50 PM | Completed. | |
| | | | The following positions were taken over :— Mr. Pinsom officer I/c Rt. Sector " Peate " " Centre " " Sutton " " Left " | |

# WAR DIARY or INTELLIGENCE SUMMARY

Army Form C. 2118.

| Place | Date | Hour | Summary of Events and Information | Remarks and references to Appendices |
|---|---|---|---|---|
| RAILWAY WOOD SECTOR ECOLE YPRES I.9.c.15.00 (ZILLEBEKE 28 NW YPRES) | 1/11/17 | | R.T. Sector<br>B5    I.11.c.00.25<br>C5    I.10.d.45.45<br>I.11.6    I.11.d.10.35<br>I.11.7    I.11.c.85.05<br><br>Centre Sector<br>I.11.2    I.11.a.10.40<br>I.11.3    I.11.d.55.40<br>I.5.4    I.5.d.50.05<br><br>Left Subsector<br>X2    I.4.d.35.50<br>B6    I.4.d.95.90<br>I.11.1    I.11.c.2.9<br>I.5.3    I.5.c.30.15<br><br>R.T. Sector H.Q's I.11.a.84.22<br>Centre<br>Coy H.Q. with 5 Reserve guns | —<br>—<br>—<br>—<br><br>—<br>—<br>—<br><br>—<br>—<br>—<br>—<br>11<br>5<br>16 |

Army Form C. 2118.

# WAR DIARY
or
## INTELLIGENCE SUMMARY

(Erase heading not required.)

Instructions regarding War Diaries and Intelligence Summaries are contained in F.S. Regs., Part II. and the Staff Manual respectively. Title Pages will be prepared in manuscript.

| Place | Date | Hour | Summary of Events and Information | Remarks and references to Appendices |
|---|---|---|---|---|
| ECOLE YPRES | 18/1/17 | | Casualties Nil. Firing Nil. | |
| | 19/1/17 | | " " | |
| | 20/1/17 | 5 AM | Anti-aircraft positions manned — at I.11.7 — I.5.4 + I.11.c.78.75. | |
| | | 4.30AM | Officer going up from Coy. H.Q. daily to look horizon. Casualties Nil — Firing nil — Frost. | |
| | 21/1/17 | | Casualties Nil — Firing Nil — Intermittent Relief | |
| | 22/1/17 | | Casualties Nil — Firing Nil — Frost. | |
| | 23/1/17 | | Firing from our right nil — Casualties Nil. Aerial activity — several planes up during the day. Anti-aircraft gun at _____ fired at enemy plane. | |
| | 24/1/17 | 8.45 P.M. | Heavy bombardment by our artillery. Casualties Nil — Firing Done Nil — Hostile artillery very active the whole day enemy appear to be registering in various spots. West flank and THE GULLY heavily shelled. Aircraft also very active. Several fights took place any several planes hostile and English forced to descend. Heavy Bombardment in front GULLY FARM — RAILWAY WOOD last half an hour. During this period enemy raided our line where it approaches the railway capturing four prisoners. The enemy left two dead in No MAN'S LAND | |
| | 25/1/17 | 5 A.M. | | |

Army Form C. 2118.

# WAR DIARY
## or
## INTELLIGENCE SUMMARY

*(Erase heading not required.)*

Instructions regarding War Diaries and Intelligence Summaries are contained in F. S. Regs., Part II. and the Staff Manual respectively. Title Pages will be prepared in manuscript.

| Place | Date | Hour | Summary of Events and Information | Remarks and references to Appendices |
|---|---|---|---|---|
| | 25/11/17 (continued) | | One Officer and one man. Casualties - Nil. Firing Done - Nil | |
| | 26/11/17 | | Casualties Nil. Firing Done Nil. Very quiet the whole day. Frost continues | |
| | 27/11/17 | | Casualties Nil. Firing Done - Anti aircraft engaged hostile planes in the morning but with no success. Day very quiet | |
| | 28/11/17 | | Casualties Nil. Firing Done Nil. ~~[crossed out]~~ Casual shelling by the enemy | |
| | 29/11/17 | | Casualties Nil. Firing Done - Nil. Enemy exploded camouflet with mine shaft 3 infantry men buried. Tremor felt at Snk HQ. Trench mor enjoue(?) at I.11.7. Flown in. Otherwise fairly quiet. | |
| | | | Firing done on night 29th/30th | |
| | | | | Rounds fired |
| | | 12 M.N. | Position        Target | |
| | | 3.30 AM | I.10.d.2.4     Level Crossing I.6.c.5.2. and Ry. cutting behind | 1000 |
| | | 8 AM    | I.11.c.0.1     Trenches on BELLEWARDE RIDGE | 1000 |
| | | 11.30 PM | | M/G |
| | 30/11/17 | 8.45 AM | Both Artillery commenced bombardment of enemy trenches – also Bn. Artillery | |
| | | 4 AM | Bombardment practically ceased | M/G |

**Army Form C. 2118.**

# WAR DIARY
## or
## INTELLIGENCE SUMMARY
*(Erase heading not required.)*

| Place | Date | Hour | Summary of Events and Information | Remarks and references to Appendices |
|---|---|---|---|---|
| | 30/1/17 | | Enemy retaliated vigorously throughout the day. The following firing was carried out commencing 4 P.M. | |

| Gun Position | Time | TARGET | Rds. |
|---|---|---|---|
| | 4 PM – 5.45 PM | Trav. Searching fire I.6.c.50.20 | 1000 |
| | 4 PM – 5.45 PM | Trav. Searching fire front I.6.c.40.50 to I.6.c.95.67 | 700 |
| | " | Area included in I.12.a.75.80, I.12.b.00.20, I.12.a.75.50 & I.12.b.00.50 | 500 |
| | 4 PM to 5.45 PM  2.45 AM to 4.15 AM | Traversing I.12.c.95.90 to I.12.d.10.46 | 1000 |
| | 4 PM – 5.45 PM | Traversing Searching round I.b.e.52 | 1000 |
| | " | J.7.a.20.60 to J.7.c.45.10 | 1000 |
| | 2.45 AM to 4.15 AM | Traversing Searching round I.b.e.52 | 750 |

# WAR DIARY
## or
## INTELLIGENCE SUMMARY

*(Erase heading not required.)*

Army Form C. 2118.

| Place | Date | Hour | Summary of Events and Information | Remarks and references to Appendices |
|---|---|---|---|---|
| ÉCOLE YPRES | 31 | | M.Gs. were directed on ground to flank & rear of bombarded Trench to prevent enemy reentering it when bombardment ceased. Sunday shelling during the day. Very quiet late evening. The following firing was done. | Inst. |

| Gun Postn | Time | Target | Rate | Officer i/c |
|---|---|---|---|---|
| I.10.c.15.35 | 11mn TO 5 AM | Area BELLEWARDE Fm. I.12.c.7.9 to I.12.d.2.3 | 1500 | LT Mult |
| I.10.a.48.58 | 9 PM TO 12.30 A.M. | Level Crossing I.6.c.5.2 harassing & searching fire. | 1500 | LT Brown |

Muhunoti.

T/ 2/Lieut. Capt.
O.C. No. 116 COY.
MACHINE GUN CORPS.

Confidential                    Vol 12

War Diary
for
the month of February 1919
116th Machine Gun Co.

Army Form C. 2118.

# WAR DIARY
## or
## INTELLIGENCE SUMMARY

*(Erase heading not required.)*

Instructions regarding War Diaries and Intelligence Summaries are contained in F. S. Regs., Part II. and the Staff Manual respectively. Title Pages will be prepared in manuscript.

| Place | Date | Hour | Summary of Events and Information | Remarks and references to Appendices |
|---|---|---|---|---|
| RAILWAY WOOD SECTOR | 1/4/17 | 5 AM | Intense Enemy Bombardment commenced. | |
| | | 5.5 AM | SOS went up. Repeatedly guns at  I.11.3  Target  I.6.a.14 | |
| | | | I.5.4  "  II.d.95.40 | |
| | | | I.11.6  "  I.12.c.9.3 | |
| | | | X 2  "  I.6.c.15.75 to I.6.c.85.85. | |
| | | 5.45 AM | Bombardment ceased. Casualties nil. | |
| | | | 1800 rds fired | |
| | 2/4/17 | 7-8 AM | Heavy frost continues. Casualties Nil. | |
| | | 8-9 PM | The following firing was done:— | |
| | | | Position  Target  TIME  Rds. |
| | | | I.11.a.13.83  Rly LINE  8-9 PM  500 |
| | | |                 "         10-11 PM  500 |
| | | | I.10.a.48.58  Level Crossing (I.6.c.5.2)  9-1 AM  1500 |
| | | | I.10.d.15.35  BELLEWARDE RIDGE  7-8 PM  }1000 |
| | | | | Area between BELLEWARDE RIDGE & WOOD S.W. ETANG  9.30-10.30 PM | |

# WAR DIARY or INTELLIGENCE SUMMARY

Army Form C. 2118.

| Place | Date | Hour | Summary of Events and Information | Remarks and references to Appendices |
|---|---|---|---|---|
| RAILWAY WOOD | 3/7/17 | 1 AM | Firing from I.11.a.13.83 Target - RLY LINE Rds 500 | |
| | | 2 AM | " I.10.a.15.35 " BELLEWARDE RIDGE YPRES AREA } Rds 500 between BELLEWARDE Fm. THODA S.W. ETAN) | |
| | | 5 PM | Relief by 117 Coy M.G.C. commenced | knl |
| | | 12:20 AM | " completed | |
| | 4/7/17 | 6 AM | 9 Gun teams proceeded to Ramparts YPRES & took up positions previously occupied by 118 Coy M.G.C. | |

Name | MAP REFERENCE
H 13 | I.14.a.78.22
F.13 | I.14.b.20.45
B.13 | I.8.d.17.45
A.13 | I.8.b.12.02
C.14 | I.8.b.02.50
A.14 | I.8.b.08.65
E.15 | I.2.d.15.30
4 YPRES | I.2.c.55.75
SALVATION CORNER | I.1.c.95.80

# WAR DIARY or INTELLIGENCE SUMMARY

Army Form C. 2118.

| Place | Date | Hour | Summary of Events and Information | Remarks and references to Appendices |
|---|---|---|---|---|
| BRANDHOEK | 4/7/17 | 4 AM | Last of Coy arrived in M.G. Camp BRANDHOEK | |
| | 5/7/17 | | Cleaning up & checking stores | |
| | 6/7/17 | | Instructed Reliefs of teams in RAMPARTS Coy Training – Revolver firing – Gas courses Reconnaissances of emergency routes by officers | M.R. |
| | 11/7/17 | 1 AM | 3 guns re taken to YPRES to assist 118 M.S Coy in a Raid | |
| | | 3 PM | 4 guns moved from RAMPARTS to assist 117 M.S Coy " " | |
| | 12/7/17 | 11 PM | Raid by 118 Bde. | |
| | 13/7/17 | 4 AM | Teams from 118 M.S. Coy return to BRANDHOEK Casualties NIL Coy Training. | M.R. |
| | 14/7/17 | 11 AM | – Raid by 115 Bde in R14 WOOD SECTOR | |
| | 15/7/17 | 4 AM | – Guns return to RAMPARTS | |
| | 16/7/17 | 4 PM | – Relieved in BRANDHOEK camp by 164 M.G Coy | |
| | | 4.30 PM | – Remainder of 116 M.G.C moved to billets in POPERINGHE | |
| | 17/7/17 | 6 PM | – Relief of teams in Ramparts commenced by 164 M.G.C. | |
| | 18/7/17 | 1.30 AM | – Teams relieved arrived in POPERINGHE | |
| | 19/7/17 | 10.55 PM | – Coy left by train via canal for BULLEZEELE | M.R. |

# WAR DIARY
## or
## INTELLIGENCE SUMMARY
*(Erase heading not required.)*

Army Form C. 2118.

| Place | Date | Hour | Summary of Events and Information | Remarks and references to Appendices |
|---|---|---|---|---|
| BOLLEZEELE | 15/9/17 | 2 PM | Arrived BOLLEZEELE | |
| | | 4 PM | Billetting complete. | |
| | 19?? | | Company Training | |
| | 23/9/17 | | | |
| | 24/9/17 | 9.12 AM | Company entrained for POPERINGHE | hw.8 |
| | | 1.45 PM | arrived POPERINGHE proceeded to ERIE CAMP 9.11.d (Belgium 28 NW). | |
| ERIE CAMP | 25/9/17 | 4 AM | Advanced Party of 1 off. 1 N.C.O. + 2 men per Gun team proceeded by Train from BRANDHOEK Stn to YPRES thence to positions in ZILLEBEKE Sector occupied by R Coy M.G.C. — carrying their guns. | hw.8 |
| | | 7 PM | Remainder of Coy. entrained to YPRES Guns sent by Road to LILLE GATE. | |
| THE BUND ZILLEBEKE SECTOR I.15.d.1.2 | 26/9/17 | 12.50 AM | Relief complete. The following positions being occupied | hw.8 |

No. of position | Name | MAP REF.
1 | HEDGE ST. | I.30.b.12.62
2 | SPY HOLE | I.24.C.93.21
3 | REDAN | I.24.C.95.35
4 | DUMP HOLE | I.24.C.70.30
5 | HALIFAX HOLE | I.24.C.60.20

# WAR DIARY or INTELLIGENCE SUMMARY

(Erase heading not required.)

Army Form.

Instructions regarding War Diaries and Intelligence Summaries are contained in F. S. Regs., Part II. and the Staff Manual respectively. Title Pages will be prepared in manuscript.

| Place | Date | Hour | Summary of Events and Information | Remarks and references to Appendices |
|---|---|---|---|---|
| THE BUND ZILLEBEKE SECTOR | 26/2/17 | | Bombardment (contd) | |
| | | | 6. OBSERVATORY HOLE — I.24.c.52.25 | |
| | | | 7. RUDKIN HOUSE N — I.24.c.15.25 | |
| | | | 8. " S — I.24.c.10.18 | |
| | | | 9. STAFFORD STREET — I.24.c.35.75 | |
| | | | " VALLEY COTTAGE — I.23.c.82.64 | |
| | | | 11. ZILLEBEKE SCHOOL — I.22.a.95.64 | |
| | | | 12A. METROPOLITAN LEFT — I.29.a.70.20 | |
| | | | — 4 Sussex Reserve at Coy/HQ THE BUND I.15.d.1.2. hut | |
| | | | Casualties NIL — firing NIL | |
| | | | Firing carried out — | |
| | | | From — Time | |
| | | | I.22.d.20.98  8–10 PM | |
| | | | 12–2 AM | |
| | | | 3.30–5.30 AM | |
| | | | | Targets | Rds |
| | | | | I.36.b.5.8 | 750 |
| | | | | I.36.b.0.4 | 750 |
| | | | | I.36.b.67 | 500 |
| | | | | I.36.a.2.30 | |
| | | | I.22.d.10.99  8–10 PM | I.36.b.0.4 | 750 |
| | | | 12–2 AM | I.36.a.6.1 | 750 |
| | | | 3.30–5.30 AM | | 750 |

# WAR DIARY or INTELLIGENCE SUMMARY

Army Form C. 2118.

| Place | Date | Hour | Summary of Events and Information | Remarks and references to Appendices |
|---|---|---|---|---|
| | 27/2/17 | | Casualties Nil | |
| | 28/2/17 | | The following indirect fire was carried out night 28/2/17 – 1/3/17 | |

Position — Target — Time — Rds

I.22.d.10.98 — I.36.b.5.8 to I.36.b.0.4 — 8.30–9.45 PM — 750
 — — 9.45 PM–10.5 PM — 750
 — — 11.30 PM–12 Mn — 500

I.22.d.10.99 — I.36.b.1.5 — " — 750
 — I.36.a.90.25 — " — 750
 — — " — 500

9.46 PM  S.O.S. went up & 5 mins of self fire along main barrage lines. Res. fired.

No. of gun — Map Reference — Target
1 — I.20.b.12.62 — MOUNT SORREL ⎱ 5750
2 — I.14.c.93.21 — THE GAP ⎰
5 — I.14.c.60.20 — I.35.a.50.60  ⎱
 — — I.29.d.20.50 Aeroplane ⎰ 1750
6 — — I.35.a.70.40
7 — I.14.c.62.25 — I.29.d.50.40 ⎱ 3x50
 — I.14.c.15.25 — THE GAP I.30.c.30.90 to I.29.d.40.50 ⎰ 2250 yds

# WAR DIARY or INTELLIGENCE SUMMARY

Army Form C. 2118.

| Place | Date | Hour | Summary of Events and Information | Remarks and references to Appendices |
|---|---|---|---|---|
| OBSERVATION RIDGE SECTOR ZILLEBEKE | 8. | | THE GAP I.34.c.10.18 I.30.c.30.90 to I.29.d.40.80 | 2750 Rds |
| | | | 12A. I.22.d.95.64 Hill 60 & IMMOVABLE ROW | 1750 Rds |
| | | | METROPOLITAN LEFT I.29.a.70.20. MT SORREL | 500 yds. |
| | | 11 AM | Bombardment ceased. Casualties O.R.s - 1 killed 1 wounded. | MR. |

TP Stephens Capt

Confidential

War Diary Vol 13
of
116th Co. M.G Corps
to
March 1917

Army Form C. 2118.

# WAR DIARY
## or
## INTELLIGENCE SUMMARY.
*(Erase heading not required.)*

Instructions regarding War Diaries and Intelligence Summaries are contained in F. S. Regs., Part II. and the Staff Manual respectively. Title pages will be prepared in manuscript.

| Place | Date | Hour | Summary of Events and Information | Remarks and references to Appendices |
|---|---|---|---|---|
| OBSERVATORY RIDGE Section | 1/3/17 | | – Very quiet day – Casualties NIL | hw8 |
| | 2/3/17 | | – Quiet day, alteration to emplacement at SPY HOLE I 24.c.93.21 completed – | hw8 |
| ZILLEBEKE | 3/3/17 | 12 MN | – Company relieved by 118 Coy. M.G.C. Sections marched back independently TO ERIE CAMP. Relief complete midnight. | hw8 hw8 |
| | 4/3/17 | 5 AM | All Coy in billets at ERIE Camp. Good relief. Casualties NIL | hw8 |
| ERIE CAMP | 4/3/17 | | – Cleaning up | hw8 |
| | 5/3/17 | | – Company Training | hw8 |
| | 6/3/17 | | – Cleaning kindred. Bathing at POPERINGHE. Coy to take to Cinema | hw8 |
| | 7/3/17 | | – Company Training. Capt. FITZGERALD left for Corps M.G. course at STEENWOORDE. Lt L.W. EVANS assumes command. | hw8 |
| | 8/3/17 | 9 AM | Prepn. of guns IC for the line. Lieut. BROWN leftmun advance | |
| | | 1 PM | party to take over from 118 Coy M.G.C. | |
| | | 4.30 PM | Remainder of Coy. left ERIE CAMP under 2/Lt EDDINGS. | |
| | | 7 PM | Limbers & Teams meet at LILLE GATE. | |
| | | | Guns IC for line take to ZILLEBEKE & unlimbered there | |

# WAR DIARY
## or
## INTELLIGENCE SUMMARY.
(Erase heading not required.)

Army Form C. 2118.

| Place | Date | Hour | Summary of Events and Information | Remarks and references to Appendices |
|---|---|---|---|---|
| | | | Posts taken up as follows | |
| | | | No.2 Section ⎰ R.B.1 I 30.b.1262  No 3 Section ⎰ 5 I 24.c.60.20 | |
| | | | " 2 I 24.c.93.21  6 I 24.c.52.75 | |
| | | | " 3 I 24.c.95.35  7 I 24.c.15.15 | |
| | | | " 4 I 24.c.70.30  8 I 24.c.10.18 | |
| | | | No. 4 Section ⎰ 9 I 24.c.35.75  No. 1 Sect ⎰ 12A I 22.d 95.64 | |
| | | | 11 I 23.c.82.64 | |
| | | | Metropolitan left I 29.a.70.20 | |
| | | | Remainder with Coy HQ at THE BUND. | |
| 8/3/17 | 9.25 pm | | Relief complete. Casualties NIL | MJE |
| 9/3/17 | | | Quiet – Casualties NIL – Inft. relieve 118 Bde. | hwR |
| 10/3/17 | | | Enemy quiet. Orders received from Bde. that no night trips to be done on account of working parties retakaka anticipated | MJE |
| 11/3/17 | | | Snow – Casualties NIL | hwR |
| 12/3/17 | 4.30pm | Kenacka Relief. No 1 sect to have No 2 sect return to HQ | MJE |
| | 8.20pm | | Relief Complete. Casualties NIL | hwR |

**WAR DIARY**
or
**INTELLIGENCE SUMMARY.**

Army Form C. 2118.

| Place | Date | Hour | Summary of Events and Information | Remarks and references to Appendices |
|---|---|---|---|---|
| | 13/3/17 | | Dull dragging day - Very little activity - Casualties NIL | WS |
| | 14/3/17 | | One enemy aeroplane on duckboards near MAPLE COPSE also 5.9's between BUND RAMPARTS | WS |
| | | | Casualties NIL - Capt FITZGERALD returned from course. | WS |
| | | | NW at Coy HQ to Bonds W/PRES. | WS |
| | 15/3/17 | | LIEUT BROWN 1 OR to A A Battery for instruction | |
| | 16/3/17 | | Bright day visibility good - aerial activity in after | |
| | 17/3/17 | | I & reaction nebel cannonant. | WS |
| | 18/3/17 | | Bright morning - enemy sent LHV + HE near Coy HP | |
| | | | Own artillery active - all day. | |
| | | | 1 OR to I Corps School of Sanitation | |
| | | | 2/Lt EDDINGS Transferred to 123 Coy M.F.C. | |
| | | | 2/Lt SIBLEY " " | WS |
| | 19/3/17 | | One slight casualty METROPOLITAN LEFT | |
| | | | Artillery moderately active during the day | |
| | | | Very windy + wet. | |

# WAR DIARY
## or
## INTELLIGENCE SUMMARY.

Army Form C. 2118.

| Place | Date | Hour | Summary of Events and Information | Remarks and references to Appendices |
|---|---|---|---|---|
| | 20/3/17 | | Quiet day. | |
| | | P.M. | Relieved by 108th A.A. Coy. Returns march back to Erie Camp independently. Relief complete by midnight. | MSR |
| ERIE CAMP. | 21/3/17 | 4.30am | All company on fatigue by 4.30 am. Good and Quiet Relief. Casualties nil. | MSR |
| | 22/3/17 | | Company baths at POPERINGHE in 3 parties. Gun Practice on range. Strong Westerly day. | MSR |
| | 23/3/17 | | Gun training on guns. Lt TRAYLEN commence GAS course. | MSR |
| | | | DIVISIONAL GAS OFFICER. Wet Windy day. | MSR |
| | 24/3/17 | | Church Parade. | |
| | | | Nos 1 & 2 Company inoculated. Lt BROWN returns from ANTI-AIRCRAFT COURSE at REININGHELST. Weather fine. | MSR |
| | 25/3/17 | | Company having Special Instruction for RANGE FINDERS. | MSR |
| | 26/3/17 | 11am | Company training. Range Practice. Preparation for entering the line. | MSR |

# WAR DIARY or INTELLIGENCE SUMMARY

Army Form C. 2118.

| Place | Date | Hour | Summary of Events and Information | Remarks and references to Appendices |
|---|---|---|---|---|
| | 2/5/17 | | Preparation for entering into the line. 118th L.G.Cy. took over trenches at BRANDHOEK for YPRES, and sections marched under section officers to ZILLEBEKE. Routine taken up as follows:— | |
| | | | (a) holbrookites { RB1. I.30.b.0. 6.  c & 3 sec. RB2 α I.22.d.9.5 on Metropolitan I.29.a.70.20 <br> RB2. I.24.a 93. 21. <br> RB3. I.24.c 90. 35.   Young Lottie I.23.c 82. 64 <br> RB4. I.24.d 70. 30.   RB.9 I.24.c 3. 75. | |
| | | | & L.2. Sect. { RB5. I.24.c 60 30.   1 howitzer <br> RB6. I.24.c 52. 25.   In Reserve at <br> RB7. I.24.c 15. 25.   ZILLEBEKE BUND <br> RB8. I.24.c 10. 15. | MR |
| | 6/5/17 | 12:30 a.m. | Relief complete. Owing to heavy shelling of railway from LILLE GATE to BUND the tackles were held up for some time. Later they had to be returned over courses to BUND. | MR |

# WAR DIARY
## or
## INTELLIGENCE SUMMARY.
(Erase heading not required.)

Army Form C. 2118.

| Place | Date | Hour | Summary of Events and Information | Remarks and references to Appendices |
|---|---|---|---|---|
| | 25/3/17 | 4pm to 4.30pm | Enemy artillery very active. BUND heavily shelled. Also RAILWAY to LILLE GATE. Smashing it in two or three places. About 40 or 50 Shells (5.9s and 7(pm)) dropped within 12 or 15 yds of HEAD QUARTERS. | |
| | | 6.40pm 6.30pm | (Shelling positions slower and continuing seven repeaters by 5.30 pm | MR |
| | 24/3/17 | | Enemy heavy artillery nearly all day. Enemy artillery active shelling in RUDKIN HOUSE burst in 5 places including M.G. positions to 4 and H.8 between 3 pm and 4 pm. | MR |
| | 28/3/17 | 1pm | Artillery activity. Enemy shelled ramparts at 1 pm about 100 shells. Ref. Warne and Ormond. Observed shoot. | MR |
| | 3/3/17 | 3 AM 5 PM | VALLEY COTTAGES shelled. Emn withdrawn to position 12 (ZILLEBEKE) until park repaired. Visibility improved during the day. Gun at METROPOLITAN LEFT fired 500 rds at enemy planes. | MR |

Confidential

Vol 14

War Diary
of
110th Machine Gun Co
for
April 1919

Army Form C. 2118.

# WAR DIARY
## or
## INTELLIGENCE SUMMARY.
(Erase heading not required.)

Instructions regarding War Diaries and Intelligence Summaries are contained in F. S. Regs., Part II. and the Staff Manual respectively. Title pages will be prepared in manuscript.

| Place | Date | Hour | Summary of Events and Information | Remarks and references to Appendices |
|---|---|---|---|---|
| OBSERVATORY RIDGE SEGOR ZILLEBEKE HQ BUND | 1/4/17 | 3 AM To 5 PM | Bombardment of Enemy lines by our artillery. Retaliation general over sector | Ref Map ZILLEBEKE |
| | | 8 PM | Intersection relief. Clearing of debris at 7 & 8 proceeding. Snow — Gun at No 7 mounted in Trench to avoid making tracks in snow to position. | MWR |
| | 2/4/17 | 4 PM – 6 PM | Bombardment of Enemy line at HILL 60 BUND shelled. | |
| | | 11 PM – 3 AM | Night firing carried out with 2 guns Targets — STIRLING CASTLE, KLEIN ZILLEBEKE — TOTAL 300 Rds Dry windy night — | MWR |
| | 3/4/17 | 1 AM | BLIZZARD — deep snow — Thaw set in — bright day — good visibility | |
| | | 5 PM | BUND shelled. | |
| | 4/4/17 | | Aerial activity increased in afternoon — also artillery active. Casualties NIL | MWR |

Army Form C. 2118.

# WAR DIARY
## or
## INTELLIGENCE SUMMARY.
(Erase heading not required.)

Instructions regarding War Diaries and Intelligence Summaries are contained in F. S. Regs., Part II. and the Staff Manual respectively. Title pages will be prepared in manuscript.

| Place | Date | Hour | Summary of Events and Information | Remarks and references to Appendices |
|---|---|---|---|---|
| | 3/4/17 | | Three forward relieved by 117 Coy MGC    RB3   I.24.c.95.35 | |
| | | |                                              RB4   I.24.c.63.33 | |
| | | |                                              RB9   I.24.c.33.70. | |
| | 6/4/17 | | Relieved Teams returned to the Bund. | |
| | | | Remaining positions relieved by 194 Coy MGC. | |
| | | | RB1 (I.30.b.20.62)   RB2 (I.24.c.98.22)   RB5 (I.24.c.60.28)   RB6 (I.24.c.57.24) | |
| | | | RB7 (I.24.c.13.26)   RB8 (I.24.c.11.24)   RB11 (I.23.c.72.60) | |
| | | | RB12 (I.23.c.11.58)   RB12a (I.22.d.87.64)   RB13 (I.22.d.23.93) | |
| | | | RB14 (I.21.b.15.19)   RB15 (I.15.d.29.30)   RB16 (I.15.c.32.63) | |
| | | | Metropolitan left I.29.a.70.20 | |
| | | | Coy HQ I.15.d.10.25 | |
| | 7th | 5AM | All Coy in Erie Camp | |
| | 8th | | Church Parades. | |
| | 9th | | Cleaning up, r.c. reconnaissance of Hooge Sector. | |
| | 10th | | Relieved 117 Coy M.G.C. in Hooge Sector. Positions taken over as follows :— | |

# WAR DIARY
## or
## INTELLIGENCE SUMMARY.

*(Erase heading not required.)*

Army Form C. 2118.

| Place | Date | Hour | Summary of Events and Information | Remarks and references to Appendices |
|---|---|---|---|---|
| | 11 | 2.30 pm | LB.1 (I.24.a.72.83) LB.2 (I.17.d.52.26) LB.3 (I.17.c.95.95) | |
| | | | LB.4 (I.17.b.65.18) LB.5 (I.17.d.30.05) LB.7 (I.23.a.52.54) | |
| | | | LB.10 (I.16.b.32.28) LB.10a (I.16.d.65.95) LB.11 (I.22.b.95.37) | |
| | | | RB.3 (I.24.c.95.35) RB.4 (I.24.c.63.33) RB.9 (I.24.c.33.70) | |
| | | | LB.12  I.22.a.05.75 ⎫ | |
| | | | LB.13  I.16.c.80.70 ⎬ Posns. to be taken up according to | |
| | | | LB.14  I.16.c.25.78 ⎪ circumstances should any break | |
| | | | LB.15  I.15.d.40.88 ⎬ through — by 4 guns on the BUND. | |
| | | | RB.13  I.22.d.23.93 ⎪ | |
| | | | R.B.14  I.21.b.15.19 ⎪ | |
| | | | RB.15  I.15.d.29.30 ⎪ | |
| | | | RB.16  I.15.c.32.63 ⎭ | |
| | | | Coy. H.Q. YPRES – SHOP HALFWAY HOUSE, ZILLEBEKE, BUND  MAP. ZILLEBEKE | |
| | | | PETROGRAD LANE | MW |
| | | | Relief Complete | |
| | | | Casualties Nil. | |

**Army Form C. 2118.**

# WAR DIARY
*or*
## INTELLIGENCE SUMMARY.
*(Erase heading not required.)*

Instructions regarding War Diaries and Intelligence Summaries are contained in F. S. Regs., Part II. and the Staff Manual respectively. Title pages will be prepared in manuscript.

| Place | Date | Hour | Summary of Events and Information | Remarks and references to Appendices |
|---|---|---|---|---|
| | 12th | | Enemy registering on C.T.S rc. | |
| | 13th | | Ramparts shelled - frequently Casualties Nil | |
| | 14th | | | |
| | 14th | 10 PM | Relieved by 68 M.G. Coy with exception of portion LB 12-15 RB 13-16 which were held by us until 15th | |
| | 15th | 5 AM | Relieved teams arrived at ERIE CAMP. Cleaning up etc. | |
| | 16th | 3.30 PM | Relief of MM Guns of No 164 MG Coy in our RT Bn front & Guns of 114 MG Coy in our left Bn front Brigade front under new distribution as follows:- | Reference Map St. JULIEN |
| | | | Map St JULIEN English Fm - LA BRIQUE | |
| | | | (a) Southern Boundary - front Trench C22.1 (inclus) - road junction C22 d 7.4 - junction of 2 H 15 SALIENT defences with the CANAL (exclusive) | |
| | | | (b) Northern Boundary - front line Trench C21.4 (inclusive) - Road C 20 a 8.6.) from PoND B COTTAGES | |

Army Form C. 2118.

# WAR DIARY
## or
## INTELLIGENCE SUMMARY
*(Erase heading not required.)*

Instructions regarding War Diaries and Intelligence Summaries are contained in F. S. Regs., Part II. and the Staff Manual respectively. Title Pages will be prepared in manuscript.

| Place | Date | Hour | Summary of Events and Information | Remarks and references to Appendices |
|---|---|---|---|---|
| CANAL BANK | | | Positions taken over from 114 Coy M.G.C. | |
| | | | C27.1 Snoh Farm C27.a.83.80 | |
| | | | C21.4 Hill Top N C21.d.10.90 | |
| | | | C21.5 " S C21.d.12.72 | |
| | | | C21.1 Clifford Towers C21.a.30.94 | |
| | | | C20.2 La Belle Alliance C20.d.05.97 | |
| | | | C20.5 Burnt Fm. C20.c.22.55 | |
| | | | C20.6 Zouave Villa C20.c.92.15 | |
| | | | C20.7 Lone Willow C20.L.9.2 | |
| | | | Taken over from 164 Coy M.G.C. | |
| | | | C26.1 Wilson's Fm. N C26.L.43.15 | |
| | | | C26.2 " E C26.d.70.85 | |
| | | | C26.3 La Brique C26.d.66.35 | |
| | | | C27.2 Threadneedle St. C27.L.14.92 | |
| | | | C27.3 English Farm C27.L.55.32 | |
| | | | C22.1 Bilge Tr. C22.c.15.15 | |
| | | | Taken over from 196 Coy. | |
| | | | Reigersburg Chateau H6.L.20.40 | |
| | | | Salvation Corner I.1.C.90.50. | |

**Army Form C. 2118.**

# WAR DIARY
## or
## INTELLIGENCE SUMMARY
*(Erase heading not required.)*

Instructions regarding War Diaries and Intelligence Summaries are contained in F. S. Regs., Part II. and the Staff Manual respectively. Title Pages will be prepared in manuscript.

| Place | Date | Hour | Summary of Events and Information | Remarks and references to Appendices |
|---|---|---|---|---|
| | | | One Section (45mm) attached to this Coy. from 118 Coy MGC. | |
| | | | Coy/H.Q. CANAL B.K. C15.a.8.2 | |
| | | | S.H.Q. Coney St. C20.d.3.4 | |
| | | | " Wilsons Fm. C26.a.7.8 | |
| | | | " THREADNEEDLE ST. C27.b.2.9 | |
| | 17th | 9.30 PM | " Hill top.  Relief complete | |
| | 17/18th | | Quiet day – v. little activity – wet. Casualties Nil | hus? |
| | 18th PM | 10-12 am | Infantry relieve 114 Bde. | hus? |
| | | 11-11.30am | Firing from VIEW FM on C14.b.30.17 – Gemmaine – 500 rds | |
| | | | " " " C20.c.62.73 on C14.b.5.9 – C9.c.25.15 – 500 rds | |
| | | | " " C20.c.58.85 Gemmaine C15.a.4.5 – C15.a.8.6 500 | hus? |
| | 19th | 3 am 4.30am | " " C20.e.62.93 on same target 100. 500 | |
| | 18th | | Transport lines moved from ERIE CAMP TO A.28.c.5.4 on Transfer to VIII Corps (16/4/17) | hus? |

2449  Wt. W14957/M90  750,000  1/16  J.B.C. & A.  Forms/C.2118/12.

# WAR DIARY or INTELLIGENCE SUMMARY

Army Form C. 2118.

| Place | Date | Hour | Summary of Events and Information | Remarks and references to Appendices |
|---|---|---|---|---|
| | 19th April | | Spasmodic Shelling<br>firing done night 19/20th<br>Gun position — Time — Target — Rds. fired<br>C.20.c.62.73    10-12 A.m    { C.15.a.4.5    500<br>                3-4.30 Am    { C.15.a.8      500<br>                              { C.15.a.7.7<br>C.20.c.59.85    10-12 MN    { C.14.a.25.45    500<br>                  3-4.30 AM    { C.14.a.45.45    500<br>                                 { C.14.a.45.75<br>VIEW FM    3-4.30    C.14.b.30.20    500<br>                              Trev. Rearnding | |
| | 20th | | Canadies N.I.<br>Enemy artillery active — Battery near JOFFRE FARM shelled with<br>about 350 heavy shells.<br>Also registration by heavy near TURCO FM.<br>Firing night 20/21 at<br>Point                     Target      Rds<br>C.20.c.62.73    10PM-12MN    C.15.a.4.5.    500<br>                  3.30AM-4.30AM    "    500<br>C.20.c.59.85                         C.14.b.w30<br>                                             C.14.b.4055    1000 | nil |

# WAR DIARY or INTELLIGENCE SUMMARY

Army Form C. 2118.

| Place | Date | Hour | Summary of Events and Information | Remarks and references to Appendices |
|---|---|---|---|---|
| | 21. | | MHV near THREADNEEDLE ST<br>Casualties NIL<br>O.M.G.O visited Battens<br>Visibility - good - quiet day.<br>During 21/22<br>Position | Time | Target<br>C.20.C.62.73 | 10-12 mn | C.15.a.4.5    Rds 500<br>               3-4 AM          "        500<br>C.20.C.59.85    10-12 mn   C.14.b.3.2   750<br>                      3-4 AM        "          250<br>C.15.C.94.55    2AM-4AM   C.15.a.60.40   750<br>                                     (CALENDAR RESERVE)<br>                                     working parties | NIL |
| | 22. | | Casualties NIL<br>Visibility high - Great aerial activity - Enemy artillery active.<br>During night 22/23<br>Position        Time        Target<br>C.20.C.65.75    10-12 mn   C.14.b.3.5.   Rds 500<br>                       3-4.30AM        "          500 | |

# WAR DIARY or INTELLIGENCE SUMMARY

Army Form C. 2118.

| Place | Date | Hour | Summary of Events and Information | Remarks and references to Appendices |
|---|---|---|---|---|
| | 22d | | Posn      Time      Target      Rds | |
| | | | C20.c.75.55   10–12mn   {C14.a.4.5}   500 | |
| | | |                  3–4.30AM                500 | |
| | | | VIEW FM.   3AM–4AM   VonKluck   500 |  |
| | | |                                  COTS. | |
| | | | Additional gun at FOCH FM. moved to VIEW FARM at denight firing & fire on S.O.S. in place of HILLTOP gun. HILLTOP guns not to fire on local S.O.S. but to be left solely for defence of HILLTOP STRONG POINT. | |
| | 23rd | | Capt Fitzgerald on leave to UK. (Special leave) Visibility high – Sunny – artillery active on both sides – great aerial activity on both sides. Lt. H.W. EVANS left for GAS COURSE 2nd Army H.Q. H.C.W. GIBBON assumed command & Lt. J.R. a Platte 2nd in command of Coy. During day 635 Rounds fired from A.A. position at enemy aircraft | |
| | | | During night 22/23 Position    Time    Target    Rds | |
| | | | 1. VIEWFARM  {10pm–midnight}  VonKluck  1250 | |
| | | | 2. C20.c.65.75   {3a.m.–4.15a.m.}  COTS. | |
| | | | 3. C20.c.75.55   do.          C14.c.20.15"  1000 | |
| | | |                    do.          C14.a.4.5.    1000 | |
| | | | 4. C26.b.37.15   3a.m.–4.15a.m.  {C15.c.9.8½,16  400 | |
| | | |                                  {C15.c.½,1 | |

| Place | Date | Hour | Summary of Events and Information | Remarks and references to Appendices |
|---|---|---|---|---|
| | 24th | | Observation Good. Enemy — Considerable aerial activity both sides — Two enemy planes brought down in their own lines by A.A. fire — One of ours was brought down by hostile A.A. fire, the machine was under control and came down in our own lines near POTSDAM FARM. — Certain amount of hostile artillery active, also T.Ms. in usual areas — During afternoon our 18 Pdrs. and T.Ms (Light & Medium) were engaged in successfully cutting wire on this front. — 4690. Rounds fired during day from our A.A. position in the line, successful in turning away enemy planes back to his own lines. About 9.50 p.m. a barrage commenced opposite WILTJE which gradually spread N. across our Divisional front. 10 p.m. enemy placed a barrage over the whole of our front. S.O.S. was put up. Our artillery's reply was quick and effective necessitating the enemy further up the S.O.S. Both here and the enemy were many red flares so enemy further up. There was consequently some misinterpretation. Enemy stopped firing 10.30 p.m. Our artillery ceased 10.45 p.m. — General stand-to between 10 p.m. + 10.30 p.m. On the S.O.S. going the Vickers in S.O.S. positions opened fire on their sight lines, held situation became about — Casualties (Bombers 1 O.R. From a S.O.S. fire — 5Pdr Rounds fired 7050 | |

# WAR DIARY or INTELLIGENCE SUMMARY

Army Form C. 2118.

| Place | Date | Hour | Summary of Events and Information | Remarks and references to Appendices |
|---|---|---|---|---|
| | 24/25th | | Routine. Right firing in addition to firing on S.O.S. call. | |
| | | | Position       Time       Target       Rds | |
| | | | 1. C.20.c.65.7½    3–4.30 a.m.   C.14 & 2.1½.16   500 | |
| | | |                                     C.14 & 6.5.7½ | |
| | | | 1. C.20.c.7.5.5½   10 p.m.–11 p.m. } C.15.a.4.5.   275 | |
| | | | 3. C.26 & 36.12   3–4.30 a.m.                  750 | |
| | | |                                 3 a.m.–4.15 a.m. { C.15.c.9.8½   500 | |
| | | |                                              { C.15.a.7½.1 | |
| | 25th | | Quiet day — very little activity in air — Dull day. | |
| | 24/25 | | Firing    Position      Time      Target      Rds | |
| | | | 1. C.26 & 36.12   1 a.m.–4.15 a.m. { C.15.c.9.8½   750 | |
| | | |                                                      { C.15.a.7½.1 | |
| | | | 2. C.20.c.6½.7½   1 a.m.–4.30 a.m. {                  1000 | |
| | | |                                                        { C.14 & 2.12 | |
| | | | 3. C.20.c.7½.5½   do                 C.15.a.4.5.   1000 | |
| | | | 4. C.21 & 93.65   do                Von Kluck Cotts   1250 | |
| | | |                             Total Rds fired at enemy aircraft during day   750 rds | |

# WAR DIARY
or
## INTELLIGENCE SUMMARY

Army Form C. 2118.

| Place | Date | Hour | Summary of Events and Information | Remarks and references to Appendices |
|---|---|---|---|---|
| | 26 | | Dull became fine later in day — Artillery on the whole quiet — Some were cutting done by our artillery — Wire parties sighted — enemy snipers put out flares from an opening tried to be handed over on relief — | |
| | 26/27 | | During the night Position of guns | |
| | | | | Front | Target | Rounds fired |
| | | | 1. VIEW FARM C31c03.85 | 10-11.45 p.m. 3-3.45 a.m. | C14 $\frac{6}{5}$ 20.10. C14 $\frac{6}{5}$ 80.20 | 1250 |
| | | | 2. C30c 6½.7½ | 10-11.45 a.m. 3-4 a.m. | C14 $\frac{6}{5}$ 2.1½ to C14 $\frac{6}{5}$ 6½.2½ | 1000 |
| | | | 3. C30 2½.5½ | do | C15 a 4.5 | 1000 |
| | | | 4. C26b. 38.12 | do | C15c 9 8½ to C15c 7½.1 | 750 |
| | 27 | | Comparatively quiet day — Some wire cutting — Considerable aerial activity in the afternoon. Relief commenced at 9.30 p.m. by 118 Coy. M.G.C., delayed somewhat by the late arrival of a section of 117 Coy. who relieved the section of 118 Coy. attached to this Coy., who in turn relieved one of this Coys. sections | |

# WAR DIARY
## or
## INTELLIGENCE SUMMARY.

Army Form C. 2118.

| Place | Date | Hour | Summary of Events and Information | Remarks and references to Appendices |
|---|---|---|---|---|
| | 28 | 1.0a<br>3.30am | Relief Complete. Sections marched independently to "S" Camp. Casualties NIL<br>Everybody in Camp ———— Cleaning up | |
| | 29 | | Church Parade ———— "S" Camp | |
| | 30 | | Transport of the Coy. left at 6.15 a.m. and joined Bde. Transport Column. Trekking in the direction of AROVES their destination on the following day. Remainder of Coy. stayed at "S" Camp — General cleaning up — Bathed in the afternoon. 117 Coy., M.G.C. arrived in the early afternoon to take over the Camp, but as the Coy. were not moving out till the following morning, they had to bivouac in adjoining fields. | Reference Maps<br>1+2E@ROUCKSA |

To H.Q.,
116th Infantry Bde.

Herewith War Diary for month of May, 1917, please.

1/6/17.
J.C. Hodson. Lieut
for O.C. No. 116 COY.
MACHINE GUN CORPS.

**Army Form C. 2118.**

# WAR DIARY
## or
## INTELLIGENCE SUMMARY
*(Erase heading not required.)*

Vol 15

CONFIDENTIAL

From 1st – 31st May 1917.

116 Coy., Machine Gun Corps.

# WAR DIARY
## or
## INTELLIGENCE SUMMARY

*(Erase heading not required.)*

Army Form C. 2118.

| Place | Date | Hour | Summary of Events and Information | Remarks and references to Appendices |
|---|---|---|---|---|
| 'S' CAMP | 1st | 1am-7:50am | Bn. marched out of 'S' Camp at 7:50 a.m., arrived at POPERINGHE ½am. Left at 9.27 a.m. arrived at ST. OMER 12.25 p.m. — 12.45 p.m. Bn. marched from St. Omer to WIZERNES and there went into billets. — Transport which had arrived at ARQUES that morning, proceeded to billets at WIZERNES and arrived there | Reference Map HAZEBROUCK 5A |
| WIZERNES | 2nd | | Réveille 4.0 a.m. — Bn. marched out of WIZERNES with its Transport at 6.0 a.m. marching via SETQUES — LUMBRES — ACQUIN to the VAL D'ACQUIN, where they went into billets, arrived at 10.0 a.m. — Weather fine & sunny. — Remainder of day was spent in cleaning up Limbers, Arms etc. | |
| LE VAL D'ACQUIN | 3rd | | Bn. marched off independently with their fighting limbers to the training area (vicinity of ZUDAUSQUES) and ACQUIN - BOISDINGHEM — Training carried out in the use of ground — cover — getting into action with the greatest possible concealment — application by examples of various forms of M.G. fire etc. Weather fine & sunny. | |
| do | 4th | | 16 guns of the Bn. fired in the Range. Some exceedingly good shooting. In the afternoon returned to training area. Weather exceedingly fine & sunny. | |
| do | 5th | | Training in open warfare — Capt. M.G.O. present. — Operations had to cease at 11 a.m. and Bn. proceeded to ACQUIN, where they were inspected by the Surgeon General, 2nd Army & Corps. Afternoon spent in cleaning up. Weather fine & sunny. Returned about 1 a.m. | |
| do | 6th | | Weather fine & sunny — Church Parade in the evening. | |
| do | 7th | | Field day. Open warfare attack various sections of Battalion to Ypres. Walks very L.P. / C.H. all sections | |

Army Form C. 2118.

# WAR DIARY
## or
## INTELLIGENCE SUMMARY
*(Erase heading not required.)*

Instructions regarding War Diaries and Intelligence Summaries are contained in F. S. Regs., Part II. and the Staff Manual respectively. Title Pages will be prepared in manuscript.

| Place | Date | Hour | Summary of Events and Information | Remarks and references to Appendices |
|---|---|---|---|---|
| VAL D'ACQUIN | 8.5.17 | | Very hot weather. Brigade field day. Attack practised by machine-guns in conjunction with Infantry battalion. Captain FITZGERALD returned from leave, assumes command of the Company. I.C.M | REF. MAP HAZEBROUCK 5.a. |
| " | 9.5.17 | | Fine weather. Company training in conjunction with infantry. Open warfare practised. Attack across the open. J.C.M | |
| " | 10.5.17 | | Company training continued. Tactical schemes carried out during the morning. Afternoon - fire control. I.C.M. | |
| " | 11.5.17 | | Brigade field day. Attack in conjunction with Infantry battalion. Open warfare conditions. C.M.G.O. present. 2 of Army Commander also present. Weather very hot. I.C.M. | |
| " | 12.5.17 | | Range practise carried out. Field firing at targets on the hill side. Shooting very good. I.C.M | |
| " | 13.5.17 | | Weather still very fine. Church parade conducted at ACQUIN and VAL D'ACQUIN. Training carried out as usual during the morning. Afternoon devoted to packing. I.C.M | |
| " | 14.5.17 | | Limbers and preparing for move. I.C.M | |
| WIZERNES | 15.5.17 | | Company march to WIZERNES arriving 10 a.m. and go into billets. I.C.M | |
| NORDPEENE | 16.5.17 | | Company march to NORDPEENE arriving at 11 a.m. and go into billets. I.C.M. | |
| WORMHOUDT | 17.5.17 | | Company march to WORMHOUDT and go into billets in the town. Arriving 11 a.m. Raining but very hot. I.C.M | |

Army Form C. 2118.

# WAR DIARY
## or
## INTELLIGENCE SUMMARY
*(Erase heading not required.)*

Instructions regarding War Diaries and Intelligence Summaries are contained in F. S. Regs., Part II. and the Staff Manual respectively. Title Pages will be prepared in manuscript.

| Place | Date | Hour | Summary of Events and Information | Remarks and references to Appendices |
|---|---|---|---|---|
| WORMHOUDT. | 18.5.17 | | Company Training during the morning. Range Control - Fire control etc. afternoon by teams in the prone & kneeling positions. Sgt Jackson won the ½ mile. Cpl Topps 4/5 in the mile. I.C.M. | REF. MAP HAZEBROUCK 5.a. |
| " | 19.5.17 | | Company Training. Programme as the morning repeated. Half-holiday in the afternoon. I.C.M. | |
| " | 20.5.17 | | Church Parade. Brigade Service held. Weather very hot. Captain F. FITZGERALD leaves for a course at CAMIERS. LIEUT. C. W. GILL assumes command. LIEUT. J. C. HOBSON, 2 i/c Coumnd. I.C.H. | |
| " | 21.5.17 | | Company training from 9 a.m. – 12.45 p.m. hot weather and heavy rain commenced, but infection during the afternoon. I.C.M. | |
| " | 22.5.17 | | Raining weather. General inspection postponed but Transport inspection during the afternoon. I.C.M. Motoring expensive to rate. Belle-peers | |
| " | 23.5.17 | 9 a.m. | General inspected the Company at 9 a.m. Fairly satisfactory. Boots all very light. General congratulated Company on their turn-out. Rest of morning devoted to training. Footwear noted in the afternoon. Company heard the best Company of the 11th Royal Sussex Regt. (3 – 2). Orders received at 11 o'clock at night to march out at 6 a.m. next morning to "D" camp between POPERINGHE and VLAMMERTINGHE. Going into Divisional Reserve. I.C.M. | |
| | | 11 p.m. | | |

**Army Form C. 2118.**

**WAR DIARY**
or
**INTELLIGENCE SUMMARY**

*(Erase heading not required.)*

Instructions regarding War Diaries and Intelligence Summaries are contained in F. S. Regs., Part II. and the Staff Manual respectively. Title Pages will be prepared in manuscript.

| Place | Date | Hour | Summary of Events and Information | Remarks and references to Appendices |
|---|---|---|---|---|
| "D" Camp REF MAP BELGIUM 28 NW B.30. central. | 24.5.17 | | Company left WORMHOUDT at 6 a.m. QMS stores left behind, from lack of transport. Arrived at "D" Camp 1 p.m. OC reports to Divl. HQ and receives instruction to 118th building replacements for transport lire. Uniform was attended to 118th Bde. | REF MAP HAZEBROUCK 5.a. and BELGIUM SHEET 28 NW |
| " | 25.5.17 | | Morning spent in adjusting Box Respirators antiseisms and practicing "Bonny" drill. Orders received for 2 coys to relieve 2 coys 118th M.G.C. in the line this evening. This orders were subsequently cancelled. 1CM. | |
| " | 26.5.17 | | Lectures by O.s.C. Aircraft, N.C.O's Section in the morning. Preparation made to relieve 2 coys 118th M.G.C. in the line this evening. Plans for looking positions to prepare 16 gun position and relieve him with 2,000 rds S.A.A. per position. In the evening Nos 2 and 4 sections took over the following positions (SALVATION CORNER, REIGERSBERG, LA BRIQUES, (2/Lt Goodall in charge) LIVERPOOL ST, NEW JOHN ST, C.28.2, C.28.6, C.28.8 (Lieut Hopfinkle in charge) Working parties completes the 16 positions with one in reserve & every took its "D" Camp about 8 a.m. | |
| " | 27.5.17 | | Working party sent up to finish position in the evening. Pte Marston, Salvation Corner, and REIGERSBERG team relieve into C.28.7 wounded. CANAL BANK 196th H.G.C. relief relieves over vacation position. 1CM and CANAL BANK. | |
| " | 28.5.17 | | In view of a shoot in conjunction with the artillery a working party goes up with all guns. Lewis force and kit for 8 of the 16 positions and place them ready for the shoot. Four of these remain at RED HEART ESTAMINET, and a Guard is left for the guns. 1CM. | |

# WAR DIARY
## or
## INTELLIGENCE SUMMARY

*(Erase heading not required.)*

Army Form C. 2118.

Instructions regarding War Diaries and Intelligence Summaries are contained in F. S. Regs., Part II. and the Staff Manual respectively. Title Pages will be prepared in manuscript.

| Place | Date | Hour | Summary of Events and Information | Remarks and references to Appendices |
|---|---|---|---|---|
| "D" Camp | 29.5.17 | | Dull day. Teams went up and took up position. Orders came through known that the start is postponed. Gun hit up stores at RED HEART ESTAMINET. Casualties – Nil. 1 C.M. | REF MAP BELGIUM SHEET 28.IV.W |
| B 30 Central | 30.5.17 | | Company received orders to relieve 117th H.R.E. with the line, after the stunt in its afternoon teams go up and take up their 8 position in THREADNEEDLE ST. Stunt commences at 6.0 p.m. – 6.14 p.m. No 2 Section [Mr 2] fells spandau from No 1 Section 28 fells without mishap. C.M & O. watches spandau from Hill Top and is satisfied. BILGE ST. THREADNEEDLE ST. IRISH FARM. No 1 Section – the relieves [2/L Stutt in charge] ENGLISH FARM. [2/L Stutt in charge] WILSON FM. N. WILSON FM. S. [Sgt Kirkwood in charge] No 4 Section relieves WILSON FM. N. WILSON FM. S. [their Place in charge] HILL TOP N. HILL TOP S. [their Place in charge] WIELTJE teams having been relieved by 117th H.R.E. takes over its platoon position. WIELTJE. FM. FOCH FARM. ZOUAVE VILLA BURNT FM. LOVE WILLOWS. CLIFFORD TOWERS. VIEW FARM. LA BELLE ALLIANCE. [Lt Brown & Lt Hippulette at CONEY ST H.Q] All relief completed by 2.30 a.m. It is many of 31.5.17. with the except of LA BELLE ALLIANCE which on relieving drew enemy fire having. Gas Attack by us during from 3 a.m. 31.5.17. did not take place owing to unstable winds. Casualties N.l. Lt H | |

# WAR DIARY
## or
## INTELLIGENCE SUMMARY

*(Erase heading not required.)*

Army Form C. 2118.

| Place | Date | Hour | Summary of Events and Information | Remarks and references to Appendices |
|---|---|---|---|---|
| CANAL BANK [HILL TOP SECTOR] C.25.a.8.2 | 31.5.17 | | A good deal of shelling during the day both by our batteries and by the Germans. Shelling continuous throughout the day. Burnt Fm shelled in the afternoon. Beautiful day. Orders received that gas attack was to take place at some hour during 1.6.17. No ranks were wounded. Casualties during the morning 2/Lt H.H. Scott. While chatting worn out & run a Pickel through his foot and was evacuated to Hospital at POPERINGHE. Company now less 16 Pistols with the one gun. 8 guns of 117th M.G.C. are attached to it. Army 2 G 196th M.G.C. Three of 26 guns. I.C.H. | REF. MAP BELGIUM SHEET 28 N.W. |

Army Form C. 2118.

WAR DIARY
or
INTELLIGENCE SUMMARY
*(Erase heading not required.)*

Vol 16

CONFIDENTIAL

WAR DIARY
of
116 Company M.G. Corps

from June 1st 1917 — June 30th 1917

A.T. Geekan /£
O.C. 116 M.G.C.

Army Form C. 2118.

# WAR DIARY
## or
## INTELLIGENCE SUMMARY.
(Erase heading not required.)

Instructions regarding War Diaries and Intelligence
Summaries are contained in F. S. Regs., Part II.
and the Staff Manual respectively. Title pages
will be prepared in manuscript.

| Place | Date | Hour | Summary of Events and Information | Remarks and references to Appendices |
|---|---|---|---|---|
| CANAL BANK [HILL TOP SECTOR] C 25 a 82 | 1.6.17 | | Great artillery activity - not immediately in our front - but all round the Salient. The German artillery are shelling a great deal in our lines of communication and batteries moved more so than they did either in the preparatory bombardments of LOOS or the Somme. Our machine guns fired 20 following fire 12 p.m. - 2 a.m. | REF. TRENCH MAP ST JULIEN. SHEET 28 NW EDITION 5 a |
| | | | <table><tr><th>Gun Position</th><th>Rounds</th><th>Times</th><th>Targets</th></tr><tr><td>C 27 a 44 56 [IRISH FARM]</td><td>1750</td><td>12 p.m. 2 a.m.</td><td>C 28 a 57 30 PILCKEM ROAD</td></tr><tr><td>C 20 c 65 66</td><td>1500</td><td>"        "</td><td>C 8 c 83 41? (C 26 b 0 25?)</td></tr></table> | |
| | | | Casualties - Nil     J.C.H | |
| d.Do. | 2.6.17 | | Bombardment of enemy lines round the entire Salient continue. The bombardment is the direction of MESSINES reached at times a great intensity. Orders received to carry out a practice barrage similar to that of the 30.5.17  117th & 118th M.G.C. occupy the position we occupied on the 30th with M.G.C. line for barrage 4.30 - 4.40 p.m. | |
| | | 4.30 p.m. | | |

# WAR DIARY or INTELLIGENCE SUMMARY

Army Form C. 2118.

(Erase heading not required.)

| Place | Date | Hour | Summary of Events and Information | Remarks and references to Appendices |
|---|---|---|---|---|
| CANAL BANK | 2.6.17 | | The Guns fired in accordance with attached Table very little retaliation. During the night very heavy firing on the right during the night. The A.C.C. activity has increased enormously. At siv 2 w.2 Snaps. Casualties - N.U. - I.O.M. Very hot and bright. Shelling continues the whole day. Night firing carried out in accordance with subjoined table. | REF TRENCH MAP ST JULIEN. SHEET 28 N W EDITION 5a. |
| [HILLTOP SECTOR] | | | | |
| C.15 a 8.2 | | | | |
| ditto | 3.6.17 | 3 a.m. | Orders received for demonstration of Artillery and machine guns to take place from 3 p.m - 3.30 p.m Our guns fired as reported yesterday. No. of rounds reported in table above under date 3.6.17 | |
|  |  | 6.15 p.m 6.30 p.m |  | |

### TABLE - OF N GUNS FOR BARRAGE 2.6.17 — 3.6.17

| GUN | POSITION | TARGET | No. OF ROUNDS |
|---|---|---|---|
| ZOUAVE WOOD | C.20 c 31.17 | Admindmedmondt & CALEDONIA WOOD & CALEDONIA LANE | 1,500 |
| WILSON FM N | C.26 b 11.12 | FORT CALEDONIA C.15 a 4.5 - C.15 a 6.3 5½ | 1,250 |
| WILSON FM S | C.26 b 11.12 | FORT CALEDONIA C.15 a 4.5 - C.15 a 7½ 8.2 | 1,750 2,000 |
| LA BRIQUE | C.26 d 7.2 9.5 | CALENDAR RESERVE C.15 b 6.6 - C.15 b 3.4 | 1,500 |
| LIVERPOOL ST | C.27 b 2.1 | CALENDAR BURRAS C.15 b 6.1 - C.15 b 8.8 | 1,500 |
| TOTAL | | | 7,250 8,250 |

| GUN POSITION | ROUNDS | TIMES | TARGETS |
|---|---|---|---|
| C.20 c 68.68 | 2,500 | 10 p.m - 2.30 a.m | C.4 c 55.49  C.9 d 38.35 |
| C.27 a 44.56 | 2,500 | 10 p.m - 3 a.m | C.29 a 57.30 |

Army Form C. 2118.

# WAR DIARY
## or
## INTELLIGENCE SUMMARY.
*(Erase heading not required.)*

Instructions regarding War Diaries and Intelligence Summaries are contained in F. S. Regs., Part II. and the Staff Manual respectively. Title pages will be prepared in manuscript.

| Place | Date | Hour | Summary of Events and Information | Remarks and references to Appendices |
|---|---|---|---|---|
| CANAL BANK | 3.6.17 | | Artillery commenced at 3 p.m. Intense from 3.15 p.m – 3.30 p.m. When gunners n at 3.15 p.m | REF MAP (Ypres) ST JULIEN SHEET 28 N.W. [Edition 5a] |
| HILL TOP SECTOR | 3.6.17 (cont.) | | Retaliation slight, lasted from Bn Hq. COLNEY ST. from 10 p.m – 3 a.m [night 3/4] | |
| [HQ C25A B2] | | | Continuous shelling of YPRES with asphyxiating and Gas shells. The wind blew the gas back on to the lines on N side of Salient. It was very strong and in places penetrated the wearers of Box Respirators. Casualties. Nil. J.E.H. | |
| ditto | 4.6.17 | | Very fine and hot. Nothing of particular note occurred during the day. Hostile shelling as usual. Our own bombardment continues. Light trig was carried out in accordance with suspended battle. | |
| | | | Very heavy firing during the night. The Germans seem very nervous. They sent up different coloured flares all night. They put up practice barrages from time to time. Any sound anywhere over each of our bombardments presumably to see whether any assault is taking place in our lines. J.E.H. | |
| ditto | 5.6.17 | | Very hot and fine. LIEUT. A.T. JACKSON, who arrived last night from 37th M. Gun Coy. | |

| GUN POSITION. | ROUNDS | TARGETS | TIMES |
|---|---|---|---|
| C.20.c.69.69 | 2,000 | TRENCH - RAILWAY C9.c.53.49 – C9.c.34.35 | 10 p.m – 2.15 a.m |
| C.27.a.44.56 | 2,500 | C.23.a.57.30 | 10 p.m – 3 a.m |

Army Form C. 2118.

# WAR DIARY
## or
## INTELLIGENCE SUMMARY.
(Erase heading not required.)

Instructions regarding War Diaries and Intelligence Summaries are contained in F.S. Regs., Part II. and the Staff Manual respectively. Title pages will be prepared in manuscript.

| Place | Date | Hour | Summary of Events and Information | Remarks and references to Appendices |
|---|---|---|---|---|
| CANAL BANK. F.5.b.9 (ento) HILL TOP SECTOR HQ. C25.A.8.2 | 5.6.17 | | took over command of the Company. Hostile shelling increasing. BRIELEN and back areas heavily shelled all day. Also POPERINGHE. Our artillery made a demonstration from 2.30 p.m - 3.10 p.m. This took place on several sectors of the Salient. A certain amount of enemy retaliation. Our anti-aircraft guns (Vickers) were in action several times during the day against low flying enemy machines. Some hundreds of rounds fired. The a.a. gun at ZOUAVE VILLA claim to have brought down a German plane. Our Vickers fired during the night in accordance with Subsidiary barrage. | REF. MAP TRENCH ST. JULIEN SHEET 2R.NW. EDITION 5 a |
| | | | | |
| | | | **GUN POSITION** \| **ROUNDS** \| **TARGETS** \| **TIMES** | |
| | | | C.20.c.64.69 \| 1000 \| C8 a 78.99 / C8 a 55.15 \| 1.30 a.m - 2.45 a.m | |
| | | | C.27.a.44.56 \| 2500 \| TRAM LINES C23.b.5.d \| 10 p.m - 3 a.m. | |
| | | | A good many planes are up during the night these last few days. Impossible to say whether hostile or British. Shelling continuous during the barrage night. Casualties - NIL. I.E.H. | |
| d[itt]o - | 6.6.17 | | Artillery activity very considerable the whole day. | |

T.J.134. Wt. W708-776. 500000. 4/15. Sir J. C. & S.

# WAR DIARY
## or
## INTELLIGENCE SUMMARY.

*(Erase heading not required.)*

Army Form C. 2118.

| Place | Date | Hour | Summary of Events and Information | Remarks and references to Appendices |
|---|---|---|---|---|
| CANAL BANK Hill Top Sector H.Q. C.25.a.8.2 St Julian | 7/6/17 | | Artillery active throughout the day. at 3.10 am attack launched on Wyschaete-Messines ridge. Cooperation on the front S of 147. 8 guns of 118 found barrage on the front C.29.a. 58.35. & C.28.c. 75.18 - C.23.c. 32.10 - C.23.c. 16.90 the cooperate guns of 116 F Coy. M.G.C. fired on the sqrs. C.16.a + C.15.b + a. from Zero to Zero + 26. Guns of 116 F Coy. M.G.C. fired as follows | |
| | | | Liverpool Sn. from C.27.a. 80.50 at. C.15.b.8.3 - C.15.b.8.8. 2500. | |
| | | | Mzouaye Villa "  C.20.c. 31.17 at C.15.b.75.30 2500. | |
| | | | New John Villa | |
| | | | Wilson Fm N C.26.b. 3.2 - C.15.a.5½.6½. 2500 | |
| | | | do. S.        do. - C.15.a.4.5 - C.15.a.3½.8½ 2500 | |
| | | | La Brique. C.26.A. 8.9 - C.15.b.6.2.     2500 | |
| | | | | Total S.A.A. 12500 |
| | | | Casualties NIL. One | |
| | | | Very hot & fine. | |
| | | | Lieut. F.G. Gordon slightly wounded remained at duty. | |
| | 8/6/17 | | Artillery quiet during the day. Hostile artillery very active during the night. At 11.9 pm Hostile gas was discharged in vicinity of St Jean - Wieltje Road. Hatchie gun Co-operated on area 22b. 23.c.a+c. | |
| | | | La Brique. C.26. A. 8.9. C.23.c.            1500 | |
| | | | Wilson Fm N+S. C.26.b. 3.2.   do            3000 | |
| | | | | 4500 |

# WAR DIARY
## or
## INTELLIGENCE SUMMARY.

*(Erase heading not required.)*

Army Form C. 2118.

| Place | Date | Hour | Summary of Events and Information | Remarks and references to Appendices |
|---|---|---|---|---|
| Canal Bank Hill Top Sector St Julien | 8/6/17 | (cont) | Threshold Sr. C.27.b.15.80 4500<br>Englist Ft. C.27.b.53.30 } on our C.23.a. 2000<br>Liverpool Tr. C.27.d.45.85 on C.22.b. 1500<br>Total. 8000<br>Casualties.<br>2/Lieut F.G. Goodall slightly wounded remained at duty. One<br>Hostile artillery was active throughout the night on front support Trenches. | |
| | 9/6/17 | | During the morning La Belle Alliance heavily shelled. Gun teams at M.G. position<br>became following Casualties.<br>Casualties<br>No. 73177 Cpl. Christmas. E.G. wounded<br>No. 70148. Pte. Parry. J.E. do<br>No. 63099 " Davies. I.I. do<br>No. 84166 " Magdalino. N. du.<br>The afternoon Canny St. & Boar lane shelled about 4.30 p.m. Our. | |
| | 10/6/17 | | During night hostile artillery active. At dawn they shelled Trenches & C.T's<br>as if trying to prevent troops assembling.<br>Night Firing<br>Irish Farm. C.27.a. 44.56 at Trench railway Von Hugel Dn. C.23.6.4. 1500 rounds. | |

**Army Form C. 2118.**

Instructions regarding War Diaries and Intelligence Summaries are contained in F.S. Regs., Part II. and the Staff Manual respectively. Title Pages will be prepared in manuscript.

# WAR DIARY
## or
## INTELLIGENCE SUMMARY

*(Erase heading not required.)*

| Place | Date | Hour | Summary of Events and Information | Remarks and references to Appendices |
|---|---|---|---|---|
| HILL TOP SECTOR. St Julian 28 N.W.2 | 10/6/17 | 6.40 pm | Hostile artillery action on Irish fm. Coney St. Junction of Boon Lane. Boundary Road Irish Farm to Coney St. & from Irish fm to English fm. 77 mm & 15 cmt. (Shelling being afternoon). Considerable 15 cmt activity around Wieltje fm about 5 pm. Hostile plane circled 2 times over the French system in front of Hill Top this afternoon at about 3000 ft, dropping a silver followed by a red flare over Billingham Tr. about 5 pm. Gun H.Q's fired from A.A. position, but plane was out of range. Evening about 6 pm. Hostile aeroplane very active over our line & chiefly WIELTJE. Hostile artillery action throughout the night. | |
| | 11.6.17 | | 2.45 am hostile artillery active. Enemy busy on front & support line. Also C.T.'s apparently anxious of an attack. Also VON BERLOT, LA BRIQUE. NIGHT FIRING. IRISH farm 2000 rounds. at Von Below fm. HILL TOP gun fired 1000 rounds. Que. A.A. Enemy artillery action from 11 am - 1 am on Hill Top. with 15 cmt & 11 cmt. 8 am - 11 am 6 Battalion round the airdrome. 15 Great action down Coney St. from Coney St. to Hill Top & to Boundary Road. 4 pm - 4.15 pm Enemy aeroplane over our lines for a short time. Bdge HQ ack ack aircraft gun fired about 100 rounds. 3.30 pm Hostile artillery action H.E. 2.13 shrapnel & 77 mm on the X fires & Thoroughfare & apparent to be Searching for a battery at C2/6b03 Gun H.Q's or 6 planes brought down by H.L 9th A.A Guns at 8.3 pm. Lieut G.R. Oates bicycle Coy. from 36th M.G. Bdge. Que. | |
| | 12.6.17 | | Hostile artillery action throughout the night. Intense from 12 - 12.30 am & 3 - 3.30 am chiefly on left division & left Cap of own Brigade. Our artillery retaliates. Gun & medium trench howitzers active. Hostile aeroplane active. Our own appears to be out of action. One of our planes brought down behind hostile A.A. guns at 8 am. Hostile planes flew over BELLINGHAM trench the morning at 4.30 am dropping Red lights & Green lights. Que | |

2449 Wt. W14957/Mg0 750,000 1/16 J.B.C. & A. Forms/C.2118/12.

# WAR DIARY or INTELLIGENCE SUMMARY

Army Form C. 2118.

| Place | Date | Hour | Summary of Events and Information | | | Remarks and references to Appendices |
|---|---|---|---|---|---|---|
| HILL TOP SECTOR. St Julian & N.W.2 | 12/6/17 | | Gun. | Map Coordinate | Target. | No of Rounds. |
| | | | Zouave Villa | C.20.c.18.15. | Hindenberg Farm. | 1500 |
| | | | La Brique. | C.26.d.70.95 | C.23.a.20.20. | 1750 |
| | | | Wilson Jn N | C.26.b.08.11. | California Avenue. | 1500 |
| | | | Wilson Jn S. | C.26.d.72.68 | California Lane. | 3000. |
| | | | Irish Ft | C.27.a.44.56. | Von Regel F. C.23.b & d. | 2000. |
| | | | Low Willow | C.20.b.8.11 | Fort Trust C.15 a.4.5 | 1000. |
| | | | La Belle Alliance. | C.20.d.99.70. | Coosie Tr Cadore Supp. | 500. |
| | | | | | Total | 19750 |
| | 13/6/17 | 2 am - 2:30 am. hostile artillery placed barrage from a line running Kemp Fort Farm north to N of La Belle Alliance, consisting of 4.2, 77 mm. & H.E. Shrapnel. This forward to the support line was repeated again from 2.45 am till 3.15 am but (N.E.) + Boar Lane. Shells rather more heavily. Aircraft 2 enemy planes flying over our line from 4.5 am - 5 am. fired at by M.G's. 1 am. few shells round La Brique Poelcan. Wilson Jn. S. & Bank Road. 2 am. shells on Willow Farm. 3.10 am. 6.30 am Enemy shelled Bent Road & La Brique with gas shells. 4 pm. Boundary Rd & Coney St. shelled. 4.40 " 3. 4.2" Shells on English Farm. | | | |

**Army Form C. 2118.**

# WAR DIARY
## or
## INTELLIGENCE SUMMARY
*(Erase heading not required.)*

Instructions regarding War Diaries and Intelligence Summaries are contained in F. S. Regs., Part II. and the Staff Manual respectively. Title Pages will be prepared in manuscript.

| Place | Date | Hour | Summary of Events and Information | Remarks and references to Appendices |
|---|---|---|---|---|
| HILL TOP SECTOR. St Julian. Sh. 28. N.W.2 | 13/6/17 | | 5 - 5.30 am  3 hostile planes over our lines driven off by M.G. fire. <br> 8 - 9.30 am  2 hostile planes patrolling within their own lines. <br> 10 - 11.30 am  2 enemy planes visited our lines at Hill Top driven off by A.A. guns. <br> 750 rounds fired by V.M.G. from A.A. mountings. <br> Our planes active all day over hostile lines. <br> Hostile artillery quieter. Target. <br> Night Firing. Target. <br> Wilson Fm. S. C.22.a.95.70  Cat Trat  3250 <br> La Brique. C.22.a.85.70      do       3750 <br> Total  7000 Rounds. | |
| | 14/6/17 | | Enemy artillery active all day. Coney St. Willows & La Belle Alliance shelled between 5 and 7 am. Threadneedle St from 3.35 - 4 pm. Wilson Fm 10 am. Heavy shelling round St Jean Cm. 11.15 am. <br> Casualties. <br> Hill Top 63041 Pte Gardner hit by a bullet fired by German gun at one of our aeroplanes more bruised than hurt. <br> During night artillery (hostile) active on Transport roads, C.T.'s & bivouacs. <br> Night Firing. Gun Position. Target. Rounds. | |

# WAR DIARY or INTELLIGENCE SUMMARY

Army Form C. 2118.

| Place | Date | Hour | Summary of Events and Information | Remarks and references to Appendices |
|---|---|---|---|---|
| HILL TOP SECTOR | 15/6/17 | 7 A | Company relieved by 117th M.G. Coy. & No 3 Sect. (3 Teams) & Team No 2 Section left in Lancashire Farm. Sects Hill Cake in command 117th M.G.C. Relief not interfered with by hostile artillery. Transport at Canal Bank being heavily shelled. 1 Sash horse killed, 1 wounded, 1 mule killed, 1 wounded. NoB20, Pte. Dalgarno. B.(driver) wounded & No 21663 Pte. Harvey B. wounded. Considering the amount of shelling the Company escaped wonderfully well. | Enc |
| | 16/6/17 | 6 p | Company arrived back in camp (S Camp) | |
| | 17/6/17 | 6 p | Day spent in refitting furniture & taking shelter from a few H.V. shells sent over during day. Enemy chiefly directed at Railway crossings & dumps situated near the camp. | Enc |
| | 18/6/17 | 7 p | Parades etc. Enemy sent H.V. shells over during day. | Enc |
| | 19/6/17 | 5 p | Parades etc. Pte. Scutt W. No 73162 wounded in leg at C. 20.1. (Lancashire Farm). Enemy sent H.V. shells round camp & two very close. Lieut Pearce reported to cope. Sgt Cain gave salut. | Enc |
| | 20/6/17 | 7 p | Parade &c. Lieut Pearce informed the Company from 39th Div. for school was left H.V. shells round camp. | Enc |
| | 21/6/17 | 7 A M | Transport (less 3 limbers No 3 Section) left for WORMHOUDT with Bde transport. | Enc |
| | | 11 AM | Coy (less 3 Teams No. 3 Sect & Lt OATES) left "S" Camp, marched to POPERINGHE STN. Vicinity of station shelled & to avoid casualties the Bde. entrained at HOUPOUTRE Siding en route for HOUIE-MOULE Training Area. | Enc |
| | | 1.45 PM | Train moved off. | |

# WAR DIARY
## or
## INTELLIGENCE SUMMARY
*(Erase heading not required.)*

Army Form C. 2118.

| Place | Date | Hour | Summary of Events and Information | Remarks and references to Appendices |
|---|---|---|---|---|
| MOULLE | 22/6/17 | 3PM | Arrived at WATTEN (HAZEBROUCK 5A) MAP 1/40000 Detrained marched to billets near MOULLE. H.Q. FRANCE – Sheet 27A SE 1/20000 Q.11.2.85.70. Men in barns. Good billets but somewhat scattered. | kwt |
|  | 23/6/17 | 2AM | Heavy Rain - Parades under Section arrangements - P.T. Rifle practices - lectures | kwt |
|  |  |  | Band of Regt arrived. |  |
|  |  | 6 AM | Reveille |  |
|  |  | 7.30AM | Coy marched to miniature Range for Rapid practices & M.G. firing Range 400yds S of E in NORDAUSQUES (MAP HAZEBROUCK 5A Sheet 1/40000 Range 400yds S of E in NORDAUSQUES) Each man fired 2 mag r an Targets - firing carried on until sunset. Major General Sir J. CUTHBERT commdg 39 Div visited Range with Brig-Gen M. L. HORNBY |  |
|  |  | 10 PM |  | kwt |
|  |  | 4 PM | Training ceased & Coy returned to Billets |  |
|  | 24/6/17 | 9 AM – 10AM | Parade for cleaning Arms. |  |
|  |  | 2 PM | Presbyt. Church Parade + R.E. |  |
|  |  | 2.30PM | Co's Inspection of Coy. C of E Parade Service – followed by a Coy. march past | kwt |
|  | 25/6/17 | 6AM | Reveille |  |
|  |  | 9 AM to 4 PM | Training on Range at NORDAUSQUES. Drawn hither Lt OATES returned from the line. | kwt |
|  | 26/6/17 | 6.30AM | Reveille - Breakfasts 7.15 AM – 9 – 10 AM Coy Parade |  |
|  |  | 11 AM | Coy left for Training area |  |
|  |  | 12 noon | Lunch on Training area |  |

# WAR DIARY or INTELLIGENCE SUMMARY

Army Form C. 2118.

(Erase heading not required.)

Instructions regarding War Diaries and Intelligence Summaries are contained in F. S. Regs., Part II. and the Staff Manual respectively. Title Pages will be prepared in manuscript.

| Place | Date | Hour | Summary of Events and Information | Remarks and references to Appendices |
|---|---|---|---|---|
| | 26/6/17 | 1 PM | — On training Area — Drill competition for prizes | |
| | | 2 PM | Pack Drill | |
| | | 2.30 PM | Inspected the Drill with arrangements for "Lift" | |
| | | 3.30 PM | Moving forward on tack 500× repeating 2000+ arranging a Barrage during taking of 4th objective | |
| | | 4.30 PM | Moving in Artillery formation to a line to be consolidated. Practice in the ordine in combination with use of R.J. | |
| | | 5.30 | Dinners cooked | |
| | | 6 PM | Stoppages — 6.30 PM Combined Drill | |
| | | 7 PM | Training ceased | |
| | | | 2/Lt H.H. Stout rejoined Coy. from C.C.S. | M.S. |
| | 27/6/17 | 5 AM | Reveille | |
| | | 6.15 | Coy. left for Training Area | |
| | | 8 AM | Sqn drill, Lewis gun & Platoon competition finished — 9.30 PM (Tea + Haversack Ration) Use of Rifle, & training trails — having companies of fire — Combined | |
| | | 1 PM | Drill — Pack Drill & Tactical Scheme | |
| | | | Thunder — | |
| | | 5 PM | Capt. J. Jackson lectured to Officers & Platoon Sergeants of Bde. on "What to teach in an hours musketry" | M.S. |
| | 28/6/17 | | Very heavy Thunderstorm. Training in Billets & Transport lines | |

Army Form C. 2118.

# WAR DIARY
## or
## INTELLIGENCE SUMMARY

*(Erase heading not required.)*

Instructions regarding War Diaries and Intelligence Summaries are contained in F. S. Regs., Part II. and the Staff Manual respectively. Title Pages will be prepared in manuscript.

| Place | Date | Hour | Summary of Events and Information | Remarks and references to Appendices |
|---|---|---|---|---|
| | 28/6/17 | 5PM | Lecture by XVIII Corps Commander Lt-Gen Sir Ivor Maxse KCB CVO DSO to 116 & 118 Bde with MILITARY HOUSE. Lessons learnt from the fighting at Arras | WR |
| | 29/6/17 | | Training Programme in Area cancelled owing to weather. Coys engaged in billet area & trained as follows — | |
| | | 9-1PM | Offrs. etc Training — Combined drill — Use of Compass — Judicator. Recognition of rangets. | |
| | | 2-7 | Baths | |
| | | | Weather fine in afternoon | |
| | | 4 AM | One section left for training area to practise Battalion attack | WR |
| | | | W/Sgt Hands Regt — cancelled on arrival. | |
| | 30/6/17 | 6 AM | Reveille — very wet. | |
| | | 8 AM | Thick lectures fired stoppages on change | |
| | | 12 Noon | One section to baths taken every 2 hrs. Remainder of day checking stores under section arrangements | WR |

Army Form C. 2118.

# WAR DIARY
*or*
# INTELLIGENCE SUMMARY

*(Erase heading not required.)*

Instructions regarding War Diaries and Intelligence Summaries are contained in F. S. Regs., Part II. and the Staff Manual respectively. Title Pages will be prepared in manuscript.

| Place | Date | Hour | Summary of Events and Information | Remarks and references to Appendices |
|---|---|---|---|---|
| | | | | |

2449 Wt. W14957/M90 750,000 1/16 J.B.C. & A. Forms/C.2118/12.

Original

Army

WAR DIARY
or
INTELLIGENCE SUMMARY

(Erase heading not required.)

Remarks and references to Appendices

116 Coy
MG/

CONFIDENTIAL

War Diary
of
116 Company M.G. Corps.
from July 1st to July 31st 1917

| Place | Date | Hour | | |
|---|---|---|---|---|

# WAR DIARY or INTELLIGENCE SUMMARY

Army Form C. 2118.

| Place | Date | Hour | Summary of Events and Information | Remarks and references to Appendices |
|---|---|---|---|---|
| MOULE | 1/7/17 | 6.30 AM | Reveille | |
| | | 9 AM | Parade for overhauling small kit & Bale filling | |
| | | 10 AM | Non-Conformist Service by YMCA Hut | |
| | | " | R.C. Service Hut Churchill | |
| | | 2.30 PM | Coy's Parade Service in Transport field | |
| | 2/7/17 | 6 AM | Reveille | |
| | | 8 AM | Coy marched from château Short Range J.28.C for Rev: Rev: Practices and Swinging Traverse practice. Parties up under Lt Hobson. Drawing cease'd gas Rd to Billets. | |
| | | 11 AM | Capt. A.T. Jackson Left for XVIII Corps Central at VOLKERINCK HOVE | |
| | | 12 noon | One NCO (Sergt Hughes) to M.G. Course at CAVIERS. | |
| | 2/7/17 | 6.30 AM | Reveille — 8.30 AM Pack animals inspected by B.S.C. 116 Bde at Bde H.Q. | |
| | | 9 AM | Nos 1,9,2 Coy's did Range Practice (correct length holding, traversing) on 100 yds | |
| | | 12 noon | Range Q 16.a. | |
| | | | Nos 3 + 4 trained in Transport field — Care of company P.T. use of company | |
| | | 2 — | Drawing out Transport field — close order drill — keeping line if fire with coys | |
| | | 4:30 | filling Belts (machine hand) | |
| | | 2 — 5.30 | 5 officers & 14 Section Sergts 1 numeros reconnoitred practice trenches. Assembled at La LONDE BOURG Estaminet. Map France Sheet 27A SE (Q35.d.2.4) maxing of trenches not complete. Trenches followed by means of map ST JULIEN 28.N.W.2. | |

**Army Form C. 2118.**

# WAR DIARY
## or
## INTELLIGENCE SUMMARY

*(Erase heading not required.)*

Instructions regarding War Diaries and Intelligence Summaries are contained in F. S. Regs., Part II. and the Staff Manual respectively. Title Pages will be prepared in manuscript.

| Place | Date | Hour | Summary of Events and Information | Remarks and references to Appendices |
|---|---|---|---|---|
| MOULE | 4/7/17 | 9AM | Reconnaissance of Practice Trenches undertaken by officers. | |
| | | 1.30PM | Haversack Ration 11AM – 11.30AM. | |
| | 5/7/17 | 9-12.30 | Bombing under Bde. Bombing officer. each man throwing live mills bombs. | |
| | | 11-12.15 | Baths + clean change of under clothing at HOULE | |
| | | 2.30 | Owing to Range being cancelled Coy carried on Training on Transport | |
| | | 4.30 | Field Range Rifle Practice, Squad Drill Batt Fatigue. Capt Jackson returned from XVIII Corps C.O. Course. | |
| | 6/7/17 | 9AM | Iving on Range – service conditions were adopted – 12" figure being used as targets. | |
| | | 1AM | Hedechons (174) To be employed for Barrage work under B.M.G.O in coming operations – took up positions at P.5.a.8.8 – O.5.b.2.8 for a Practice Barrage on Belts Q.7.d.o.9 – Q.7.a.b.3. Owing to a telephone break down no Barrage fire was carried out | |
| | | 3.30 | Cleaning guns rc | |
| | | 4.30 | | |
| | 7/7/17 | 8AM. | Training in accordance with Provisional Bde. Order re Active Operations commenced. Guns have been disposed of as follows "Barrage work" 8 Guns at disposal of the B.M.G.O for "Barrage work" 6 Guns allotted to 13 Bn R.S. Regt for defence of ST. JULIEN ~ WINNIPEG 2 " " " 14 " " " " SPRINGFIELD | 11.60p.t A1/1 |

# WAR DIARY
or
## INTELLIGENCE SUMMARY

Army Form C. 2118.

| Place | Date | Hour | Summary of Events and Information | Remarks and references to Appendices |
|---|---|---|---|---|
| | 7/1/17 | | Lots drawn by L. Officers as to Tasks - result as follows:- | |
| | | | No. 1 Sectn - Rt. section Barrage | |
| | | | " 2 " - " " - attached to 13th Sussex for defence of ST. JULIEN | |
| | | | " 3 " (Less 2 guns) " " " " WINNIPEG | |
| | | | " " " " " 14th Hants " " SPRINGFIELD | |
| | | | " 4 " - Left section Barrage | |
| | 8/1/17 | 8 AM | Nos. 2 & 3 sections on Practice trenches with Bde. | |
| | | | " 1 & 4 " drawing in vicinity of Billets - Squad Drill - Barrage drill - P.T. | |
| | | 2 PM | Limber & Pack Drill - map & compass - P.T. | |
| | | | 32 men (8 p. Gr. in Bde) attached to Coys. for training prior to acting as Carriers in active operations. | |
| | | | Separate training in M.G. given to those under Lt STOTT. | |
| | 9/1/17 | 10 AM | Non conformist Service in Y.M.CA hut. | |
| | | 39 M | C of E parade in Transport field - Rev. Neville TALBOT. | |
| | | 8.30 AM | No.1 Sectn. proceed across Rds. Q 18.c 4 9 en route for Practice trenches | |
| | | 8.40 | " 2 " & 2 guns of No 3 " " " " " " together | |
| | | | with 13th R.S. Regt. | |
| | | 9 AM | " 3 Sect. (2 guns) joined 14th Hants. Regt. at Q 18.c.4 9 en route for Practice area | |
| | | 8.40 | " 4 Sect. to Practice Trenches for Barrage work | |

Oct. J.

# WAR DIARY
## or
## INTELLIGENCE SUMMARY

Army Form C. 2118.

| Place | Date | Hour | Summary of Events and Information | Remarks and references to Appendices |
|---|---|---|---|---|
| | | | Nos. 1 & 4 advanced rear of 4th, 12th R.S.R against the Blue line & took up posts for putting a barrage 400x beyond the Black line | |
| | | | All details concerning barrage carried out by means of flags & drum – (Artillery Barrage) | |
| | | | Attached men under Lt Stott in Transport field | |
| | 10/11/17 | 8.30 | Drawing on practice trenches with Battalion – 730 p.c inspected full rounds. Attached men on transport field under Lt Stott | |
| | | 4 pm | Lt L.W Evans proceeded to Volkerinchove to X111 Corps course – clerks for 3 days – 14 horse | |
| | | | Announcement re. return of Coy. | |
| | 11/11/17 | 9 am | Attached men to range at Q.10.C.4.5 for M.S firing | |
| | | | Remainder participated in Bde. Practice attack over trenches. | |
| | | 10 am | Object of Trg – to give practice to Junior officers + N.C.O's in commands. re concerted arranged intrinsic digging practised | |
| | | | All details of barrage. Barrage, etc | |
| | | 6 pm | Lecture in general. Topics of Training by Captain Jackson model trenches laid out in transport field – Bde front in active operation | |
| | | AM 9–1 PM | Cadre Anneal or [?] Practice Trenches | A.T.F |

# WAR DIARY
## or
## INTELLIGENCE SUMMARY.
*(Erase heading not required.)*

Army Form C. 2118.

| Place | Date | Hour | Summary of Events and Information | Remarks and references to Appendices |
|---|---|---|---|---|
| MOULE | 12/7/17 | 3.30 AM | Humanity reported made Paraded To Bake HP. | |
| | | 4.30 AM | Greatest increase light at 4.10 AM | |
| | | 8.30-9.30 | Inspection of Kit — Stores — Limber Packing &c in Transport lined | |
| | | 9AM-5PM | 'Silent Period' — all ranks to obtain some sleep | |
| | | 6PM | Lecture on forthcoming operations — from note map made at XVIII Corps Course of Instruction. | |
| | | 10.30 PM | Nos 2 & 3 Sections marched off toward their respective Bns for Training on Practice Trenches — Divisional attack | |
| | 13/7/17 | 4.10 AM | Zero for attack practice | |
| | | 8 AM | No. 1st Section left for 'B' Range & carried out a practice Barrage at 2200 yds. Half of the men observed during ranging — proof very good — ground immediately behind Targets untenable — observers into huts for Barrages of 1915 mins. Attacked to trying Report by Lt Holson. Great interest taken by all ranks. Increased Confidence gained. | A.J.J. |
| | | 10 AM | | |
| | | 10 AM | Nos 2 & 3 Sections returned from Training | |
| | | 6 PM | Lecture by Capt Jackson, for content operation & Range cards from (2/Lt HRS Crosser MGC joined as Reinforcement) | |

# INDIRECT OVERHEAD FIRE.

No. 11 **B** M.G. Coy.　　No. 1-4　　Sections A-1-S　　Date 13.7.17　　Map used Tilques. Tr. Area.　　Officer i/c Firing Lieut. J.C. Holden

| Gun No. | Target | Range to Target in Yards | ELEVATION — Contours in Yards — Gun A | ELEVATION — Contours in Yards — Target | V.I. in Yards | Q.E. in Minutes Table 3(A) or 3(B) | Range from Q.E. in Yards Table, Col. 2 | Contour of own troops in Yards B | Range to own troops in Yards | Traj. Height in Yards Table 2 C | Clearance obtained by Note (1) below | Clearance required in Yards | Compass Bearing or D.D. Reading | Time of firing | No. of rounds fired | Checked by | REMARKS General |
|---|---|---|---|---|---|---|---|---|---|---|---|---|---|---|---|---|---|
| 1 | Barrage from O.7.a.09 – O.7.a.6.3 Refresne Wood. Tilques Training Area. | 2,250 | 55ˣ | 44ˣ | 11 | -7' | 6°24' | | | | | | 133½° - 135° | 10.30 - 11.0½ | 500 | ✓ | |
| 2 | " | " | " | " | " | " | " | | | | | | 135° - 136° | " | " | | |
| 3 | " | " | " | " | " | " | " | | | | | | 136° - 137° | " | " | | |
| 4 | " | " | " | " | " | " | (7000) (2000 dk) | | | | | | 137° - 138° | " | " | | |
| 5 | " | 2225 | " | " | " | " | 6°16' | 5.5. | | | | | 138° - 139° | " | " | | |
| 6 | " | " | " | " | " | " | 6°16' | " | | | | | -139° - 140° | " | " | | |
| 7 | " | " | " | " | " | " | 6°16' | " | | | | | 140° - 141½ | " | " | | |
| 8 | " | " | " | " | " | " | 6°16' | " | | | | | 141½ - 143° | " | " | | |

NOTES.— (1) Clearance in yards = A − B plus or minus C according as trajectory tables give positive or negative values of C.
(2) Immediately before firing Q.E. must be corrected, if necessary, for atmospheric influences. See Table 5.
(3) For lateral wind allowance. See Table 4.
(4) If obstruction exists between gun and target, and its highest point cannot be seen, ascertain if shots will clear by substituting "obstruction" for "own troops" in clearance columns above, and find clearance by rule in Note (1). Minimum clearance required equals half height of cone for range to obstruction.

## Barrage Scheme

| | | | | |
|---|---|---|---|---|
| E | Battery | = | 116th Coy. | 8 guns. |
| F | Do | = | 145th Coy. | 8 guns. |
| G | Do | = | 145th Coy. | 8 guns. |
| H | Do | = | 117th Coy. | 8 guns. |

E & H assemble with their Bdes.
F & G on ground representing HILL TOP.

After capture of BLUE line, move to —

| LOCATION | | TARGET | |
|---|---|---|---|
| C.32.b.75.60 | from | C.12.a.20.05 to C.12.c.55.40 | 1800 rounds per hour |
| to C.32.b.85.40 | +5 hours | C.12.a.99.72 to C.12.b.60.30 | 3750 rounds per hour |

Times after ZERO + 5 hours will be according to the rate of advance during the practice.

On the capture of the GREEN DOTTED line E. & H. Batteries will cease fire and move forward to carry out barrage as below from the time our troops leave the GREEN DOTTED line, thereafter times will be according to the rate of advance in the practice.

Location E about C.7.b.10.70
Targets C.7.d.10.10 to D.7.c.55.60 3300 rounds per hour.
D.7.a.90.85 Do

# WAR DIARY
## or
## INTELLIGENCE SUMMARY.
(Erase heading not required.)

Army Form C. 2118.

| Place | Date | Hour | Summary of Events and Information | Remarks and references to Appendices |
|---|---|---|---|---|
| | | | Various stages of the line prepared & posted & made certain BOLT Bays which are trademarked with asgn according to line (Red Blue &c) | |
| | 14/7/17 | | Forward dump & being done. Aeroplane photographs shown to O.T.'s Heavy showers in the morning — very hot in afternoon Whole Coy. 10 Training area for Divisional attack no. 2 93 Sections with B⁶ (B⁶ R Sussex Regt & 14ᵗʰ Hants Regt.) for defence of 'Black' line Zero 11 A.M. — Orders received from Bde. allotting different tasks to Sections — 4 guns (No 2 Sect.) to 13ᵗʰ Sussex for defence of ST. JULIEN 2 guns to 13ᵗʰ Sussex for defence of BLACK LINE — 2 to 14ᵗʰ Hants for defence of BLACK line. Coy H.Q. in Pill Box in vicinity of "Hill Top" F^m (Map ST. JULIEN). Late moved to MOUSE TRAP F^m Instructions re Tasks of 8 Barrage guns received as attached. Positions taken up. Guns laid on respective targets Phone could not be read owing to interference with Bde Comm Bugg. A.T.S. | |

# WAR DIARY
## or
## INTELLIGENCE SUMMARY.
(Erase heading not required.)

Army Form C. 2118.

| Place | Date | Hour | Summary of Events and Information | Remarks and references to Appendices |
|---|---|---|---|---|
| | | | Men in Quarters packed in readiness waiting. | |
| | | 4 PM | marched home | |
| | | | Orders received for advanced party to A 30.c (Belgium 28 NW) Camp | |
| | | | Total Remainder in readiness | |
| | 15/7/17 | 7.45 | Cof E Holy Communion in PM Stores | |
| | | ra. 9.30 AM | R.C Service HOUSE Church | |
| | | 10 AM | Nonconformist Service in YMCA hut | |
| | | noon | Cof E service in Transport field. | |
| | 16/7/17 | 4.30 PM | Reveille | |
| | | 6 AM | Vacated Billets marched to WATTEN Stn entrained with 1st R.S.R 114th Hants | |
| | | 8.19 | Train left — detrained at HOUPOUTRE SIDING near POPERINGHE. | |
| | | | Marched to Z Camp — arrived 1.30 P.M. Camp at all occupied by 5th R.S Regt. (48 Div. Pioneers) | |
| | | 8 AM | Transport left with Bde. transport & travelled via WORMHOUDT - night spent there. | |
| | | | Stores by lorry from MOUILE. | Q.76 |

Army Form C. 2118.

# WAR DIARY
## or
## INTELLIGENCE SUMMARY.
(Erase heading not required.)

| Place | Date | Hour | Summary of Events and Information | Remarks and references to Appendices |
|---|---|---|---|---|
| Z Camp | 17/7/17 | | Coy Training in Camp — Inspection — Squad Drill — Gas Drill & Lecture Physical Training — Coy Parades. 2–5 Silent Period for rest. | |
| | | 1.30 PM | 2 N.C.O.s + 20 men went by G.S. wagon to CANAL BANK to work on M.G. Emplacements under O.C. 32nd M.G. Coy | |
| | | 4 PM | 4 Gun Teams went to Hill Top Section to relieve 4 Teams of 118 Coy M.G.C. Personnel by G.S. wagon to VLAMERTINGHE Sance on foot. Guns by Limber to VLAMERTINGHE thence by Pack mules. Lt. Hobson in charge | |
| | | | Capt. A.T. Jackson visited model of Corps Front with Brigadier S.C. + Bde Major — C. Camp. A.30 cartridge Belgium 28 N.W. Lt STOTT went to CANAL BANK to arrange re SAA dump in preparing of features | |
| | 18/7/17 | 6.30 | Reveille — Lt Doyle relieved Lt. Hobson for a while hence to go on leave | |
| | | 8.45 | Coy Training — Gun Cleaning — Gun Drill — Lecture on "own attack" | |
| | | 11.45 | Inspection of Kit + C | |
| | | 2–5 | Silent Period. | A.T.9 |

# WAR DIARY
## INTELLIGENCE SUMMARY.
*(Erase heading not required.)*

Army Form C. 2118.

| Place | Date | Hour | Summary of Events and Information | Remarks and references to Appendices |
|---|---|---|---|---|
| Z CAMP | 19/1/17 | 8.30 | Officers & N.C.O's visited Model Trenches - Coy front - in 'C' Camp a 3 O Centre | |
| | | | Remainder of Coy Trenching Billets - | |
| | | | Gunners - Horsemanagement grooming, watering & under 17 O.R.Ts | |
| | | 12.45 | Attachedmen Gun Drill &c under C.S.M | |
| | | | Cold evening. | |
| | | | Fatigues commenced one months furlough. | |
| | | 5.30 PM | Officers & warrant NCO 13th R.Sussex Regt. in/for coming of rations attached conference held by Col having Commdg 13th R.S. 13-Z Camp. | |
| | 20/1/17 | 9.45 | Coy Training - Inspection - Lecture & Drill - Gun Drill &c | |
| | | 11.45 | Steel Helmets marked with yellow cross on Gun support - G.O.C. Bde approved of Coy Sign on limbers - Red square with Green cross Gunn in Centre | |
| | | 2-5 | Rest Period - men today in Billets | |
| | | | Requirements & Teams me tone & Pack Mule | |
| | | | Water carriers for pack animals completed - commenced putting rear portion of each limber with Rocks for Petrol Tins. | |
| | | | Collected surplus stores for storing in POPERINGHE | A.T.S. |

A5915  Wt. W14422/M1160  350,000  12/16  D. D. & L.  Forms/C/2118/14.

# WAR DIARY
## or
## INTELLIGENCE SUMMARY.
(Erase heading not required.)

Army Form C. 2118.

| Place | Date | Hour | Summary of Events and Information | Remarks and references to Appendices |
|---|---|---|---|---|
| Z Camp | 21/7/17 | 4 AM | Reveille | |
| | | 8.45 | Coy training – C.O's Inspection – Gas Drill – Instruction by C.O. | |
| | | 11.45 | General points on m.g. of guns in active operations – covering fire &c | |
| | | 2-5 | Silent Period | |
| | | | During Demoralizing attacks of men not going into action – all subt. guns stores were dumped in the Rue, store POPERINGHE – RUE TETE D'OR | |
| | | 9.30 PM | Relief of 4 Gun Teams in the line under Lt. Doyle – commenced. One section of 228 m.g. Coy relieved them. Guns &c stored at CANAL BANK under Lt. STOTT. Lt. Doyle & Teams proceeded to 'C' Camp on completion of Relief & stayed at Jes. School for the night – arriving there 4 A.M. No casualties during tour in line though Enemy artillery active & Gas shell used considerably whilst in the line. Each gun fired 3000 r⁰s per night. Harassing fire on enemy approaches &c. | A.1.9 |

# WAR DIARY or INTELLIGENCE SUMMARY

Army Form C. 2118.

| Place | Date | Hour | Summary of Events and Information | Remarks and references to Appendices |
|---|---|---|---|---|
| Z Camp | 21/7/17 | 5AM | Reveille - Lt Evans & one NCO left as advance party to "C" Camp A.30 c.Tive (BELGIUM 28 NW) to take over camp for Coy. 11 Tents & 8 Bivouac shelters for Offrs. & O.R's near R.H.Q. XVIII Corps H.A. H.Q. | |
| | | 7.40AM | Coy & Transport ready to move from Z Camp - delayed start owing to traffic on the road - marched through ST. JAN TER BIEZEN | |
| | | No. | Via Switch Rd starting POPERINGHE - POPERINGHE - VLAMERTINGHE Rd. & "C" Camp A.30.d.1.6 (BE 19.1 um 28NW) | |
| | | 10.30 AM | Coy. arrived in Camp | |
| | | 2PM | Mule pack mules fetched from Kit of Teams (relieved 21/7/22) | |
| C Camp | 23/7/17 | 10.0AM 6.30AM | from CANAL Bk daylight Pack grenades A.D.M. & working party attd to 32 Inf'y returned to Coy. Highly praised by DM.50 for work done Reveille | |
| | | 8.45 | Co's Inspection & Training & filling belts & on Transport lines | |
| | | 9.45 | under Section officers | |
| | | 10AM | Const. of Engraving on top of Kit in the Coy. Postponed owing to one man being late | |
| | | | A.30.d.4.5 | |
| | | 11AM | The CO. Rect offrs marked the model with the Tank Officers att'd to the Bde | G.T.J |

# WAR DIARY
## or
## INTELLIGENCE SUMMARY.
*(Erase heading not required.)*

Army Form C. 2118.

| Place | Date | Hour | Summary of Events and Information | Remarks and references to Appendices |
|---|---|---|---|---|
| Camp | 25/5/17 | 2-5 | Silent Period. | |
| | | | Lt Hobson returned from leave to BOULOGNE | |
| | | | Shelling less on Back areas. Gas shells still being used by enemy in | |
| | | | large quantities. Our artillery actively bombarding | |
| | | | Rations drawn for 2 days — also 100 extra water Bottles 50 Helmets | |
| " | | | Belt Box carriers & 16 YUKON PACKS | |
| | | | Very Hot + dry | |
| | 29/5/17 | 6.30 AM | Reveille — enemy artillery quiet in vacinity of this camp during | |
| | | | night 23/24 | |
| | | 8.45 | Checking of stores — Equipment etc in Transport field | |
| | | 12.45 | | |
| | | 10 AM | Court of Enquiry held in Gas School C Camp on reference | |
| | | | of ots of Coy when taken over on June 3. 1917 by Capt | |
| | | | At JACKSON | |
| | | | President — Major CASSY M.C. 12th R.S. Regt | |
| | | | Witnesses — Lt Evans Lt Higginbottom CQMS Sergt T. Andrews (Transport) A.J. |

# WAR DIARY
## or
## INTELLIGENCE SUMMARY.
(Erase heading not required.)

Army Form C. 2118.

| Place | Date | Hour | Summary of Events and Information | Remarks and references to Appendices |
|---|---|---|---|---|
| | | | No Reply. The advances were principally throughout in fighting | |
| | | | from 10 Nov. 16 not replaced – most important items | |
| | | | 1 Rangefinder, 1 watch, 1 Telescope, 16 Mount Browning, 7 Binoculars | |
| | | | 8 Compass magnetic. | |
| | | 2–5 | Slept & Messed | |
| | | 5.30 | Lecture to whole Coy by CO. Instructions re the Battle. | |
| | | | Means of getting up SAA water &c — Routes of HQ — communications | |
| | | | [illegible] | |
| | | 9 PM | 1 Offr & 5 men proceeded to CANAL BK to carry up 15 Petrol | |
| | | | Tins of water for MG. water dump at CROSS Rd Farm C2r C.3.7. | |
| | | | (BELGIUM 25NW). NCO & 3 men confer for Battle in KT rations | |
| | | | Two drawn at RED HART ESTAMINET | |
| | | 9 AM | All officers reconnoitred Route to CANAL BK via the CHEMIN | |
| | | | MILITAIRE & QUEENS Rd — newly laid 'roads & tracks | |
| Camp | 25/7/17 | 6.30 AM | Reveillé — quiet night in camp | |
| | | 8.45 | CO's Inspection | |
| | | | Heavy rain necessitated removing in TENTS | A.T.F |

Army Form C. 2118.

# WAR DIARY
## or
## INTELLIGENCE SUMMARY.
(Erase heading not required.)

Instructions regarding War Diaries and Intelligence
Summaries are contained in F. S. Regs., Part II.
and the Staff Manual respectively. Title pages
will be prepared in manuscript.

| Place | Date | Hour | Summary of Events and Information | Remarks and references to Appendices |
|---|---|---|---|---|
| | 25/1/17 | 9.30 PM | 4 Camero who took Patrol Pm to forward dump reft his base unable to reach cross RDS Fm. | |
| | | 10.45 | to T HILLTOP dugouts — Offr & 3 men. Grad. Gas in line necessitated wearing of | |
| | | | masks for 3–4 hrs | |
| | | 12 noon | Order received cancelling move of advance party to CANAL BANK until further notice | |
| | | | due to have left 6PM | |
| | | | Lt. Brown returned from leave UK. Camp & vicinity quiet. | |
| | | 2–5 | Silent Period | |
| | 26/1/17 | 8.45 | CO's Inspection — Gun Drill & T Transport kits & preparation for operations | |
| | | 12.45 | | |
| | | 2–5 | Silent Period. | |
| | 27/1/17 | 8.45 | all ranks to 39th Div Sp. School for testing of SBR to fit in lachrymatory | |
| | | 11 AM | gas. | |
| | | 11–1 | Preparation in Transport field — each man with his own load | |
| | | 1–5 | Silent Period | |
| | | 5–7 | Sections on model of ground overwhich attack is to take place. | |
| | | 5PM | Lt EVANS 2/Lt CROSER & 1 NCO as advance party to CANAL BANK | R.T.Y |

**Army Form C. 2118.**

# WAR DIARY
## or
## INTELLIGENCE SUMMARY.
*(Erase heading not required.)*

Instructions regarding War Diaries and Intelligence Summaries are contained in F. S. Regs., Part II. and the Staff Manual respectively. Title pages will be prepared in manuscript.

| Place | Date | Hour | Summary of Events and Information | Remarks and references to Appendices |
|---|---|---|---|---|
| | | | Coy Comdrs ordered to move at 2 hrs notice. L.T. was advised from CANAL BANK — accommodation naturally very limited. Rumour that Enemy had withdrawn to beyond STEENBEEK | |
| | 28/7/17 | | Packs of parties to move up to CANAL BANK. Operation Order No 6 issued as follows:— | |
| | | | REF MAP ST. JULIEN 1/10000 | |
| | | | 1. In accordance with 116 Inf Bde Order No 146 of 26/7/17 the 116 MG Coy (less Transport) will move to CANAL BANK | |
| | | | 2. All sections will place necessary Tm equipment for forthcoming operations on one of their fighting limbers — also two Camp Kettles + 1 for H.Q. | |
| | | | The rations for X + Y days | |
| | | | Services. Two of Drinking water will be taken for section. | |
| | | | Coy Cooks will accompany the Coy to CANAL B.K. | |
| | | | 3. Coy will fall in 9.20 PM for inspection march to Drill ground A, B, C by 9.30 PM | R.T.Y |
| | | | 4. Order of March Nos 4 3 2 1 Sections | |

M9415 Wt. W1142/M1180 350,000 12/16 D.D. & L. Forms/C./2118/14.

# WAR DIARY
## or
## INTELLIGENCE SUMMARY.
(Erase heading not required.)

Army Form C. 2118.

| Place | Date | Hour | Summary of Events and Information | Remarks and references to Appendices |
|---|---|---|---|---|
| | 25/7/17 | | 5. Reporting fatigue wagons under Sergt T. Graham will beat Brickground at 9.25 PM under Transport Sergt. Each wagon will follow its Sect. | |
| | | | 6. Starting point – YMCA hut – Time of passing 9.35 PM – 50 yds distance between sections | |
| | | | 7. Route – CHEMIN MILITAIRE & QUEEN'S RD No smoking | |
| | | | 8. Fatigue wagons will return to Transport lines on completion of move under T. Sergt. | |
| | | | 9. Camp to be thoroughly cleaned before leaving. | |
| | | | 10. Hammer personnel detailed to remain with [illeg] behind will proceed to the wagon lines. Move under the Officer i/c lines. | |
| | | 9.35 PM | Coy formed up in accordance with above – delayed owing to other troops not yet clear. Quiet en route until MACHINE Fm reached # S. en route Coy. experienced several narrow escapes but managed to reach the CANAL BANK and limbers got unloaded into billets without [illeg] | |
| | | | Casualties – Enemy fired 9.2 shells on to CANAL BANK. | R.T.F. |

Army Form C. 2118.

# WAR DIARY
## or
## INTELLIGENCE SUMMARY.
(Erase heading not required.)

Instructions regarding War Diaries and Intelligence Summaries are contained in F.S. Regs., Part II. and the Staff Manual respectively. Title pages will be prepared in manuscript.

| Place | Date | Hour | Summary of Events and Information | Remarks and references to Appendices |
|---|---|---|---|---|
| CANAL BANK | 29/7/17 | 3AM | Coy. allin dug outs. | |
| No 90 dug out | | | Sorty of Stores during the day. 2 Officers & N.C.O's made a reconnaissance | |
| | | 5PM | of their assembly positions — Guard returned from Dunzen Hill | |
| | | | To P. one man left in charge | |
| | | | A large amount of S.A.A. which caused uneasiness — Issued to B.A.N.R. — | |
| | | | one man only gassed | |
| | 30/7/17 | | Final Preparations — 16 Canvas from Bde. carrying bag dividing equally between | |
| | | | The Two Barrage Sections — 1 o.t. | |
| | | 5AM | Hot meal served Prior to leaving for assembly positions | |
| | | 8.45 | Mongolian avan/Higgins Rt. subsection of No 3 Sect under Lt Higginbottom | |
| | | | & Left subsection under Sergt. Kirkwood to assemble in rear of 13th R.S. Regt | |
| | | | 4/4. Br. Harris res'pts respectively | |
| | | | Routes — Rt. Subsect. Bridge 2A – track via PITTSBURG, to LA BRIQUE – THREADNEEDLE ST. | |
| | | | TO JUNCT OF THREADNEEDLE & ENGLISH TR.; w/ ENGLISH TR. TO BRIDGE — Overland | |
| | | | TO CAVAN TR. & assembly position | |
| | | | Assembly fask = Rt. subsect in rear of 13th Sussex who assembled as follows:— | A.T.S. |

# WAR DIARY
## or
## INTELLIGENCE SUMMARY.
*(Erase heading not required.)*

Army Form C. 2118.

| Place | Date | Hour | Summary of Events and Information | Remarks and references to Appendices |
|---|---|---|---|---|
| | | | Between C.21.d.75.00 & C.27.b.95.65. | |
| | | | Black ref: No 3 Left BLACK LINE - (Canopus System) | |
| | | | Left subsect - Room Route - Bridge 3 - Track - via C.2.s.d.85.75 to | |
| | | | C.26.a.75.40 to - IRISH FM. - TOWER POST - FINCH ST to hostile | |
| | | | Assembly - rear of 14 Platoons who assembled at C.21.d.6.6. | |
| | | 9.15PM | No. 2 Sect under Lts Brown & Stuart Left CANAL BANK & proceeded via | |
| | | | R.T.robats route of No 3 Section assembled in rear of 13th R.S. Regt. | |
| | | 10PM | Nos 1 & 4 sects under Lt Nolan & Lt Doyle approx (Barrage fring) formed | |
| | | | 'E' Battery under Lt Nolan as comdr. & assembled in rear of 13th Sussex | |
| | | | Battery | |
| | | | 414 hands about C.27.b.90.70 | |
| | | 7PM | Capt T. A. T. Jackson moved to HILL TOP to join Bde HQ | |
| | | 11PM | Lt Evans left 10/1 on Coy HQrs at HILL TOP Funnel dug out No 4. | |
| | | | 2/Lt Crozier & 2 cooks remained at CANAL B.R. for an aggregate rate R. | |
| | | | the following instructions were issued to sect officers under | |
| | | | OPERATION ORDER No 4 | |
| | | | The Rt subsection will form up (as above) in rear of the 13th R.S. Regt & follow | |

# WAR DIARY
## or
## INTELLIGENCE SUMMARY.
*(Erase heading not required.)*

Army Form C. 2118.

| Place | Date | Hour | Summary of Events and Information | Remarks and references to Appendices |
|---|---|---|---|---|
| | | | Them is to BLACK LINE 5 mins of arrival with so on to reach objective. 5 mins to of to Capture. Posn will be selected near Muy of CANTEEN Tr. barrage crossfire on bayn bearing N & NE. Left & section will follow my & bay 5 to BLACK LINE & select positions in communication Tr. (or just off it) N of CANOPUS SUPPORT one gun front N & one E. as nearly as possible. Tr Subsect Commdr will get into d with Coy on his Left. No 2 Sect. will assist in defence of ST. JULIEN. Next subsect proceeding to S. side of Hill 19. barrage crossfire N & E & to LEFT subsect to TO NW portion of the village. barrage crossfire N & E. Nos 1 & 4 Sects will proceed to MOUSE TRAP Fm. separate "B" barrage, ready to fire at zero + 2 hrs. At Zero + 4.05 hrs. Barrage Sects will cease fire - & proceed to Cy. t. 20.70 & be ready to create "E" barrage at Zero + 6.20. AT Zero + 7.16 they will cease fire but remain under 2 hrs. a/o A.T.f. | |

# WAR DIARY or INTELLIGENCE SUMMARY

Army Form C. 2118.

(Erase heading not required.)

| Place | Date | Hour | Summary of Events and Information | Remarks and references to Appendices |
|---|---|---|---|---|
| | | | Capture of SOLID GREEN LINE. When the cover under orders of O.C. 116 Bde Gunners were unmolested until dusk, a few rifle operations HQRs well made east Hill Top dugouts at 7pm rifle later. Move to vicinity of Junction of CALF RESERVE & CALF AVENUE — Dumps near I.2.a. 1.9. C.21.d.4.3. C.21.c.8.6. C.22.c.3.7. & C.16 central. As soon as B. attached me reach MOUSE TRAP FM. WR Bert Boss Hayward Humphreys return to CROSS RES. FARM under Lt. STOTT taken up 16 horses SAA. This must therefore until Zero & the Communication by runners – Matthews & man chargeable. Equipment &c. was carried as in attached table. Barrages are to be created as given in following page 'B' Barrage. | |

| Battery | LOCATION | FIRING FROM ZERO to | FIRING ZERO to | Targets | Rate of fire | Remarks |
|---|---|---|---|---|---|---|
| E | C.21.c.7.6.50 | 2.00 | 3.40 | C.11.d.30.05 to C.12.c.55.40 | 180rds/hour | At Zero + 4.05 E Battery will cease the advance to |
| | | 3.40 | 4.05 | D.7.c.24.50 to C.12.c.72.12 | 3.750 | targets for 'C' Barrage |

# WAR DIARY
## or
## INTELLIGENCE SUMMARY.
*(Erase heading not required.)*

Army Form C. 2118.

| Place | Date | Hour | Summary of Events and Information | Remarks and references to Appendices |
|---|---|---|---|---|
| "C" Barrage | | | | |

| Battery | Location | Firing From Zero Hour | Firing To Zero Hour | Targets | Rate of fire | Remarks |
|---|---|---|---|---|---|---|
| E | C.17.b.20.70 | 6.20 | 6.52 | D7.b.50.40 to D7.c.50.70 | 3500 rds p.b. | at Zero + 7.16 E Batty will cease firing on barrage & will remain on last named barrage target until slow by B Capt'd. doto. "Green Line" |
| | | 6.58 | 7.16 | D7.b.99.78 to D7.a.90.16 | 3500 rds " | |

| | 3/1/17 | 3.50 AM | Zero Hour | |
| | | | At Zero the Sections followed the Infantry according to instructions. | |
| | | | They were subjected to heavy shelling in assembly position & during their advance. | |
| | | | No 2 Section sustained several casualties on arrival at Dotted Blue | |
| | | | Line there being only Lt Brown, 1 Sgt, 1 Sgt, 1 Cpl, 1 Dvr, 2 Gnrs & a | |
| | | | Trptr with other Welts. The Sergeant Lt Brown & 3 men were then | |
| | | | wounded & Lt Stuart & 3 men reported to OC 13th Anzac & joined | |
| | | | Coy HQ in CALF RESERVE — 9 AM. | A.T.J. |

… Army Form C. 2118.

# WAR DIARY
## or
## INTELLIGENCE SUMMARY.
*(Erase heading not required.)*

| Place | Date | Hour | Summary of Events and Information | Remarks and references to Appendices |
|---|---|---|---|---|
| | | Zero | No 3 Section left assembling points an(d) moving to heavy shelling & menw of 13th R.S.R | |
| | | | 44th Batts & passed CWAN at Zero | |
| | | | Passed Red Line together – subsequently much lost slightly & several carriers & my Head Blue Line reached & 13th RS subsect found self in gap between Division on our Rt. & 13th RS Regt with a small party of mixed Infantry. He pressed on & pushed on. Holding 4 M.G. in turn at C.23.a.9.5.60 opened fire at platitude this caused the infantry to cease fire Lt Higginbottom got the Infantry to clear the M.G. crews out (New Improvement). The subsection was seen in line with the Infantry. They had several good targets of retreating boch – one at ST JULIEN Rd & CANTEEN REDOUBT – his reached & guns placed at C.18.a.0.1. & C.17.d.9.1. front at opposite Bank of STEEN BEEK & ST JULIEN | |
| | | 2 P.M | Lt Higginbottom met Lt Douglas in C.17 of S Tr. & at that time the Higginbottom left subsection caused Lt Higginbottom to remove his guns to C.17 d.33. One gun of the left subsection under Serjt T. Kenwood reached its objective. R.T.f. | |

# WAR DIARY
## or
## INTELLIGENCE SUMMARY.
*(Erase heading not required.)*

Army Form C. 2118.

| Place | Date | Hour | Summary of Events and Information | Remarks and references to Appendices |
|---|---|---|---|---|
| | | | Moved into position at eng to 2.5. incorporating the Black LINE with Corps. 2 Blues Regt. | |
| | | 3.25 AM | BARRAGE "ZERO". After 30 seconds jerkier & immediate rapid fire. Zero they answered schrol casualties | |
| | | 5 AM | Go on to Rd pressured to the BUFFS Rd. This was followed under M.G. fire for 10 mins. Thought to be MOUSETRAP Fm. Lt Hobson collected teams | |
| | | | Fog very thick. Day advanced forward to clearer parts. Found enemy at Pn. 1 & decided they were not at MOUSETRAP Fm — 3 men killed | |
| | | 7.45 AM | 3° from 91st Wing on ST. JULIEN | |
| | | 8.15 AM | Guns moved forward to CANOPUS Tr for "C" Barrage | |
| | | 8.45 AM | Reached CANOPUS system | |
| | | 9 AM | Lt Hobson killed whilst crossing Parapet | |
| | | | Sgt Murphy then O/C assisted by Cpl Gray & who remainder of Barrage Such — 4 guns on left & 8 bells, 4 gun on Saa — Lt Drayfs decided | |
| | | | a barrage useless & chose S.O.S. Posn in CANOPUS TR. | |
| | | 11.45 | Wireless officer informed Lt Drayfs of expected counter attack | A.T.4 |

The page missing after photocopying.
29/7/98.

# WAR DIARY
## or
## INTELLIGENCE SUMMARY.
(Erase heading not required.)

Army Form C. 2118.

| Place | Date | Hour | Summary of Events and Information | Remarks and references to Appendices |
|---|---|---|---|---|
| | | | He decided to wait for direct targets as parties of our troops not accurately known. | |
| | | 12.20 PM | OC 118 MGC (OC "C" Coy Barrage Guns) sent word for guns to cover from St. Julien Church to ALBERTA. | |
| | | 6.30–9 | Our Artillery put up heavy Barrage. | |
| | | | Total Casualties on 31st | |
| | | | 1 Off. killed (Lt Hotson)  1 Off wounded (Lt Brown) | |
| | | | O.R.s killed 4 — O.R.s wounded 19 | |
| | | | O.R.s missing 4. | |

A.T. Jackson, Captain
O.C. 116 M.G. Coy

# WAR DIARY
## or
## INTELLIGENCE SUMMARY.

**Army Form C. 2118.**

CONFIDENTIAL

WAR DIARY
of
116 Coy. M.G. Corps.

August 1st — 31st 1917.

Army Form C. 2118.

# WAR DIARY
## or
## INTELLIGENCE SUMMARY.
(Erase heading not required.)

Instructions regarding War Diaries and Intelligence Summaries are contained in F. S. Regs., Part II. and the Staff Manual respectively. Title pages will be prepared in manuscript.

| Place | Date | Hour | Summary of Events and Information | Remarks and references to Appendices |
|---|---|---|---|---|
| CAIF RESERVE TR. | 1st | | Coy HQ. in CAIF RESERVE TR. near Bde forward STN. Everywhere deep in mud but to rising. Missing men reporting by one's & two's. Rations brought up by packmules via cross country TRACK & taken to CAPTOUS TR along ST. JULIEN RD. Enemy artillery fairly active — one man wounded near VAN HEULE Fm. Instructions received from Bde to allot 4 guns to each of the two O.Pim. the BLACK LINE. | |
|  | | 8 P.M. | Rations for 2nd arrived — Capt Jackson went to CANAL BK to meet DM.G.O. | |
|  | 2nd | 10 A.M. | Gun teams in BLACK LINE came to Coy HQ for rations & water. Runners re relief | |
|  | | Noon | Orders to arrange relief by 117 M.G.C. commencing 3.P.M. | |
|  | | 4 P.M. | Relief postponed | |
|  | | 6 P.M. | Capt Jackson retd. & arranged relief with 117. 4 guns & left in line for relieving Coy. | |
|  | | 8 P.M. | Relief commenced | |
|  | | 11 P.M. | S.O.S. went up & heavy bombardment. | |

Army Form C. 2118.

# WAR DIARY
## or
## INTELLIGENCE SUMMARY.
(Erase heading not required.)

Instructions regarding War Diaries and Intelligence Summaries are contained in F. S. Regs., Part II. and the Staff Manual respectively. Title pages will be prepared in manuscript.

| Place | Date | Hour | Summary of Events and Information | Remarks and references to Appendices |
|---|---|---|---|---|
| | | 10 AM | Coy HQ closed at CALF RESERVE. | |
| | | | Gun teams moved independently to CANAL BK | |
| | 3rd | 3 AM | Teams & ally at CANAL BK. Poor accommodation very muddy | |
| | | | Two wounded men whoever wounded 3/7/17 to Hospital | |
| | | | Gun men many on journey down | |
| | | | Guns carried out | |
| | 4th | 6 AM | Orders received to move to School Camp (L.30. Central) Sheet 27 | |
| | | 7.30 AM | Transport came for stores. | |
| | | 9 AM | 17 troyles went by Bus from Reigersburg CHATEAU as advance | |
| | | | party to School Camp | |
| | | 11.30 AM | Coy paraded & marched to Asylum Siding, YPRES ventrained at | |
| | | 12 noon | to POPERINGHE. | |
| | | 1.30 PM | Detrained marched to School Camp. 3 Huts + 10 Tents. | |
| | | | Very muddy wet. | |
| | 5th | | Cleaning up equipment - Church Parade | |
| | | | 21 men attached to Coy from bde carrying coy | |

# WAR DIARY
or
# INTELLIGENCE SUMMARY.

Army Form C. 2118.

| Place | Date | Hour | Summary of Events and Information | Remarks and references to Appendices |
|---|---|---|---|---|
| | 6th | 6 AM | 4 Guns & Pitched from CANAL BR. previous Ex't TO 117 MGC | |
| | | 9 AM | Gun cleaning & checking Kit | |
| | | 11 AM | CO's Inspection | |
| | | | 10 men non attached from Bde. carrying Company | |
| | | 12 noon | Lt Doyle & NCO left for new Billets as advance party | |
| | | | Ground drying rapidly. | |
| | | 2-5 | Cleaning Guns Stores &c | |
| | | | Afternoon a draft of 1 offr 1 NCO & 7 men joined us from Cdn. MG Base Depot (Belgium & France) Sleeting | |
| | | 10.30 PM | Practice Gas alarm | |
| | 7th | | Cleaning Gunstores & packing Limbers — Dry day | |
| | 8th | 4.30 AM | Reveille | |
| | | 6.30 AM | Coy paraded & marched to HOPOUTRE SIDING | |
| | | 9 AM | Entrained — remainder of Bde. | |
| | | 10 AM | Detrained at CAESTRE — Motor Buses to Billets — compact — allotted in a barn remainder in tents — rain during leleure | |
| | | | Billets at LES 4 FILS D'AYMON — 5 allotted to Coy | |

# WAR DIARY or INTELLIGENCE SUMMARY

Army Form C. 2118.

| Place | Date | Hour | Summary of Events and Information | Remarks and references to Appendices |
|---|---|---|---|---|
| BILLETS X 4 c 4.4. (Bilg & Dunc Sheet 27) | 9th | | Transport proceeded by Road - arrived 1.30 PM. Dinners on arrival in Billets | |
| | | 9 AM | Paraded & marched to field at Bde HQ. for inspection by G.O.C. | |
| | | | 39 Bn. No inspection but addressed on development of Bde in | |
| | 10th | 12 Noon | recent operations. Very flattering comment. | |
| | | 5 AM | Lt Oates & 1/Lt Crosser proceeded by Bus to VOORMEZEELE to reconnoitre HOLLEBEKE Sector prior to relief | |
| | | 10.35 AM | Inspection by General Plumer & held at Bde HQ | |
| | | 12 Noon | C.O. & N.C.O. to VOORMEZEELE to reconnoitre | |
| | | | Gun cleaning & Drill — Reinforcements 2 ORs | |
| | 11th | Noon | Lt Evans & N.Co visited HOLLEBEKE Sector & made arrangements re relief of 4 guns 122 Coy & 1 gun & MM.G Battery | |
| | | | 7 Reinforcements | |
| | | | Coy. Training & prep. for move. | |
| | 12th | 4.30 AM | Reveille | |
| | | 8.30 AM | Coy left in Buses proceeded via METEREN & BAILLEUL TO | |

# WAR DIARY
## or
## INTELLIGENCE SUMMARY.

*(Erase heading not required.)*

Army Form C. 2118.

| Place | Date | Hour | Summary of Events and Information | Remarks and references to Appendices |
|---|---|---|---|---|
| RIDGE WOOD | | | RIDGE WOOD N.5.a (Map France 28 S.W.). Accommodation taken over from 140 Coy. Infants tents. Ordes for advance party tomorrow to hive. | |
| RIDGE WOOD | | 6.30PM | No.2 Lt Oats & 10 Nos. 1 left for line. | |
| | | 8.30PM | Orders to relieve 4th M.M.G Battery received. Guides to hand at 122 Bde HQ at 10PM — SPOIL BANK. | |
| N.S.a. | | 9.30PM | Lt Drayfer & 4 guns Teams, Lt Crozier & 3 Teams & Lt Stott & 3 Teams left for line. | |
| | | 11.30PM | Jeanmann. Bde HQ SPOIL Bk. No guides for 1,2,3,4,5,6 | |
| | 13th | 12.30AM | Lt Drayfer's relief of 4 Barrage guns completed | |
| | | 2.30AM | Guides for 1,2,3,4,5,6 arrived — Shelling heavy at Bde HQ 4 Casualties including 2 guides. | |
| | | 5AM | Offr of 4th MMS guided Teams to 4,5,6. relief completed. Relief of Teams 1,2,3 taken by Lt Evans to HQ 4th MMS. Reft there until dusk. | |

**Army Form C. 2118.**

# WAR DIARY
## or
## INTELLIGENCE SUMMARY.
*(Erase heading not required.)*

Instructions regarding War Diaries and Intelligence Summaries are contained in F. S. Regs., Part II. and the Staff Manual respectively. Title pages will be prepared in manuscript.

| Place | Date | Hour | Summary of Events and Information | Remarks and references to Appendices |
|---|---|---|---|---|
| DAMSTRASSE O 4 c.3.3 | 13 | 8.30 AM | Relief of 11, 3 posts commenced | |
| Map | | 10.30 AM | Relief complete. | |
| WYTSCHAETE | | | Coy & remainder of Coy. (including No 3 Sect=) at RIDGEWOOD. | |
| | | | following dispositions now of guns &c. | |
| | | | Map Reference | |
| | | | No. of Post | |
| | | | 1     O.6.c.27.17 | |
| | | | 2     O.5.c.75.15 | |
| | | | 3     O.11.a.10.45 | |
| | | | 4     O.5.c.15.70 | |
| | | | 5     O.S.c.20.20 | |
| | | | 6     O.S.c.25.10 | |
| | | | Two Barrage guns.  O.4.a.6.6.  'A' Battery | |
| | | | Coy H.Q.  O4 c.3.3. — | |
| | 14 | | Capt Jackson ntd to Coy H.Q.  SBR's for 2hrs 12.30 – 2.30 AM | |
| | | | Artillery active. | |

**Army Form C. 2118.**

# WAR DIARY
## or
## INTELLIGENCE SUMMARY.
*(Erase heading not required.)*

Instructions regarding War Diaries and Intelligence Summaries are contained in F. S. Regs., Part II. and the Staff Manual respectively. Title pages will be prepared in manuscript.

| Place | Date | Hour | Summary of Events and Information | Remarks and references to Appendices |
|---|---|---|---|---|
| | 14th | | No 2 Sect made Lt. Higginbottom relieved 'C' Battery on left Bank Canal — Jos Barragework attd to 228 MGCoy | |
| | 15th | | HQ shelled at night | |
| | 16th | 4.45AM | Some activity — S.a.a carried to posn. 6 Boys to each + 40 to Barrages M G Barrage & Joint Barrage fino — 4.45 – 5.15AM Zero hour of opertions on our left — heavy bombardment 7000 rds on O12.d.15.95 to O12.c.75.25. Heavy shelling | |
| | 17th | | OC 111 Coy MGC (B7 Dn) came to HQ re Relief Reconnaissance | |
| | | | 10/ft. 7000 R's new for cements | |
| | 18th | 9am | Heavy shelling 5.9's near HQ. 9 – 2.30PM | |
| | | 4PM | Relief of coy by 111 Coy due for tonight Cancelled | |
| | | 9PM | 2nd Lieut Flinn relief took place | |
| | | 12PN | | |
| | 19th | 4AM | 6 scouts on Enemy tracks to approaches. | |

Army Form C. 2118.

# WAR DIARY
## or
## INTELLIGENCE SUMMARY.
(Erase heading not required.)

| Place | Date | Hour | Summary of Events and Information | Remarks and references to Appendices |
|---|---|---|---|---|
| | 19 | 2/A | Enemy Planes bombing | |
| | | 13 AM | Lt M Symington 14 guns in action from C Battery to ground army Buses MD | |
| | 20 | | Guns mounted in St. ELOI Craters O.2.d.10.60. Heavy there — 6 men gassed. Whistling near dugout. Artillery active on both sides — Gas shells used. Armd Coy HQ Coy & R.E. Officer about looking for making Tunnel dug outs? N.9 enfaccaeys | |
| | 21st | | Battery active 7-11 am. Ammuncanc dbls. fixed at Coy H.P. OC 117 Coy visited cmp. Journey abt. Relief for 22/23. Lt. Hyg [illegible] O/C wagon lines vice Mr. Stuart to No. 1 sect. at ST.ELO! CRATERS. Army Nl. | |
| | 22nd | 3PM | Relief of Coy by 117 Coy NfC commenced | |
| | | 10PM | Relief complete — Casualties NIL Coy moved by sections on completion of Relief to RIDGE WOOD | |

# WAR DIARY
## or
## INTELLIGENCE SUMMARY.
*(Erase heading not required.)*

Army Form C. 2118.

| Place | Date | Hour | Summary of Events and Information | Remarks and references to Appendices |
|---|---|---|---|---|
| GROVE WOOD | 23rd | 9AM | Cleaning up + saddlebag + sound Tests v Bombing | |
| | | | Two guns mounted at front N.5.C.15. N.5.C.20.55 for anti-aircraft purposes — continuously | |
| | 24th | 5PM | Two guns movements cont. for a.a purposes | |
| | 25th | | Special complement of Lewis guns in Coy. | |
| | | | Cleaning + testing of musket &c | |
| | 26th | 5.45 AM | Relief of 118 Coy in left Sector — BATTLE WOOD — commenced | |
| | | | 12 guns in line — | |
| | | 10.40 PM | Relief completed. | |
| | | | Dispositions as follows— | |

| Right Group | | Centre Group | | Left Group | |
|---|---|---|---|---|---|
| No | | No | | No | |
| 8 | 0.5.c.68.15 | 2 | 06.a.58.20 | 11 | I.35.b.51.51 |
| 9 | 0.5.c.49.69 | 3 | I.36.c.28.13 | 12 | I.36.a.50.34 |
| 10 | I.35.d.20.30 | 4 | I.36.d.35.30 (SHP) | 13 | I.36.a.49.57 |
| 17 | 0.5.a.24.56 | 5 | I.36.d.40.40 | 18 (SHP) | I.35.a.72.82 |

Army Form C. 2118.

# WAR DIARY
## or
## INTELLIGENCE SUMMARY.
*(Erase heading not required.)*

Instructions regarding War Diaries and Intelligence Summaries are contained in F. S. Regs., Part II. and the Staff Manual respectively. Title pages will be prepared in manuscript.

| Place | Date | Hour | Summary of Events and Information | Remarks and references to Appendices |
|---|---|---|---|---|
| THE BLUFF T34.C.4.1 | 27 | | Wet — Ground in bad state | |
| | | | Reports in terrible condition | |
| | 28th | | Capt A.T. Jackson — on leave to Paris. | |
| | 29th | | Trench Routine — Enemy fairly quiet — very wet weather etc | |
| | 30th | | " " | |
| | | | O/R of 175 Lunelly by R.R. visited No 18 posts. decided at was moonlight considerable. | |
| | | | No 1 Sector relieved posts 10, 11, 12, 13, 18. | |
| | 31 | 7PM | Pte Oguald wounded in arm by sniper shot at Coy HQ. | |
| | | | Summary of Evidence taken | |
| | | | Bright day — increased aerial activity — enemy planes flying low — 500 rds fired at hostile aircraft. | |

W Suann Lt
o/c 116 M/G Coy
1/9/17

Original

Army Form C. 2118.

WAR DIARY
or
INTELLIGENCE SUMMARY.
(Erase heading not required.)

Vol 19

CONFIDENTIAL

WAR DIARY

of

116 Coy M.G. Corps

from Sept 1 – 30. 1917

# OPERATION ORDERS
## by
## CAPTAIN A.T. JACKSON
## COMMANDING 116 MGC

COPY No 10

REF MAP ZILLEBEKE 1/5000
SHEET 28NW Edition 6A

17/9/17

1. At ZERO hour on ATTACK day, the 117th Infantry Bde will attack the enemy on the 39th Divisional front.

2. The 116th MGC will co-operate as follows:—

No 1 and 4 Sections will assist in holding the line prior to and during the attack, and repel Counter-Attacks should occasion arise.

They will occupy the following positions:—

No 1 Section — R.1.2.3.4. Situated in I.29.d.

No 4 —,,— F.1.2. Situated in J.25.c. and S.1.2 Situated in I.30.d. a & c.

No 2 and 3 Sections will occupy the Barrage Emplacements constructed in vicinity of J.25.c.20.85. No 2 Sec.

occupying the Northern four beams will be numbered from the right (SOUTH)

The GROUP of 8 Guns will be commanded by Lieut. Fitzambleton and will be known as GROUP 2A (E BATTERY)

Lieut Sturt will command No 2 Sec
2/" Glendinning " No 3 do

3. The Group Commander (at J.15.d.30.85) will be in touch with the DMGO at LARCH WOOD on the buried cable.

4. Firing details are shown on APPENDIX A. They include calculations for all squares within gun range ready for "Switching".

5. A repair shop has been established in a dug-out at I.29.d.85.50

6. Ammunition in belts and bulk, water for drinking rations lubricating oil spare parts &c are being placed in the Battery HQ.

7. The Coy will assemble in its Battle Positions on D day
Detailed instructions will be issued separately

8. The ground in front of the Battery will be fixed, so to keep stragglers out of the Gun Danger Zone.

9. In the event of the S.O.S. signal being received after operations, all M.G.s will open fire on their final Barrage lines at the rate of one belt per gun in two minutes for 10 minutes, and thereafter, 50 rounds a minute until the situation is clear.

10. Detailed instructions for the Gunners are given in Appendix "B".

A. T. Jackson
Capt<sup>n</sup>
OC 116 MGC

Copy No 1 39<sup>th</sup> Div    Copy No 8 C.Q.M.S.
      2 116 Inf Bde          9 File
      3 OC No 1 Sec       10 Spare
      4 "     2 "
      5 "     3 "
            4 "
      7 Sgt Major

## "E" BATTERY

| No of Gun | TARGET | COMPASS BEARING | QUADRANT ELEVATION | DEGREES TRAVERSE | FIRING FROM TO | RATE OF FIRE per Gun |
|---|---|---|---|---|---|---|
| 1 | | | | | | |
| 2 | J 27 C | 105° | | | | |
|   | WOODED | 15 | 6° 10' | 4° | | |
| 3 | AREA | 109° | | | Issued Separately | |
| 4 | | | | | | |
| 5 | J 33 B | 114° | | | | |
|   | ALASKA | 15 | 9° | 3° | | |
| 6 | HOUSES | 117° | | | | |
| 7 | J 33 A | 123° | | | | |
|   | KENT | 15 | 5° 5' | 5° | | |
| 8 | FARM | 128° | | | | |

## "E" BATTERY SWITCH TARGETS

| TARGET | | Q.E. | BEARING | FROM ZERO | TARGET | | Q.E. | BEARING | FROM ZERO |
|---|---|---|---|---|---|---|---|---|---|
| J32 A | 1 | 5°5' | 90° | | J33 A | 1 | 4°40' | 117° |
| | 2 | 6°15' | 91° | | | 2 | 5°45' | 118° |
| | 3 | 4°40' | 97° | | | 3 | 5°15' | 123° |
| | 4 | 6°10' | 97° | | | 4 | 6°35' | 123° |
| J32 B | 1 | 8°10' | 93° | | J33 B | 1 | 8°0' | 115° |
| | 2 | 10°0' | 93° | | | 2 | 10°0' | 116° |
| | 3 | 7°45' | 98° | | | 3 | 8°50' | 118° |
| | 4 | 10°0' | 98° | | | 4 | 11°0' | 119° |
| J32 C | 1 | 4°15' | 103 | | J33 C | 1 | 5°45' | 129° |
| | 2 | 5°15' | 104 | | | 2 | 7°15' | 130° |
| | 3 | 4°10' | 110 | | | 3 | 6°30' | 133° |
| | 4 | 5°15' | 109 | | | 4 | 8°30' | 133° |
| J32 D | 1 | 7°30' | 104 | | J33 D | 1 | 7°30' | 125° |
| | 2 | 10°0' | 104 | | | 2 | 10°55' | 128° |
| | 3 | 7°35' | 109 | | | 3 | 10°55' | 129° |
| | 4 | 10°0' | 108 | | | 4 | | 127° |

## "E" BATTERY

| No. of Gun. | TARGET | COMPASS BEARING | QUADRANT ELEVATION | DEGREES TRAVERSE | FIRING FROM TO | RATE OF FIRE per Gun. |
|---|---|---|---|---|---|---|
| 1 } 2 } 3 } 4 } | J27c WOODED AREA | 105° to 109° | 6°10' | 4° | | Issued Separately |
| 5 } 6 } | J33B ALASKA HOUSES | 114° to 117° | 9° | 3° | | |
| 7 } 8 } | J33A KENT FARM | 123° to 128° | 5°5' | 5° | | |

## "E" BATTERY SWITCH TARGETS

| TARGET | | QE | BEAR-ING | FROM ZERO | TARGET | | QE | BEAR-ING | FROM ZERO |
|---|---|---|---|---|---|---|---|---|---|
| J27 A | 1 | 5°5' | 90° | | J 33 A | 1 | 4°40' | 117° | |
| | 2 | 6°15' | 91° | | | 2 | 5°45' | 116° | |
| | 3 | 4°40' | 97° | | | 3 | 5°15' | 123° | |
| | 4 | 6°10' | 97° | | | 4 | 6°25' | 123° | |
| J27 B | 1 | 8°10' | 93 | | J 33 B | 1 | 8°0' | 116° | |
| | 2 | 10°0' | 93 | | | 2 | 10°0' | 120° | |
| | 3 | 7°45' | 98 | | | 3 | 8°50' | 118° | |
| | 4 | 10°0' | 98 | | | 4 | 11°0' | 129° | |
| J27 C | 1 | 4°15' | 103 | | J 33 C | 1 | 5°45' | 127° | |
| | 2 | 5°15' | 104 | | | 2 | 7°15' | 134° | |
| | 3 | 4°10' | 110 | | | 3 | 6°35' | 135° | |
| | 4 | 5°15' | 109 | | | 4 | 8°30' | 133° | |
| J27 D | 1 | 7°20' | 104 | | J 33 D | 1 | 9°20' | 125 | |
| | 2 | 10°0' | 104 | | | 2 | 10°55' | 123 | |
| | 3 | 7°35' | 109 | | | 3 | 10°55' | 129 | |
| | 4 | 10°0' | 108 | | | 4 | - | 127 | |

# WAR DIARY
## or
## INTELLIGENCE SUMMARY.

Army Form C. 2118.

| Place | Date | Hour | Summary of Events and Information | Remarks and references to Appendices |
|---|---|---|---|---|
| BATTLE WOOD SECTOR 2 (BLUFF Tunnels) | 1. | | Trench Routine Inst Reps of positions checked | |
| | 2. | | Advance parties of 117 M.G. Coy. came to the line | |
| | 3. | 3.30 P.M | Relief by 117 M.G.C. commenced | |
| | | 10 P.M | Relief complete. Teams returned to RIDGE WOOD CAMP N.5. Central | |
| | 4. | 12.15 AM | all ranks to Bamboo encamp | |
| | | | Cleaning up &c. | |
| | 5. | | Inspection & testing of S.B.R's in gas chamber. | |
| | 6. | | Coy training – Checked stores – lecture by O.C. as a petance | |
| | 7. | 10 AM | One man of 9 under age to have – two to relief of 118 MG Coy in SHREWSBURY FOREST Sec. ion | |
| | | 4 PM | 1st Section left RIDGE WOOD for line others following at shown intervals | |
| | | 10.30 PM | Relief Complete | |
| LARCH WOOD Tn. C.15.55 | | | Dispositions as follows 2 AA. at N.P. | |
| | | | I.30.c.88.10, I.30.a.85.00, I.13.d.18.30, J.25.a.60.68, J.25.a.50.37 | |
| | | | J.25.a.35.25, J.25.b.45.95, J.25.b.26.80, J.25.b.30.72, J.25.c.78.36 | |

# WAR DIARY
## or
## INTELLIGENCE SUMMARY.
(Erase heading not required.)

Army Form C. 2118.

| Place | Date | Hour | Summary of Events and Information | Remarks and references to Appendices |
|---|---|---|---|---|
| | 8 | | 9.25.C.80.60 Qu at HQ. I.29.C.15.85 Reconnaissance on enemy tracks carried out throughout S/9 | |
| | 9 | | One fatal cast. of shaken by shellfire | |
| | 10 | | Manoeuvres | |
| | 11 | | LARCH WOOD shelled – Gas shells | |
| | 12 | 10AM | 5 reconnoitred by 117 M.G.C + proceeded to CHIPPEWA CAMP Remainder of Coy relieved by 117 M.G.C | |
| | | | Shelling – 3 casualties on convoy out | |
| | | | L.t Stubbs reconnoitred line to construct emplacements | |
| CHIPPEWA CAMP | 13 | 4–6 | Baths | |
| | | PM | M.G. Gunnery remedial | |
| | 14 | noon | Orders received to reinforce Lieutenant by 1 P.M | |
| | | 1 P.M | whole 117 Inf Bde | |
| | | 4.30 | Teams moved up to SHREWSBURY FOREST SECTOR | |
| | | 10.30 | Relief complete | |
| | | | L.t Hunt & men out of doors working emplacements I.S/N Barrage fire | OC |

**Army Form C. 2118.**

# WAR DIARY
## or
## INTELLIGENCE SUMMARY.
*(Erase heading not required.)*

| Place | Date | Hour | Summary of Events and Information | Remarks and references to Appendices |
|---|---|---|---|---|
| | 15 | 8AM | Harassing fire on enemy tracks with 9 guns throughout night Practice Artillery Barrage & M.G. at zero time | |
| | | 4PM | do | |
| | 16 | 10AM | Harassing fire on Enemy tracks by night – mine guns Practice Barrage | |
| | | 6PM | " " 13th R.S. Regt | |
| | | | Harassing fire on enemy tracks + communications during the night | |
| | | | 4 guns relieved by teams from 124th bty Coy and by 122 Coy | |
| | | | 3, 4, by 122   11, 83, 54, 59, by 122 Coy – 41st Divn. | |
| | | | one to come JACKSON'S Dump at 8 + 11 AM | |
| | | | late parade costumes | |
| | 17 | 11AM | Relief complete by guns relieved into Bde Reserve at Coy HQ | O.T.7 |
| | | 5.30AM | Practice Barrage | |
| | | 3PM | " | |
| | | | McLeatts left Coy + assumes of duties with 117 MGC | |

Army Form C. 2118.

# WAR DIARY
## or
## INTELLIGENCE SUMMARY.
*(Erase heading not required.)*

| Place | Date | Hour | Summary of Events and Information | Remarks and references to Appendices |
|---|---|---|---|---|
| | 17 | | Commenced rolling Belt Boys 70 Barrage Positions Cavalho one. | |
| | | | Harassing fire on Enemy Tracks throughout the night — 30000 rds | |
| | 18 | 8 AM | Army Barrage 8 guns cooperated on enemy Trackes | |
| | | 2 PM | Completed mounting of Control on Plateale | |
| | | | Saigne a 9 day 1er No 1 | |
| | | | Enemy aircraft active — engaged by our MG 11457th | |
| | | | 2/Lt Kolo came to camp H.Q. & 2/Lt Montgomery joined Co | |
| | | 8.30 M | Practice Army Barrage | |
| | | | Droops of MG Bde moving up the line | |
| | 19 | 7 AM | 116 Bde relieved 117 Bde MG | |
| | | | All guns in Battle Positions — 2 at Mt Sorrel (SOS) 2 in front line & Reserve Posts ZWARTELEN (ad) & 8 in Barrage Positions under Lt Higginbotham Battery commander | a.Y |
| | | | Barrage fire controlled by phone — by DAJO at Bde HQrs | |

Army Form C. 2118.

# WAR DIARY
## or
## INTELLIGENCE SUMMARY.
*(Erase heading not required.)*

Instructions regarding War Diaries and Intelligence Summaries are contained in F.S. Regs., Vol. II. and the Staff Manual respectively. Title pages will be prepared in manuscript.

| Place | Date | Hour | Summary of Events and Information | Remarks and references to Appendices |
|---|---|---|---|---|
| Lapech | 19 | | 4 guns in position E of Barrage position orders for Attack issued & attended - & su. Int Tops TS | |
| WOOD | 20 | 5.40AM | Zero. Barrage put down in attached Table | |
| | | 6.24 | Intense fire — 6.24 — 7.8 slow 7.8/7.8 — 7.32 intense 7.32 — 9.53 protective — 9.53 — 10.15 Intense 10.15 — 10.53 (slow) The guns then remained in position ready to switch on to enemy massing for counter attack. Already SMLG very accurate Conj with in.s.cycs barrage. Shallower & especially to MJ Coys. concerned & barrage covered 17 Bde. Enemy clothing seen through at times but our C.S. not effective - not effective chiefly dim out. | |
| | 21 | AM | orders from Adam To camp NG6 | |
| | 22 | 6AM | orders to go to all ests | O.T. |
| | | 10.15AM | bn. less LieuT JACKSONS BOMB proceeded To Camp NG6 | |

# WAR DIARY
## or
## INTELLIGENCE SUMMARY.
(Erase heading not required.)

Army Form C. 2118.

| Place | Date | Hour | Summary of Events and Information | Remarks and references to Appendices |
|---|---|---|---|---|
| | 22 | | Men billeted in afts. | |
| | 23 | 10 AM | Church Parade — Cleaning guns re. | |
| | | 7 PM | Orders received to relieve 7 mg Coy in DUMBARTON LAKES Sector ZILLEBEKE 1 od. + 3 guns of 68 MG Coy in same area. Relief completed 4h. Heavy shelling — 4 OR 12 Killed 4 OR W. | |
| | | | Enemy bombarded MT. SORREL all day | |
| | 24 | | Heavy shelling. OS wounded. | |
| | 25 | | 1 gun tripod destroyed — 6 ORs wounded in front line | |
| | 26 | 5.50 AM | 39 Div attacked TOWER HAMLETS Ridge — 118 RT — 116 LT. | |
| | | | 116 Coy held Rahure — no news all day | |
| | 27 | 5 AM | Reports from Sect. offrs. — one team missing believed prisoners 117 WT reconnected front line but did not move forward — 112 W | |
| | | | one gun destroyed — Teams buried — Evening quiet | |
| | | | Rations + water got up under officers parties | |
| | | | Two guns sent to MENIN Rd. 1 destroyed on route | A1 |
| | 28 | | Relieved by 111 MG Coy — complete 9 PM | |

Army Form C. 2118.

# WAR DIARY
## or
## INTELLIGENCE SUMMARY.
*(Erase heading not required.)*

| Place | Date | Hour | Summary of Events and Information | Remarks and references to Appendices |
|---|---|---|---|---|
| | 28 | 10PM | Lorries conveyed men from BUS HOUSE near SHRAPNEL CORNER to FRONTIER Camp M.13.c.9.9. | |
| | 29 | 3AM | all company in camp. Resting &c. all day. | |
| | 30 | 8-9AM | Baths — Cleaning & football | |

A. T. Jackson
Captain
OC. 116 M.G.C.

Army Form C. 2118.

# WAR DIARY
## or
## INTELLIGENCE SUMMARY.
*(Erase heading not required.)*

Vol 20

War Diary
116 M.G. Coy.
CONFIDENTIAL
Oct 1st — Oct 31st 1917

Original

# WAR DIARY
## or
## INTELLIGENCE SUMMARY.
(Erase heading not required.)

Army Form C. 2118.

Instructions regarding War Diaries and Intelligence Summaries are contained in F. S. Regs., Part II. and the Staff Manual respectively. Title pages will be prepared in manuscript.

| Place | Date | Hour | Summary of Events and Information | Remarks and references to Appendices |
|---|---|---|---|---|
| MT. KOKEREKE | 1 | Am 9-11 | Mustering & cleaning of all stores | |
| | | 11.45 | Co's inspection — Recreation in aft. football — | |
| | | | Draft of 40 arrived good type of men. | |
| | 2 | 9 Am | Co's inspection issue of clothing — Coy Training | |
| | | 2.30 Pm | Inspection of Btn. by G.O.C. 39th Bn "M" | |
| | 3 | | Coy Training 9-1 Rumoured — P.T. lectures — 2/Lt Pritchard joined Coy | |
| | 4 | 8 AM | Capt Jackson left to take over duties as instructor in Anuna | |
| | 5 | 9 AM | Inspection — 10 AM — 11 AM — Gas demonstration & gun instruction in tents | |
| | 6 | | Very wet — route march & gun instruction | |
| | 7 PM | | NAHARA Lt. E. ROTHWELL joined Coy & resumed command | |
| | 7 | 11 AM | Church Parades — Very wet all day | |
| | 8 | 9 AM } 10 AM } | Co's inspection — staffing — PT — march discipline — ED. | |
| | | 2 — | Co's address — filling of equipment | |
| | | 3 | Lecture N.C.O's & off. Rooks Matinee | |
| | 9 | 9 AM | Route march 8 miles & in order | |

Army Form C. 2118.

# WAR DIARY
## or
## INTELLIGENCE SUMMARY.
(Erase heading not required.)

Instructions regarding War Diaries and Intelligence Summaries are contained in F. S. Regs., Part II. and the Staff Manual respectively. Title pages will be prepared in manuscript.

| Place | Date | Hour | Summary of Events and Information | Remarks and references to Appendices |
|---|---|---|---|---|
| | 9 | 2 PM | Revolver Instruction — Sqn drill &c | |
| | 10 | | Training near Billets | |
| | 11 | 9-1 | " | |
| | | 2-5 | Revolver firing on Range | |
| | 12 | 5.30 | Route march — 10 miles — very wet am/pm | |
| | | 2-4 | Revolver firing & Drill &c | |
| | 13 | 9-1 | Coy training — orders received to move at 2 PM 14th to camp at NQ l.ca.Im | |
| | | 11 PM | move orders cancelled | |
| | 14 | 8 AM | Co. Sect. officers to line. Reconnaissance prior to Relief of MG Coy in TOWER HAMLETS Sector | |
| | | | In the field 2/Lt G MONTGOMERY killed during reconnaissance | |
| | 15 | | Coy Training — Prep for line | |
| | 16 | 11 PM | Coy less details entrained at FRONTIER Camp for Dehune | |
| | | 2 PM | Transport details moved to BEAVER Camp N.15.a (Sheet 28) | |
| | | 5.30 PM | Relief of 63 MG Coy commenced — TOWER HAMLETS SECTOR | |

# WAR DIARY
## or
## INTELLIGENCE SUMMARY.
(Erase heading not required.)

Army Form C. 2118.

| Place | Date | Hour | Summary of Events and Information | Remarks and references to Appendices |
|---|---|---|---|---|
| Coy HQ CANADA TUNNELS | | | Relief successful - no casualties. Bell-Boys Infants Take one 15" nine & one 1 at Coy HQ in reserve. Guns divided into 3 groups each under an officer. G. Battery 6 guns. Map Refs. T.19.b.80.05 (2 guns) T.19.d.6.5 (2 guns) T.19.d.60.65 (2 guns). H. Battery 4 guns. MAP REFS. JAFFA TR (Support Line) T.26.a. ends. I & J Batteries 5 guns. Map Refs. T.20.c.8.3 (2) T.21. central (3). Relief complete at 9.10 pm. Company numerous & found difficulty in finding their Battery positions & guns to duckboard tracks being destroyed. Mounted Orderly & Rations | |
| | 17 | | | |

# WAR DIARY
## or
## INTELLIGENCE SUMMARY.
*(Erase heading not required.)*

Army Form C. 2118.

| Place | Date | Hour | Summary of Events and Information | Remarks and references to Appendices |
|---|---|---|---|---|
| | | 6.30 pm | Enemy laid ours to heavy shelling in previous traffic | |
| | | 7.0 pm | Others to move Coy HQ next day to HEDGE STREET TUNNELS - Pte Chalmers gassed. | |
| | 18 | 2.40 am | Warned before to co-operate with Artillery in barrage from 5.30 to 6 am as enemy attack expected. Batteries warned to "Stand to". | |
| | | 1.35 am | Pte Williams (No 1 Section) wounded. Batteries fired as above orders. | |
| | | 11 am | Pte Glendinning wounded. 130 & 7 Ambulance. | |
| HEDGE STREET TUNNELS | 19 | 3 noon | Coy HQ moved to HEDGE STREET TUNNELS, 9 established by 2.30 pm | |
| | | 11 am | C.O. toured the battery front lines. | |
| | 20 | 3.30 pm | Relief orders received. 7.30 "9" Battery fired on S.O.S. | |
| | | | O.C. in ca[n]ary ward in tears over | |
| | | 3.35 pm | One Sec of No 1 Section landed. | |

# WAR DIARY
## or
## INTELLIGENCE SUMMARY

Army Form C. 2118.

| Place | Date | Hour | Summary of Events and Information | Remarks and references to Appendices |
|---|---|---|---|---|
| WILLEBEEK Sheet 28 M9d.7.5 | 21 | 8.30 am | Relief complete - no casualties | |
| | | 9.30 | All men in camp at N.9.d.7.5 (Sheet 28) | |
| | | 11.30 | 2/Lt Evans proceeded on leave | |
| | 22 | 8.45 am | Tool Inspection | |
| | | 10.0 | C.O. 2/8 Cay arranged to discuss forthcoming operations | |
| | | | Tents arranged for protection against strafing | |
| | | 5.40 pm | 5th/Alpha Battn relieved from line | |
| | | | Enemy Aeroplanes bombed vicinity of camp | |
| | | 9 am | Reveille | |
| | | 9.30 | C.O.s Inspection | |
| | | 10.30 | Checking & reloading from Kit | |
| | | 11.30 | Baggage Drill | |
| | | 12 | P.T. | |
| | | | Belt filling | |
| | | 12.30 | Gas Stripping | |
| | | | C.O. visits Brigade HQ re 7th & 39th Div | |
| | | | to meet DMGOs N.Q. T.O.C. 2/8 Cay re impending | |

# WAR DIARY or INTELLIGENCE SUMMARY

Army Form C. 2118.

| Place | Date | Hour | Summary of Events and Information | Remarks and references to Appendices |
|---|---|---|---|---|
| | 23. | 9 pm | Operation map & range tables received. Operation orders issued. E.A's again bombing but not in vicinity of camp. | |
| | | 9 am | C.O.s inspection. Preparing for line. Men to baths. Orders to move up the line on 24th inst. received. (Battalion attached to 9th Division then Res.) | |
| | 24 | 12.30 pm | Company moved off at 10.45 a.m. to relieve 228 & 229 Coys in the TOWER HAMLETS SECTOR, taking over "A" & "B" & "D" Batteries. Coy HQ in HEDGE STREET TUNNELS. | |
| HEDGE ST TUNNEL | | 2.30 pm | C.O. arrived HEDGE STREET at 2.30 pm. Eight Pigeons & Lofts taken over. "D" Battery relief complete | No Casualties |
| | | 2.45 | "B" " " | |
| | | 2.55 | "A" " " | |
| | | | Map References. "A" Battery (4 guns)  J.25.B.3.8. | |
| | | | "B" " (4 guns)  J.25.a.55.30. | |
| | | | "D" " (8 guns)  J.25.a.35.80. | |
| | 25.6. | 5.50 am | Three O.R.s wounded at D Battery. One gun damaged. C.O. visited all Batteries. Battery positions improved by the C.R.E. trenches dug, duckboards laid. Total time used on outdoor work, Telephone wires displaced. | |

FIRING REPORT  116 M.G.Coy.  26 Oct 1917  5.43 a.m to 8.18 a.m.

| Battery | Gun | Belts | Rounds | Remarks |
|---|---|---|---|---|
| "A" | 1 | 20 | 5000 | Gun fired very well. 2 slight overjerks & 1 Broken Lock Spring. |
| | 2 | 1 | — | Punctured Barrel casing. Returned to D.A.D.O.S. Gas gun did not arrive in time. |
| | 3 | 22 | 5500 | Fired very well. 2 Separated Cases. |
| | 4 | 19 | 4750 | Fired extremely well. No stoppages. |
| "B" | 1 | 20 | 5000 | ⎫ |
| | 2 | 22 | 5500 | ⎬ Gun fired very well indeed. |
| | 3 | 20 | 5000 | ⎭ |
| | 4 | 3 | 750 | Crank pin worked out causing prolonged stoppage. |
| "D" | 1 | 20 | 5000 | No trouble |
| | 2 | 20 | 5000 | do |
| | 3 | 19 | 4750 | A few No 4 Stoppages - Worn trigger bar suspected |
| | 4 | 19 | 4750 | A few No 3 Stoppages |
| | 5 | 19 | 4750 | Muzzle Attachment blew off, but carried on. |
| | 6 | 19 | 4750 | No stoppages. |
| | 7 | 21 | 5250 | 1 Extractor Broke & 1 Firing pin |
| | 8 | 21 | 5250 | A few stoppages. Bad ammn suspected. |
| | | Total | 71,000 | |

26/10/17
E. Nothnell Lt
O.C. 116 M.G.C

26° Oct 1917

## Barrage Table of Battery (No 2 Battery 1st Gun)

| N° | Position of Target | Gun Range Correct Wind Mini/Min | Tang¹ Corr¹ Mini/Min | V.I. | Q.E. | Time Before Opening | M/S Bearing | Change | Times & Rates of Fire (All Guns) |
|---|---|---|---|---|---|---|---|---|---|
| 1 | Target | 2400 | 57 | 32 | — | 25m 20' 10" | 117° | 19° 30' | 200ˣ | from +3ʰ +4ʰ 10ʲᵘ to 4/min<br>+4ʰ +5ʰ 6 rds per min<br>+5ʰ +6ʰ 8 rd/m 4/min<br>+6ʰ +10ʰ 4 rd/m<br>+10ʰ +20ʰ 20 rds per min<br>All guns remain on Battery |

### (For Zones of Battery Shifting Barrage from Barrage Line) (whichever also S-S. Line) as ordered

| N° | Position of Target | Gun Range Correct for Wind Mini/Min | Tang¹ Corr¹ for Wind Mini/Min | V.I. | by E. | Time Before Opening | M/S Bearing | Change | Times & Rates of Fire (All Guns) |
|---|---|---|---|---|---|---|---|---|---|
| 1 | Target | 2500 | 57 | 40 | -11 | 2° 30' | 110° | 30° | 39ˣ | S-cal-S |
| 2 | | 2500 50'+2 1710 | 46 | 45 | -11 | 3° 30' | 111° | 30° | 42ˣ | 1st 10min +4 rds/min 2 min<br>20 rds per min |
| 3 | | 2750 +99 1900 | 9a | 50 | -11 | 3° 30' | 113° | 30° | 62ˣ | Fire will then cease unless situation is<br>very obscure, when fire will be reopened<br>at 3rds per gun until the situation is clear |
| 4 | | 2550 +99 2200 | 9a | 45 | -19 | 4° 30' | 113° | 30° | 85ˣ | |

+0.46.40 -310.47   E Jordan

## BARRAGE TABLE "B" BATTERY (Hostile Barrage Lines)

| No of Gun | Position of Gun | Position of Target | Range | Gun Contour Metres | Target Contour Metres | V.I. | Q.E. | True Bearing | Mag Bearing | Mag Clearance | Traverse Rates of Fire (Full Gun) |
|---|---|---|---|---|---|---|---|---|---|---|---|
| 1 | J25a 55.30 | J27a 90.95 | 2200 | 50 | 45 | -5 | 5°10' | 94° | 106°30' | 76* | |
| 2 | do | J2761.0 | 2250 | do | 45 | -5 | 5°30' | 93°30' | 106° | 88* | From +3 to +15 |
| 3 | do | J2762.0 | 2350 | do | 42 | -8 | 6°10' | 93° | 105°30' | 96* | 1 Blt in 4 min |
| 4 | do | J2764 5.05 | 2400 | do | 40 | -10 | 6°30' | 93° | 105°30' | 106* | |

At Z+15, change to lines assumed. – This is also your SOS line

| No of Gun | Position of Gun | Position of Target | Range | Gun Contour Metres | Target Contour Metres | V.I. | Q.E. | True Bearing | Mag Bearing | Mag Clearance | Traverse Rates of Fire (Full Gun) |
|---|---|---|---|---|---|---|---|---|---|---|---|
| 1 | J25a 55.30 | J27a 90.55 | 2250 | 50 | 40 | -10 | 5°30' | 99°30' | 112° | 94* | +15 to +44 – 1 Blt in 4 Min |
| 2 | do | J272a 05.55 | 2350 | do | 40 | -10 | 5°30' | 99° | 111°30' | 109* | +44–+76 – 20 rds per min |
| 3 | do | J27d 2.6 | 2350 | do | 38 | -12 | 6°0' | 98°30' | 111° | 112* | +76 – +110 – 1 Blt in 4 Min |
|  |  |  |  |  |  |  |  |  |  |  | +110 – +136 – 20 rds per min |
| 4 | do | J27d 4.6 | 2400 | do | 38 | -12 | 6°30' | 98° | 110°30' | 125* | SOS (after Z+136) |

1st +10 min – 1 Blt in 2 min
2nd +10 – ,, – 20 rds per min

Gas will then cease unless the situation is very obscure, when fire will be maintained at the rate of 20 rds per min until the situation is clear.

E. Mitchell Lt.
O.C. No 1 G.C.Y.

23-10-17

# WAR DIARY
## or
## INTELLIGENCE SUMMARY.

(Erase heading not required.)

Army Form C. 2118.

| Place | Date | Hour | Summary of Events and Information | Remarks and references to Appendices |
|---|---|---|---|---|
| | | 5.30 p.m | 2Lt D.M.G.O visited C.O. re future operations & announced Zero as 5.40 a.m tomorrow | |
| | 26 | 12.30 a.m | Casualty report received from "A" Battery – 4 O.Rs Killed and 4 O.Rs wounded – all No 2. Section Teams made up from "B" Battery & spare numbers and gun teams | |
| | | 5.40 a.m | Zero - all guns fired S.O.S lines out to original | |
| | | 8 a.m | O.C. Division changes S.O.S lines & promised relief of Company | |
| | 27 | 7 a.m | Relief orders received from D.H.Q. 7th Division – To be relieved as follows:- "A" Battery to run (Dram) "B" " " relieved by 4 June 22 m.g.C "D" " " " " 220 m.g.C. Relief complete at 12.45 pm. O.C. left HEDGE ST TUNNELS at 4 p.m. Company reached CHAMPION CAMP at 5.30 p.m. No casualties. Between gun equipment handover | |
| CHAMPION CAMP. | 28 | 6 a.m | 1 Sgt & 10 O.Rs left camp for HEDGE ST & VOORMEZEELE to | |

# WAR DIARY
## or
## INTELLIGENCE SUMMARY.

Army Form C. 2118.

(Erase heading not required.)

| Place | Date | Hour | Summary of Events and Information | Remarks and references to Appendices |
|---|---|---|---|---|
| | | | Collected guns & tripods & all boxes handed over in exchange by 22 & 220 M.G. Coys. | |
| | | 9.30am | Parade. Cleaning equipment & guns & protecting tents against bombing. Warning order received to move to CHIPPEWA CAMP tomorrow. No Strict sent on to take over. | |
| | | 6pm | Men from HEDGE ST TUNNELS with guns, tripods & all boxes. | |
| | 29.9 | 9am | Company preceded by march route to CHIPPEWA CAMP – arriving there at 10.25 a.m. | |
| CHIPPEWA CAMP | | | C.O. visited Battalion Commanders re future operations. | |
| | | 3pm | G.O.C. Brigade visited the Camp. All Ranks protected against bombs. Four military medals awarded. | |
| | 30 | | Parade. | |
| | | 9am | CO's Inspection – Rifle Order. | |
| | | 9.30 | Re-organizing teams rebuilding guns stores etc | |

**Army Form C. 2118.**

# WAR DIARY
## or
## INTELLIGENCE SUMMARY.
*(Erase heading not required.)*

Instructions regarding War Diaries and Intelligence Summaries are contained in F. S. Regs., Part II. and the Staff Manual respectively. Title pages will be prepared in manuscript.

| Place | Date | Hour | Summary of Events and Information | Remarks and references to Appendices |
|---|---|---|---|---|
| | | 11 am | Range drill. | |
| | | 12.0 | Physical Training. | |
| | | 12.30 | Reconstruction | |
| | | 2 pm | Stripping | |
| | | 3.0 | Re-Loading of Limbers. | |
| | | | Draft of 9 men arrived. Mostly men over forty-first time. | |
| | 31 | 8.30 am | Route March | |
| | | 1 pm | Foot Inspection | |
| | | 2.30 | Stripping | |
| | | 3.30 | Billet Inspection by C.O. | |
| | | E. | As bombed vicinity of camp at 5.15 a.m. | |

G H Higginbotham Lt
Fr O.C. 116 M.G.C.

H.Q.,
7th Division.

4. 11. 17.

My dear Clokey,

Would you please convey to all Officers, N.C.Os. & men of the 116th M.G.Coy. my sincerest thanks for the very great assistance they gave me in the battle of the 26th Oct. and for the help they gave me before the 26th in holding the line.

They carried out the tasks given them in a most excellent manner, and I was extremely pleased with their work.

Lieut. Rothwell was extremely good & helped me in every way possible — as well as looking after my bodily comforts when I was stationed at Hedge Street.

Yourself, too, I wish to thank for all the help you gave me especially as regards the ammunition supply.

I hope I may have the chance of repaying you at some future date.

May the best of luck be with you.

I am,

Yours very sincerely,

(sd) J.C.M.MATHESON.
D.M.G.O., 7th Division.

-------------------------------------------------------

G.1842

Officer Commanding,
116th M. G. Company.

--------------

For your information.

Captain.
a/Brigade Major,
116th Infantry Brigade.

9/11/17.

Original

Army Form C. 2118.

Vol 21

# WAR DIARY
## or
## INTELLIGENCE SUMMARY.
(Erase heading not required.)

War Diary

1st to 30th November
1917

116th Coy M.G. Corps

# WAR DIARY
## or
## INTELLIGENCE SUMMARY.
*(Erase heading not required.)*

Army Form C. 2118.

| Place | Date | Hour | Summary of Events and Information | Remarks and references to Appendices |
|---|---|---|---|---|
| CHIPPEWA CAMP | 1st | | Parade. | |
| | | 7.30 a.m | Foot Rubbing Drill | |
| | | 9.0 a.m. | CO's Inspection - Drill Order | |
| | | 9.30 | Intensive digging renovation of M.Gs emplacements | |
| | | 11.0 | Barrage Drill | |
| | | 12.0 p.m | Inwards Games | |
| | | 12.30 | Review Instruction | |
| | | 2.0 p.m. | Packing limbers, preparing to move to new Lands. | |
| | | | D.S. unit | |
| | | 3.0 p.m. | Shipping day by declaration. Eridus & Pumira under O.C | |
| | | 6.0 p.m. | N.Cos marching in S.B.R. (Gas Troops will be carried Lifelines). | |
| | | 7.30 p.m | Foot Rubbing Drill. Staff Lettering Party for duty (Snow Party) | |
| | 2 | 5.30 a.m | Early morning March | |

# WAR DIARY
## or
## INTELLIGENCE SUMMARY.
(Erase heading not required.)

Army Form C. 2118.

Instructions regarding War Diaries and Intelligence Summaries are contained in F.S. Regs., Part II. and the Staff Manual respectively. Title pages will be prepared in manuscript.

| Place | Date | Hour | Summary of Events and Information | Remarks and references to Appendices |
|---|---|---|---|---|
| | | 9 am | C.O's inspection Red Huts | |
| | | 9.15 am | Bayonet drill | |
| | | 10.0 am | Swedish games | |
| | | 10.30 " | Route march & instruction | |
| | | 11.45 | March to baths at AZEBROUKE | |
| | 3 | 2.45 | Coy of a supply Column on pl. Blue & No. 2 Cos. under Lt. Coffey Coy. attached to an Eng. on Pioneer work |  |
| | | 9.13 | C.O.s inspection | |
| | | 9.30 | Bayonet drill | |
| | | 9.30 | C.O's & C.O Battle Coms. ordered to Reco. of relief. | |
| | | | 1st Rows relieves from Reserve. Orders received to relieve 118 mfg C in the line tomorrow. | |
| | 4 | 9.30 am | C.O's inspection of billeting order. | |
| | | | Entrained for the line at 2pm from Hts at CHIPPAWA CAMP | |
| | | | to relieve 118th mfg O. Six funds at C Battery – relief complete | |
| | | | at 5.30pm. Two funs in JAVA TRENCH – relief complete 5pm | |

# WAR DIRY or INTELLIGENCE SUMMARY.

Army Form C. 2118.

| Place | Date | Hour | Summary of Events and Information | Remarks and references to Appendices |
|---|---|---|---|---|
| HEDGE ST TUNNEL | | | Three guns in AMBROSE STUTE FARMS. Two guns on MENIN ROAD & one at DUMBARTON LANES. Wires relief complete 7.20 p.m. Coy H.Q. established at HEDGE ST TUNNELS at 4.40 p.m. No casualties. Orders received to co-operate in operations at 4 am | |
| | 5.11.17 | | "B" Battery to fire "B" Battery co-operates in operation by firing from 4.50 to 5.10 am on barrage line. 13750 rounds fired. D.M.G.O. visits H.Q. C.O. to "B" Battery to check barrage line. Verbal orders received from DHQ regarding future operations. | |
| | 6. | 6.3 am | BASSWOOD farm fixed at ranged fire, 1500 rounds IMA TRENCH 3 guns & "G" Battery 1 gun fired in co-operation with artillery from 6 am to 6.45 am firing 21,000 rounds. F.g. Battery guns slightly wounded. No wire received | |

Copy 13

Operation Order No. 5.

M.E. Robinson Lieut S.
116 Coy M.G Corps.   7-11-17

Ref: Map. SHREWSBURY FOREST.

I. The 119th M.G Coy will relieve 8 guns of the 116th Coy on the night of the 8/9th inst in the TOWER HAMLETS SECTOR.

II. The guns at "C" Battery & the TAVA TRENCH guns will change places with the guns of 119th Coy now at "A" & "B" Batteries as follows:—
  (a) Two guns now at TAVA TRENCH & two guns of "C" Battery under LT OUTLER will change place with the guns of 119 Coy now at "B" Battery. LT OUTLER will make his own arrangements as to time of moving.
  (b) Four guns of "C" Battery under 2/LT PRITCHARD will relieve 4 guns of "A" Battery (119 Coy). 2/LT PRITCHARD will also make his own arrangements as to

time of moving.

**III** The teams at "A" & "B" Batteries will consist of three men per team with one spare at Battery H.Q. All spare men will be sent down to Bgde H.Q. immediately & post of as complete.

**IV** 2/Lt PRITCHARD will make arrangements for his 4th team, at present at PAYTIS FM, under Lt STURT, to be met at junction of "A" & "B" tracks by a guide at 5 p.m. as they come down "A" track after being relieved from PAYTIS FM by "C" Coy. This team will join "A" Battery. Lt STURT will give instructions to this team to look for the guide at junction of "A" & "B" tracks.

**V** These two batteries will come under command of O.C. 228th Coy as soon as relief is complete.

**VI** <u>Rations for these 2 Batteries (A & B)</u>

will send a party every evening to the end of the sleeper track at MT SORREL at 2.15 pm daily.

VII. Torpedo & Bell Boxes will be exchanged & Lt CUTLER & 2/LT PRITCHARD will forward their TRENCH STORES LISTS & HANDING OVER CERTIFICATES to Coy HQ as soon as relief is complete.

VIII. Petrol Tins at JAVA TR & "G" Battery will be conveyed to "A" & "B" Batteries. No petrol tins will be taken over there from 117 Coy.

IX. Reports. The usual reports will go in to 228th Coy HQ from "A" & "B" Battery Commanders

X. Guides from Lt STORT, 2/LTS CROSSER & HALE will meet Coy on the sleeper track at MT SORREL at 4 pm. Two Guides only from each officer will be necessary & they will guide the relieving teams to their respective section HQ

from whence they will be
taken to the Gun positions.

XI. Relief Tins will be handed
over filled at each Gun
position. Section Officers
will see that all tins are
filled up at Cup H.R on the
morning of the 8th inst.

XII. All maps, lines of fire
map refs of S.A.A. dumps
will be handed over
together with Trench Stores
lists & receipts obtained.

XIII. The Transport Officer will
arrange to have two empty
limbers on the end of the
sleeper track at NIT S.A.A Res.
at 5.45 pm. (8th)

XIV. All teams when relieved,
will load their Guns &
Gun kit on these limbers
& proceed to SHRAPNEL CORNER
where they will entrain
for CHIPPAWA CAMP.

XV. 2/Lt GABBEY will meet the limbers at 5.45 pm & see that all Gun Kit is loaded up before the limbers move off.

XVI. If the limbers are not at the end of the sleeper line 2 teams will proceed down the track until they meet it.

XVII. Officers will complete & hand in their receipts etc at Coy HQ on their way out.

XVIII. Guides must be given full written instructions containing names of their officers & gun positions.

XIX. ACKNOWLEDGE.

Issued at 10 pm 7/4/7.  
Lt Higginbottom M  
for O.C. 116 T.M.B.

Copy 1 to O.C.  Copy 9 to T.O.
" 2. 2/Lt Carden  " 8. 116 Bde HQ
" 3. Lt Stait  " 9. 39 D. M.G.O.
" 4. 2/Lt Crossan  " 10. O.C. 117 Coy
" 5. 2/Lt Hale  " 11. C.S.M.
" 6. 2/Lt Pritchard  " 12. File

Addendum No. 1 to Operation
Order No. 5.

Para VI. For 4 pm daily
read 2.15 pm daily.

Para X as far as the words
"will be necessary" is
cancelled as guides will
be provided from Bty HQ

Signallers. Pte Beechey will
be attached to 'A' Battery &
Pte Hill to 'B' Battery. They
will report to their respective
batteries at dusk & if the
relief has not taken place
by that time, they will
wait at the Battery position

G. Higginbottom Lt
For O.C. 116 Bde R

Copies as before

# WAR DIARY
## or
## INTELLIGENCE SUMMARY.
*(Erase heading not required.)*

Army Form C. 2118.

| Place | Date | Hour | Summary of Events and Information | Remarks and references to Appendices |
|---|---|---|---|---|
| | | | that TUTZ COTTS fire was believed knocked out. Confirmed at 9.30 pm Three O.Rs Killed & five discharged. Ten intensely discharged. One O.R Killed, one wounded remained duty at HEDIN Rd Guns, S.A.A. moved up to SNA TR & "G" Battery during the night. | |
| | 7 | | Relief orders received for 8th unit - 8 June to stay in. 2 O.Rs slightly wounded at "G" Battery. O.C 117 Coy to CHQ re relief. Harassing fire from "G" Battery 9.30 pm 6 rounds, 1750 rounds. Relief Orders received from Brigade. Operation Orders for relief issued at [illegible] copy | |
| | 8 | | O.C 117 Coy to take over at 3.35 pm Relief complete at 8.35 pm One O.R wounded. Arrived CHIPPAWA CAMP 11.40 pm. 19 Reinforcements (Can) men | |
| | 9 | 9.30 am | Guns & cleaning etc. Inspection of Barrels by O.C | |

Army Form C. 2118.

# WAR DIARY
## or
## INTELLIGENCE SUMMARY.
(Erase heading not required.)

Instructions regarding War Diaries and Intelligence Summaries are contained in F. S. Regs., Part II. and the Staff Manual respectively. Title pages will be prepared in manuscript.

| Place | Date | Hour | Summary of Events and Information | Remarks and references to Appendices |
|---|---|---|---|---|
| | 10. | | 7.30. Foot Rubbing drill. 9 am C.O.s Inspection in D.Coy. 9.30 a.m. Cleaning overhauling firearms. 2.30 p.m. Phys. Training 6.30 p.m. Foot Rubbing. Recreation in afternoon. | |
| | 11. | | Church Parade 11.15 am. | |
| | 12. | | Orders to move received. 7.30 Foot Rubbing. 9.30 a.m. C.O.s Inspection (marching order) 10 a.m. Reorganizing of Sections 11.0 P.T. 11.30 O.C.s lecture to N.C.Os & Sec. Commanders. Drafts of O.R.s received - 3 O.R.s Company now included. | |
| | 13 | | 6.45 a.m. Foot Rubbing. 8.45 Coy paraded in full marching order & moved to DEAD DOG FARM. Transport remained at CHIPPEWA CAMP. | |
| DEAD DOG FARM. | 14 | | Coy H.Q. moved to BEDFORD HOUSE, Adv Coy HQ at HEDGE St TUNNEL. Details remained DEAD DOG FARM. The 6 guns in the line relieved by the 6 guns relieving. Orders from Bde to receive "A" Battery 6 in my Coy. | |

A6945 Wt. W14422/M1160 350000 12/16 D. D. & L. Forms/C./2118/14.

# WAR DIARY
## or
## INTELLIGENCE SUMMARY.
*(Erase heading not required.)*

Army Form C. 2118.

| Place | Date | Hour | Summary of Events and Information | Remarks and references to Appendices |
|---|---|---|---|---|
| | 15. | | Battery. Two extra Gun teams sent up. Orders received for men at DEPOT O.O.B ready to move to RIDGE WOOD. Men relieved from line had baths. | |
| | 16. | | S.A.A. sent up to INFANTRY & "J" Battery by pack animals during the night. | |
| | 17. | | Nightly R.F.A. shelled to prevent enemy registering. 1150 rds | |
| | 18. | | I.A.A. taken by pack animals from MT SORREL to INFANTRY & "J" Battery. Harassing fire 1000 rds | |
| | 19. | | Harassing fire carried out – 2000 rds (rifle) Extra fifle ordered) – 2000 rds (rifle) | |
| | 20. | | | |
| | 21. | | Practice on S.O.S. lines carried out – 2000 rds | |
| | 22. | | Harassing fire 2500 Harassing fire during day trip at 6000 rds. | |
| | 23. | | Harassing fire carried out during day night 35,000 rounds. Orders to clear details from RIDGE WOOD to CONFUSION CORNER. Clearing for relief on | |

A6945 Wt. W14422/M1160 350,000 12/16 D.D.&L. Forms/C./2118/14.

# WAR DIARY
## or
## INTELLIGENCE SUMMARY.
(Erase heading not required.)

Army Form C. 2118.

| Place | Date | Hour | Summary of Events and Information | Remarks and references to Appendices |
|---|---|---|---|---|
| | | | Sept 26/26th received. | |
| | 24. | | During night of 23rd sent 22,950 rds harassing fire | |
| | 25. | | Harassing fire 144/100 rounds. Relieved by 90 MgC. Relief complete by 6 pm. Entrained on light railway for FUZEVILLE ZEVECOTEN at 8.30pm. Camped at ZEVECOTEN | |
| ZEVECOTEN | 26 | | Advanced party sent to WINNIZEELE for billets. Movement Orders to entrain at OUDERDOM received | |
| | 27 | | Paraded 2.30 pm entrained at OUDERDOM. Returned GODEWAERSVELDE marched to billets on STEENVOORDE — RWELD ROAD (T.35.6.2.4 - Sheet 27) Arrived billets at | |
| | | 6.30 pm | All men in barns. | |
| | 28 | | General cleaning up of clothing & equipment. | |
| RWELD. | 29 | | Baths for men from 7 - 9 am at STEENVOORDE. | |
| | | 10.30 | Kivés & inspection of clothing. S.B. Rs, Iron Rations etc | |
| | | 11.30 | Cleaning arms & limbers | |

# WAR DIARY
## or
## INTELLIGENCE SUMMARY

*(Erase heading not required.)*

Army Form C. 2118.

| Place | Date | Hour | Summary of Events and Information | Remarks and references to Appendices |
|---|---|---|---|---|
| | 30. | 12.30pm | Inspection of Guns & Kit by C.O. Football in afternoon. C/O to demonstration at Le Touquet. 9am CO's Inspection in F.S. order. 9.45 Elem: gun drill 10.45 S.B.R. drill. 11.15 Barrage drill. | |

E.J. Munce Capt
O.C. 116 M.G.C.

Original

Army Form C. 2118.

**WAR DIARY**
*or*
**INTELLIGENCE SUMMARY.**
*(Erase heading not required.)*

Vol 22

116 M.G. Company
War Diary
Dec 1st to 31st
1917

E. Tothwell Capt.
O.C. 116 M.G. Coy.

Army Form C. 2118.

# WAR DIARY
## or
## INTELLIGENCE SUMMARY.
(Erase heading not required.)

Instructions regarding War Diaries and Intelligence Summaries are contained in F. S. Regs., Part II. and the Staff Manual respectively. Title pages will be prepared in manuscript.

| Place | Date | Hour | Summary of Events and Information | Remarks and references to Appendices |
|---|---|---|---|---|
| RWELD. | 1 | 8a | Foot Rubbing Drill | |
| | | 9am | Route March - F.M. Order | |
| | 2 | 7pm | G.O.C's inspection of Transport | |
| | | 7.30am | Foot Rubbing Drill | |
| | | 10.45 " | G.O.C's inspection of Coy in Drill Order | |
| | | 11.30 " | Church Parade | |
| | 3 | 7 am | Foot Rubbing Drill | |
| | | 9 " | Nos 1 & 2 secs washing equipment. Nos 3 & 4 Secs arranging kit | |
| | | 10 " | Change over | |
| | | 11 " | Cleaning Guns, spare parts etc | |
| | | 12.30 pm | CO's inspection of Guns & Gun Kit | |
| | | 2 pm | Cleaning limbers & harness | |
| | 4 | 7 am | Foot Rubbing Drill | |
| | | 9 " | Route March in F.M. Order | |
| | | 2 pm | Foot inspection | |
| | | 3 | Stoppages | |

Army Form C. 2118.

# WAR DIARY
## or
## INTELLIGENCE SUMMARY.
(Erase heading not required.)

Instructions regarding War Diaries and Intelligence Summaries are contained in F. S. Regs., Part II. and the Staff Manual respectively. Title pages will be prepared in manuscript.

| Place | Date | Hour | Summary of Events and Information | Remarks and references to Appendices |
|---|---|---|---|---|
| | 5 | 6.30 a.m. | Foot Rubbing Drill | |
| | | 9 " | C. O. Inspection in F. M. Order | |
| | | 9.30 " | Gun Drill by Sections | |
| | | 10.30 " | Swedish Games | |
| | | 11.0 " | Infantry Drill | |
| | | 12.0 p.m. | Packing ver Park'g Limbers | |
| | | 3 " | Limber Painting | |
| | | | Football in Afternoon. Each man doing three | |
| | | | 1 min rounds boxing daily. | |
| | 6 | 6.30 a.m. | Foot Rubbing Drill | |
| | | 9.0 " | C. O. Inspection in F. M. Order | |
| | | 9.30 " | Gun Drill by Sections | |
| | | 10.30 " | Swedish Games | |
| | | 11.0 " | Infantry & S.B.R. Drill. | |
| | | 12 p.m. | Packing verPark'g Limbers | |
| | | 2 p.m. | Limber Painting. | |

**Army Form C. 2118.**

# WAR DIARY
## or
## INTELLIGENCE SUMMARY.
*(Erase heading not required.)*

Instructions regarding War Diaries and Intelligence Summaries are contained in F. S. Regs., Part II. and the Staff Manual respectively. Title pages will be prepared in manuscript.

| Place | Date | Hour | Summary of Events and Information | Remarks and references to Appendices |
|---|---|---|---|---|
| | | | Football & Boxing as usual. Lt Evans | |
| | | | left from Course at Counin. O.C on leave GHQ | |
| | 7 | 5.45 am | Foot Rubbing Drill | |
| | | 6.45, 7.45, 8.45 | Parties to Baths | |
| | | 9.30 | Arm Drill wearing S.B.Rs | |
| | | 10.30 | Batt. Swedish Games. | |
| | | 11.0 | Bett Firing | |
| | | 12.15 pm | COs Inspection in F.S Order | |
| | | 2 | Limbir Cleaning & Painting | |
| | | | Boxing & Football as usual. | |
| | 8 | 6.30 | Foot Rubbing Drill | |
| | | 9 am | C O's Inspn in F D Order. 9.30 am | |
| | | | Combined Drill. 11.0 Swedish Games | |
| | | 10.10 am | Order Drill | |
| | | 11.30 | Lecture 1.15 pm Parking Limbers, stripping & cleaning | |
| | | | Guns. Afternoon – Football & Boxing | |
| | 9 | 7.30 | Foot Rubbing Drill. 11 am CO's Inspection – Bellboots | |
| | | 10.30 | Non-Coms numb. Parade. 11.30 CofE Parade. | |

# WAR DIARY
## or
## INTELLIGENCE SUMMARY.
*(Erase heading not required.)*

Army Form C. 2118.

| Place | Date | Hour | Summary of Events and Information | Remarks and references to Appendices |
|---|---|---|---|---|
| | | 11 am | Transport moved to LUMBRES area staying one night at MAISON BLANCHE (CASSEL-STONOR RD) next day will move on to the LUMBRES area. Orders received for Coy to move 10th entraining at GODEWAERSVELDE. | |
| | 10 | | The Coy moved to Bielek in the LUMBRES area. Paraded 9.45 am to march to GODEWAERSVELDE where it entrained at 12.35 pm. 21 detrained at NIEULLES. L52-13 EQUIN at 7 pm reached its billets in LART at 7.45 pm. Billets very scattered but fair. | |
| LART | 11 | 9 am | Cleaning up Billets, clothing & equipment. 2.15 pm Kit Inspection by Section Officers. | |
| | 12 | 7.15 | Foot Rubbing. 9 am Co's Inspection in Drill Order. 9.30 Close Order Drill. 10.10 Boxing & Swedish Games. 11.0 Lecture by CO. 12.0 Revolver & Rifle Drill. | |

# WAR DIARY
## or
## INTELLIGENCE SUMMARY.
*(Erase heading not required.)*

Army Form C. 2118.

| Place | Date | Hour | Summary of Events and Information | Remarks and references to Appendices |
|---|---|---|---|---|
| | 13 | | 12.30 S.B.R drill 2.15 Foot Inspection & Rubbing Football & Boxing in afternoon. Pay at 2.45. | |
| | | 7.0–7.15 | Foot Rubbing. Saw L.B.R drill 9.30 C.O.s Inspection in Drill Order 10.10 Gun Drill 11.10 Boxing & Indoor Game 12.0 Lecture by C.O. 12.30. Skipping. Afternoon – Football & Boxing. 8.45–9 p.m. Skipping & Rubbing. 12 Reinforcements arrived – half sent men out. | |
| | 14. | | Foot Rubbing 7.0 – 7.15 am. Saw Route March Co LUMBRES & back. Foot Inspection at 12.45 pm. Football & Boxing on round. | |
| | 15. | | Coy Training on Parade Ground – Inspection by Brigadier | |
| | 16 | AM 9.30 | Non Com. Service | |
| | | 10 | RC " | |
| | | | 11.15AM. C of E Service. – Lt W.H. Hooper joined as Reinforcement | |
| | 17 | 7AM | Coy Musketry Range carried out M.G. swing & Rapid Reserve practices 8.30 – 11.30 AM – short range. | |

# WARY DIARY or INTELLIGENCE SUMMARY

Army Form C. 2118.

| Place | Date | Hour | Summary of Events and Information | Remarks and references to Appendices |
|---|---|---|---|---|
| | 17. 18. | | Baths at SENINGHEM Standing | |
| | 19. | 8 AM | Arrived 2nd Army musketry Range but nothing until noon | |
| | | 12 – 3.30 PM | Musketry practices at 300x falling plates. | |
| | 20. | | Baths & Coy Training — football in aft. | |
| | 21. | 9 – 1 | Coy training — Boxing — Tug of war — Snowball games &c | |
| | 22. | | Inspection of Transport by Brigade Major | |
| | | 2.15 | Coy football team beat C coy Hants Regt. Major 4 – 1 Tug of war team beat B coy Hants but beaten by C Coy Hants | |
| | 23 | | Church parade | |
| | 24. | 1 – 3 | Inspection of Sections Transport mt F.M.O. by CO — Capt Rothwell from leave | |
| | | 9.45 | Inspection of Coy Transport by Major Syd. Feetham commdg 39th Bn. | |
| | | | P.M. played rugger tie to Sergt Andrews rept Quilter stag &c visited by man Beresford. The Turn out had no fewer 15 – 10 pad | |
| | 25. | | Football team beat D Coy Hants 1 – 0. Church services — Xmas Dinner — Roast Pork, Plumpuddings &c Holiday | |

# WAR DIARY
## or
## INTELLIGENCE SUMMARY.
*(Erase heading not required.)*

Army Form C. 2118.

Instructions regarding War Diaries and Intelligence Summaries are contained in F. S. Regs., Part II. and the Staff Manual respectively. Title pages will be prepared in manuscript.

| Place | Date | Hour | Summary of Events and Information | Remarks and references to Appendices |
|---|---|---|---|---|
| | 26th | | Coy Training — 9.30–12.30 on Parade ground | |
| | 27th | | Coy " " | |
| | | 1–3 | Baths — Coy Football Team played Divl M.T Drivers in Final | |
| | | | of Dela Group — lost 4–0 | |
| | 28th | 9–11.30 | Firing on short range | |
| | 29th | 9.45 | Transport left for forward area. | |
| | 30th | 2AM | Coy marched off to WIZERNES & Entrained at 7.30AM | |
| | | 1.30AM | Coy detrained at ELVERDINGHE marched to SIEGE CAMP | |
| | | | Good accommodation | |
| SIEGE CAMP | 31st | | Cleaning up Camp | |
| ELVERDINGHE | | 9AM | 2 offrs. M.N. Co reconnoitred renfront. | |
| BELGIUM 28 N.W. | | 3AM | Transport arrived. | |

E Gohnen Capt
O.C. 116 Coy.

# WAR DIARY
## or
## INTELLIGENCE SUMMARY.

Vol 23   Army Form C. 2118.

Confidential

116 M.G. Coy

WAR DIARY

Jan 1st — 31st 1918

W. Evans Lt.
for O.C.
116 M.G. Coy

# WAR DIARY
## or
## INTELLIGENCE SUMMARY.
*(Erase heading not required.)*

Army Form C. 2118.

| Place | Date | Hour | Summary of Events and Information | Remarks and references to Appendices |
|---|---|---|---|---|
| SIEGE Camp | 1 | | Coy Training - Foot Drill - Rifle Exs - Repelling Bolts - O.T. Wk at Fort | |
| | 2 | | Coy Training - Gun Drill - O.T. Stoppages | |
| | 3 | | Div. Front reconnoitred by 5 officers & 9 O.Rs. | |
| | | | Bombing Planes active morning & night. | |
| | 4 | | Coy. Drawing 9-1 Gas Chamber. Wear S.B.Rs 2.30-3.15. Hard Frost continues | |
| | 5-6 | | Coy. Training 9-1 P.M. Hard Frost continues. | |
| | | | Church Service | |
| | 7 | | Reconnaissance of Reserve Gun positions by Co Y Lt Oates. | |
| | | | Bunny horses killed by shell - 118 Bde. | |
| | | | Shave - Frost at night. | |
| | 8 | 11AM | Lt. Oates & 4 Gun Teams left for Frue to relieve 118 M.G. Coy. at GENOA FM. D.I.C. 37.25. 25rms VON TIRPITZ D.7. b. 32. 67 | |
| | | 1.30PM | Coy left SIEGE CAMP for Support area CANAL BANK EAST | |

Army Form C. 2118.

# WAR DIARY
## or
## INTELLIGENCE SUMMARY.
*(Erase heading not required.)*

Instructions regarding War Diaries and Intelligence Summaries are contained in F. S. Regs., Part II. and the Staff Manual respectively. Title pages will be prepared in manuscript.

| Place | Date | Hour | Summary of Events and Information | Remarks and references to Appendices |
|---|---|---|---|---|
| | 8 | 12 p/m | Relief complete. | |
| | 9 | | Gun cleaning - Belt overhauling - improving area - Men held to UK leave | |
| | 10 | | Coy training & work on Transport lines - Reconnaissance of Battery positions for support guns mainly to N + East. | |
| | 11 | | Divine Service & work on Horselines | |
| | 12 | | Full C.O. parade - G.O.C. 8 Div inspected Transport | |
| | 13 | | Church Parade 9.15 AM - officers NCOs Reconnoitre the line. Material drawn for improvement of area. | |
| | 14 | | 2 S.A.A. dumps 50,000 each made at CORNER COT to Reserve Battery Posts | |
| | 15 | | Reconnaissance of line | |
| | 16 | | Coy relieved 118 M.G. Coy in WESTROOSEBEKE Sector - 16 guns in line - Coy HQ ALBERTA. Set up to R SH (M). weather very bad - Position very wet. | |

# WAR DIARY
## or
## INTELLIGENCE SUMMARY.

*(Erase heading not required.)*

Army Form C. 2118.

Instructions regarding War Diaries and Intelligence Summaries are contained in F. S. Regs., Part II. and the Staff Manual respectively. Title pages will be prepared in manuscript.

| Place | Date | Hour | Summary of Events and Information | Remarks and references to Appendices |
|---|---|---|---|---|
|  | 17 |  | Very satisfactory tour in spite of conditions in line. Frostbite |  |
|  | 18 |  | Teams relieved by 98 Coy night 18/19th. Then onwards every |  |
|  | 19 | 9 hr | 1 Dick 1 wounded, 1 acc. wounded only. |  |
|  | 20 |  | 20 Trench feet cases |  |
|  | 21 | 4 PM | Relieved by 106 Coy. |  |
|  |  | 8 AM | 105 juniors left by Train from WIELTJE Sdg for School Camp. |  |
|  |  | noon | Remainder of Coy entrained. |  |
| School Camp | 22 | 3.30 | Baths re-cleaning up. |  |
| L.3C | 23 |  | Inspection & issue of new clothing. |  |
| Sheet 28 | 24 |  | Transport Camp |  |
|  | 25 | 5.30 PM | Coy to 39 Bve Canteen POPERINGHE |  |
|  |  | 7.30 PM | Advance Part left for MERICOURT |  |
|  | 26 | 6 AM | Reveille |  |
|  |  | 7.45 AM | Coy left for PROVEN Stn entrained at 9.30 & Transport |  |
|  |  | 9.30 PM | Coy detrained at MERICOURT L'ABBE' marched to SAILLY le SEC |  |
|  |  |  | TO BILLETS (AMIENS 10000) |  |

# WAR DIARY
## or
## INTELLIGENCE SUMMARY.
*(Erase heading not required.)*

Army Form C. 2118.

| Place | Date | Hour | Summary of Events and Information | Remarks and references to Appendices |
|---|---|---|---|---|
| SAILLY LE SEC | 27 | | Dull thirsty - settling down - fixing up usual latrines & cleaning own range - rental left behind | |
| (AMIENS) 1/100,000 | 28 | | Beautiful Sunny day - Gun Drill - Foot Rubbing - Stoppages - Volleys | |
| | 29. | | C.O. + I off - reconnoitered new line. Coy prep for line | |
| | 30. | 2AM | Reveille. 3AM Breakfast | |
| | | 4AM | Coy marched vit VAUX SUR SOMME to CORBIE - entrained 7AM. 9 detrained at PERONNE marched to Test Camp at HAUT ALLAINES | |
| HEUDECOURT FRANCE 57 SE | 31. | 2AM | Entrained on light Railway to hut | |
| | | 4AM | Detrained at HEUDICOURT. Coy Relieved 27 M.G. Coy in GOUCHE WOOD SECTOR - 12 Guns in line 4 in Reserve in HEUDICOURT. Early Relief - Low visibility | |

Murray
D. Pilkington

# WAR DIARY
## or
## INTELLIGENCE SUMMARY.
*(Erase heading not required.)*

Army Form C. 2118.

Vol 24

War Diary
116 M.G. Coy.
Jul. 1st – 28th 1918

J Munro Lt
for O.C. Coy

Army Form C. 2118.

# WAR DIARY
## or
## INTELLIGENCE SUMMARY
*(Erase heading not required.)*

Instructions regarding War Diaries and Intelligence Summaries are contained in F. S. Regs., Part II. and the Staff Manual respectively. Title Pages will be prepared in manuscript.

| Place | Date | Hour | Summary of Events and Information | Remarks and references to Appendices |
|---|---|---|---|---|
| HEUDICOURT | 1 | | Twelve Guns in position in The BelleSector – GOUZEAUCOURT (CENTRE) SECTION – | |
| Ref. GAUCHE WOOD 1/10,000. | | | R1 – X.7.c.18.45 – S.O.S lines X8.a.4.4 – X8.a.8.5. | |
| | | | R2 – W12.b.98.05    S.O.S    X2.b.3.4 | |
| | | | R3 – X.7.a.19.80    Direct Targets | |
| | | | R4 – X.1.d.4.4 – Direct fire from GAUCHE WOOD | |
| | | | R5 – X.1.d.2.6    "    " | |
| Adv. C.H.Q. | | | R6 – W.8.a.7.2    S.O.S lines X8.C.15.80 – X8.C.45.90. | |
| | | | R7 – W12.d.55.05    "    "    X8.C.40.65 – X8.C.40.55 | |
| W12.b.61.7 | | | R8 – W12.b.72.15 | |
| | | | R9 – W12.b.68.25 } | |
| | | | R10 – W12.b.62.80 }    "    "    R32.C.53. TO R32.b.9.8 | |
| | | | R11 – W12.b.62.85 | |
| | | | R12 – W12.d.45.65    "    "    X2.b.15.50 | |
| | | | Four guns in Reserve in HEUDICOURT. | |
| | 7PM | | Harassing fire on enemy Tracks &c commenced carried on through night – four R7. | |

# WAR DIARY
## or
## INTELLIGENCE SUMMARY
*(Erase heading not required.)*

Army Form C. 2118.

| Place | Date | Hour | Summary of Events and Information | Remarks and references to Appendices |
|---|---|---|---|---|
| | 2 | | Clearing up emplacements & checking references alternative positions for 10 & 11 commenced. Usual harassing fire. | |
| | 3 | | Night firing party for R.F. commenced — emplacements improved at R 8 & 9 — S.A.A. increased at positions. Bombs sent up to GAUCHE WD. positions. Harassing fire on R. Tracks throughout night. | |
| | 4 | | Improvements at positions continued — Coy HQ dug out floorboarded — new dug outs sandbagged. Latrine Bays made at HEUDICOURT & new Dugout completed at HEUDICOURT. | |
| | 5 | | Latrines made at positions in line where not already completed — alternative positions for 10 & 11 completed & S.A.A. reserves commenced. Usual harassing fire on R7. | |
| | 6 | | Emplacements made at REVELON Fm. to be occupied by reserve Sects in case of attack | |

# Army Form C. 2118.

# WAR DIARY
## or
## INTELLIGENCE SUMMARY

*(Erase heading not required.)*

Instructions regarding War Diaries and Intelligence Summaries are contained in F. S. Regs., Part II. and the Staff Manual respectively. Title Pages will be prepared in manuscript.

| Place | Date | Hour | Summary of Events and Information | Remarks and references to Appendices |
|---|---|---|---|---|
| | 7 | | Trench Routine. Improvements to Emplacements. Harassing fire | |
| | 8 | | do | |
| | 9 | | do  L to A to 5th Army Infantry School | |
| | 10 | | do  3/Lt G Hale to M.B.T. course | |
| | 11 | | do | |
| | 12 | 12 noon | Field hutting put in at R12 night firing position Zero line obtained - | |
| | | | CO. to D/174 RJA for 2dys course. | |
| | | | Accommodation at R12 increased - latrine screened | |
| | | | Start partisans MG shafts from tunnels at R1, R2. | |
| | 13 | | Harassing fire from R12, R7. | |
| | 14 | 12 noon | CO returned from RJA course | |
| | | | 4 trans to D/174. RJA. | |
| | 15 | | | |
| | 16 | | | |
| | 17 | | Trench Routine | |

**Army Form C. 2118.**

# WAR DIARY
## or
## INTELLIGENCE SUMMARY
*(Erase heading not required.)*

Instructions regarding War Diaries and Intelligence Summaries are contained in F. S. Regs., Part II. and the Staff Manual respectively. Title Pages will be prepared in manuscript.

| Place | Date | Hour | Summary of Events and Information | Remarks and references to Appendices |
|---|---|---|---|---|
| | 17 | | Head cover made at R.6. Trench deepened at R.8 & 9 — Rivetting at Western to 10 M.1. Usual harassing fire. | |
| | 18. | | Beet Butts increased at positions to 16 for 3mm — S.a.a as received. Harassing fire and R. Tracks re throughout night. | |
| | 19 | | Usual Routine & repairs | |
| | 20 | 4 AM | Raid by 13th R.S.R. on enemy post — no assistance regd. Head cover to R.9 & Rivetting. Harassing fire as usual | |
| | 21 | 4.55 | 9 guns (SOS) reflected to S.O.S. before artillery opened. 9,000 rds fired — all quiet 6 AM. Sap continued at Coy. H.Q. Accommodation at R.8 & 9 commenced — elephants put in for. | |
| | 22 | | Usual Routine | |

# WAR DIARY
## or
## INTELLIGENCE SUMMARY

*(Erase heading not required.)*

Army Form C. 2118.

Instructions regarding War Diaries and Intelligence Summaries are contained in F. S. Regs., Part II. and the Staff Manual respectively. Title Pages will be prepared in manuscript.

| Place | Date | Hour | Summary of Events and Information | Remarks and references to Appendices |
|---|---|---|---|---|
| | 23 | | Loopholes, etc made for R1 – Cutting at face of position completed. Tunnel portion for R1 reacted. Dugouts at C.H.Q. strengthened. Reserve water to all positions. | |
| | 24. | | Usual Routine – working party from Reserve H.Q. to R8 & 9 on dugouts. | |
| | 25. | | Usual Routine – working party to R8 & 9. Action of Reserve guns changed – 2 to a joint W16 d 85.85 for temporary forward guns under Bde.O. Orders. 1 to W21. d. 1. 3. 1 to W15. d. 21. 35. | |
| | 26. | | Fitting of dugouts at R8 & 9 – continuation of work on emplacements at R1 & R2. Putting positions in Auchy W.D. Usual harassing fire. | |

**Army Form C. 2118.**

# WAR DIARY
## or
## INTELLIGENCE SUMMARY
*(Erase heading not required.)*

Instructions regarding War Diaries and Intelligence Summaries are contained in F. S. Regs., Part II. and the Staff Manual respectively. Title Pages will be prepared in manuscript.

| Place | Date | Hour | Summary of Events and Information | Remarks and references to Appendices |
|---|---|---|---|---|
| Line Msp | 27 | | Enemy artillery very active during day & night — Mule Track shelled 7.30 P.M. 1 O.R. wounded whilst on duty, 2 mules wounded. Continued work on dugouts — harassing fire as usual during the night. | |
| | 28 | 9 AM 5.15 AM | Advance Billetting Party left for BRAY AREA. 18500 rds. fired in cooperation with raid by our left Bde. Targets R32.b.6.48, R17.c.27.05, R32.d.3.7 Relief by 27 M.G.Coy on night 27/28 cancelled — The 34th Division taking over its Battle front. Casualties — 1 O.R. wounded. | |

M Brandt
p O.C.
116 M.G.Coy.

# 39TH DIVISION
## 116TH INFY BDE

LT! TRENCH MORTARS

JLY - SEP 1916

116 L.T.M.B.

July, August, &
September 1916

Confidential

Fras Leary

116 McKinnon Gun Coy
from 1st August 1915 to 31st August 1916

## 116th Light Trench Mortar Battery

4 guns fired from our own lines during the bombardment, while the infantry were going over, & after they had reached the German lines. Of these 4 guns, No 1 (the right hand gun), fired 72 rounds during the bombardment when it was put out of action by a shell which buried the base plate completely & made the emplacement untenable.

Further firing from this gun was impossible during the remainder of the operations.

No. 2 gun (emplacement No. 8), fired 17 rounds during the bombardment; this was the total number of shells with this gun.

No. 3 gun (No. 5 emplacement), fired ~~200~~ 150 shells; about 50 during the bombardment, on the German front & support lines. to the left of the sector on which the attack was launched. The gun was put out of action for a short time by dirt thrown up by a shell which clogged the barrel. The barrel was cleaned & firing continued.

Nº 4 gun (emplacement 6), fired 150 rounds approximately on the same points as number 3 gun, but it fired more on the German support line.

Four guns were intended to be set up in the German second line. Of these 4 guns, Nº 1 gun reached a point between the German first & second lines; but the officer in charge of Nº 1 & 2 guns had been killed, & the N.C.O did not know where to go to & could find no place in which to set up the gun.

Under
^ Heavy shell fire, the gun was brought back in tact, but the base plate was subsequently lost in our own lines.

No 2 gun reached the German sap where the N.C.O in charge + 3 men were wounded by a shell which buried the gun completely, with cleaning rod, satchel etc.

No 3 gun: The officer in charge of 3 + 4 guns went over the parapet at 3.15 with the fourth wave, + immediately got wounded. Meanwhile the N.C.O in charge of the detachment who were with the gun, was killed by a shell, which also damaged the legs of the gun rendering it useless. This gun, therefore, never left our own lines.

N⁰ 4 gun: ~~N⁰ 3 + 4 guns were~~ N⁰ 3 + 4 guns were under the same officer who was wounded immediately on going over the parapet. The N.C.O left with the detachment did not know where to take the gun to, & as heavy shelling was in progress, the detachment + gun did not leave our own lines.

6.

Guns lost & out of action.

1 complete gun buried in German sap.

1 gun out of action owing to having lost base plate.

1 gun out of action owing to legs being damaged.

S.F. Farrer.
2nd Lieut.
116 Light T.M.B.

July 1st.

N.B. There are really only 2 guns out of action, as the base plate belonging to the guns whose legs are smashed can be used for the gun which has lost its base plate.

116 Light Trench
Mortar Battery

Report of operations on
June 30th

Army Form C. 2118

# WAR DIARY
## or
## INTELLIGENCE SUMMARY
*(Erase heading not required.)*

Instructions regarding War Diaries and Intelligence Summaries are contained in F. S. Regs., Part II. and the Staff Manual respectively. Title Pages will be prepared in manuscript.

| Place | Date | Hour | Summary of Events and Information | Remarks and references to Appendices |
|---|---|---|---|---|
| Cuinchy | 2.7. | | **B. Casualties** | |
| | 11.7. | | Temp Capt L. H. Rayner evacuated to 32. C.C.S. (wounded.) | |
| | | | 1353 L/Cpl. A. E. Hurrell (12th R. Suss R.) wounded — by premature rifle grenade. | |
| | | | 1654 Pte V. C. Amey ( — wounded | |
| Ferme de Bois | 21.7 | | 3941 Cpl. R. Bush (13th R.Suss.R) wounded by defective Stokes' shell | |
| | 21.7 | | 1154 Pte E. J. Brown (11th R.Suss R) slightly wounded | |
| | | | **C. Changes in personnel.** | |
| 11th R Suss R. | 6.7. | | 2nd Lieut F. G. Armitage reported for duty vice 2nd Lieut Turner (killed in action) | |
| 14th Hants | 7.7. | | ——— A. E. Browne Rose (in hospital.) | |
| 13th R.Suss.R | 19.7. | | ——— J.W. Barrow Lieut Titley (wounded) | |
| 12th R.Suss R | | | ——— R.H. Gillett (attached). | |

S. J. Turner 2nd Lieut
Aug. 6th '16. 116/T.M.Bty

Army Form C. 2118

# WAR DIARY
## or
## INTELLIGENCE SUMMARY

*(Erase heading not required.)*

Instructions regarding War Diaries and Intelligence Summaries are contained in F. S. Regs., Part II. and the Staff Manual respectively. Title Pages will be prepared in manuscript.

| Place | Date | Hour | Summary of Events and Information | Remarks and references to Appendices |
|---|---|---|---|---|
| | | | **A. Operations** | |
| Cuinchy | 10.7 | 7am to 7am | The left 4 guns fired 74 rounds in retaliation to minenwerfers. + 2 guns fired 50 rounds each (11.45 p.m.) | |
| | 11.7 | 7am to 7am 12th | The right 4 guns fired 13 rounds then we sprung 2 small mines & 2 guns fired 50 rounds each 11.45 p.m. Two guns on left section (Brickstacks) fired 30 rounds. | |
| | 13.7 | 1.15am 12.30am | Left 4 guns fired 29 rounds retaliation to minenwerfers. One gun on right section fired 42 rounds on Mine Point. | |
| Givenchy de Bois | 22.7 | 12.30 a.m. 1.30am | 3 guns on night section fired 168 rounds on German front & support lines on the Boars Head. 3 Guns on left section fired 26 rounds during Battalion fire operations. | |
| | 23.7 | 11.30 p.m. 5pm | 2 Guns on Left fired 58 rounds on German defences in the Seven Sisters. 4 night section fired 200 rounds (50 per gun) on German wire at S.16.a.5.6½. | |
| Festubert | 28.8 | 12 mid | 2 guns fired 85 rounds on German wire in front of Pope's Nose. | |
| | 30.8 | 1.30 a.m. | 2 ——— From Kinkeroo. | |
| | | | 2 ——— 52 | |
| | | | 2 ——— Ruined Trench. | |
| | | | 2 ——— 50 | |
| | | | 2 ——— 220 ——— Barnton T on the Pope's Nose. | |

39/Vol I

Confidential

War Diary
of
116" Siege Howitzer Battery
from
1st July to 31st July 1916

**SECRET**

39. Vol 2.

Army Form C. 2118

116th Bde. Trench Mortar Battery
August

# WAR DIARY
## or
## INTELLIGENCE SUMMARY
(Erase heading not required.)

Instructions regarding War Diaries and Intelligence Summaries are contained in F.S. Regs., Part II. and the Staff Manual respectively. Title Pages will be prepared in manuscript.

| Place | Date | Hour | Summary of Events and Information | Remarks and references to Appendices |
|---|---|---|---|---|
| Givenchy | | | Operations. | |
| | 7.8.16 | 5.30 a.m | In Givenchy section from 6.8.16 to 10.8.16. 60 shells fired from 3 guns on points A.10.c.2½.2. A.10.c.1½.1½. A.9.d.9½.5. Casualties. Killed 14360 Pte Teague J. 14th Hants 13004 " Skilling R. 14th Hants 1676 " Daughtry.O 12th Royal Sussex 1367 " Lambert.S 12th Royal Sussex Wounded 12747 Pte Ducker E.J. 14th Hants 12878 " Bowers T.J 14th Hants | Attached to 116th Brigade L.T.M.B. |
| Harrel Section | 30.8.16 | | | |

S.P. Farrer.
2nd Lieut.
116/T.M.Bty

116/T.M.Bty (Hsp) WAR DIARY. SEPT. 1916. Vol 3

| PLACE | DATE | HOUR | Summary of Events & Information | Remarks |
|---|---|---|---|---|
| HAMEL | 3.9.16 | 5.10am | During the operations of this date, 2 Stokes guns went over with the 2nd wave of infantry. Both these Guns failed to reach the German lines in one case because the 2nd wave got buried back & in the other because the ammunition carriers got lot. One Gun was subsequently taken out of Hamel from a shell hole in no mans land close to German front line. One of the guns did not come over with the infantry was also set up in a shell hole & these 2 guns fired about 260 rounds on enemy communication trenches before returning when the General withdrawal was ordered. 7 Stokes Guns fired 1075 shells on different parts of the German front & support lines, & 14 guns have fired on S.O.S. in enemy lines every night. 2nd Lieut. Flu Bannon wounded remaining. (13th R Surr R.) | |
| AUCHONVIL-LERS & REDAN SECTIONS. | 26.9.16 | 1.45 to 4.55 p.m | CASUALTIES. 3.9.16.<br>1006 Cpl H J Buxton. killed.<br>2744 S/Cpl J.G. Naskell, wounded.<br>4705 Pte A Walters wounded.<br>3638. Pte R. Newnham wounded.<br>155.  —  C. Brooker wounded<br>1879.  —  E. Dreyfuss wounded & missing<br>3372 —  A. Ayling wounded remaining. | 2624. Pte A.A. Bennett, wounded & missing<br>12931. — J.A. Haskell, wounded & missing<br>946. Pte. J.E. Walker missing<br>3708 — S. Palmer. ——<br>1316 — C. Fay ——<br>Signed |

www.ingramcontent.com/pod-product-compliance
Lightning Source LLC
Chambersburg PA
CBHW080803010526
44113CB00013B/2314